Resource Management
at the International Level

Resource Management
at the International Level

The Case of the North Pacific

Oran Young

Frances Pinter Ltd., London
Nichols Publishing Co. New York

Copyright © Oran Young 1977

Published in Great Britain in 1977 by
Frances Pinter (Publishers) Limited
161 West End Lane, London NW6

Published in the U.S.A. in 1977 by
Nichols Publishing Company
Post Office Box 96
New York, N.Y. 10024

ISBN 0 903804 25 5

Printed by A. Wheaton and Co. Ltd., Exeter

PRINTED IN GREAT BRITAIN

Young, Oran R.
Resource Management at the International Level

Includes index
1. Natural resources—Bering Sea region
2. Environmental protection—Bering Sea region   I. Title
HC737 B47Y68 1977   333'.009164'51   77–24320
ISBN 0 89397–027–1

for mushuna, with love

CONTENTS

PREFACE

This essay is about the management of natural resources and the maintenance of environmental quality at the international level. It concerns itself with the special economic, political, legal, and organizational problems that arise when resources are exploited by two or more states or when resource exploitation involves activities cutting across two or more sovereign jurisdictions. In dealing with these issues, I have chosen to focus my attention on the following key concepts. In the first instance, I attempt to develop the idea of international resource regions as appropriate managerial units in the realms of resource management and environmental quality. In addition, I emphasize the concept of a regime as a system of governing arrangements for a given social structure or region.

This work takes the form of a theoretical case study. That is, the argument proceeds in the form of a detailed examination of the problems of resource management arising in a particular resource region. The case in question is Beringia, a region encompassing the marine areas to the north and to the south of the Bering Strait together with the associated coastal littorals of eastern Siberia and western North America. At the present time, patterns of resource usage in this region are changing rapidly. Therefore, certain factual statements contained in this essay will undoubtedly be out of date by the time the essay is available in printed form. However, I believe the basic thrust of the argument contained in the essay will remain relevant to the Beringian region during the foreseeable future. Moreover, there is no reason to conclude that changes in specific circumstances in Beringia will lessen the applicability of the conclusions of this study to other international resource regions.

I began work on this project during the autumn of 1973 at the instigation of the Center for Northern Studies. At the time, I was looking for a promising area in which to apply various concepts associated with the literature in the realm of public choice, and the Center was in the process of clarifying its long-term interests in Beringia. During the winter of 1973–1974, I was further stimulated to pursue this project by a request from the Center of International Studies at Princeton University to formulate my ideas about regimes for Beringia in the form of an essay for a volume on lawmaking in the global community. Since that time, I have made two extensive field trips to Alaska to gather materials for this study: one during the summer of 1974 and a second during the summer of 1975. Accordingly, the detailed factual material in the essay reflects conditions in Beringia as of the end of the summer of 1975.

I should like to take this opportunity to express my appreciation to numerous individuals who have helped me with various aspects of this project. Above all, I owe substantial intellectual debts to Steven B. Young, director of the Center for Northern Studies, and to Eugene H. Buck, director of studies of the Arctic Environmental Information and Data Center. In addition, the following individuals freely contributed information, insights, and advice: Gordon Bennett, Lester Brockett, John Burns, Michael Conroy, Francis Fay, Robert Friedheim, Jeffrey Hart, Donald Hood, Toshio Isogai, Barbara Johnson, Garth Jones, Robert Meyer, Daniel Middlemiss, Michael Nicholson, Nicholas Onuf, Walter Parker, Robert Weeden, Norman Wilimovsky, Esther Wunnicke, and Mark Zacker. I was also fortunate in having the help of two research assistants during various phases of the project: M. Catherine Hawes and François Vieillescazes.

Beyond this, I wish to acknowledge the support of various institutions in conjunction with my work on this project. At one time or another, crucial financial support came from the Center for Northern Studies, the World Order Program at the University of Texas, the University Research Institute at the University of Texas, and the Rockefeller Foundation. Institutions that were of great help to me in other ways include the Princeton Center of International Studies, the University of Alaska at Fairbanks, the Arctic Environmental Information and Data Center, and the Natural Resources Library located in the Anchorage office of the Bureau of Land Management.

It is a pleasure to acknowledge the assistance of all these individuals and institutions; I am grateful to them all for their help.

O.R.Y.
Austin, Texas
1 November 1975

CHAPTER I

RESOURCE MANAGEMENT IN AN INTERNATIONAL REGION

This essay is about the management of natural resources and the maintenance of environmental quality at the international level. It explores a group of economic, political, legal, and organizational issues that arise when sovereign states seek to utilize natural resources efficiently and to distribute the proceeds equitably while minimizing the resultant damage to non-economic values (e.g. the preservation of the physical habitat). To this end, the essay directs attention to three inter-related clusters of questions.

To begin with, it probes the utility of focusing on international regions in efforts to cope with problems of resource management affecting two or more sovereign states. To what extent can mutual or or collective gains be obtained by transcending national perspectives and thinking of international regions as unified managerial units? Are there compelling reasons for stopping at the level of the region rather than treating the entire global system as the appropriate managerial unit in the context of resource problems? This essay examines these questions in depth through a theoretical case study of a single well-defined international region. The case in question is Beringia, a region whose significance is presently growing rapidly as a source of important natural resources such as fish, oil, and natural gas.[1] Though the substantive material examined in the study relates entirely to the Beringian case, the conceptual framework developed and the general conclusions concerning international resource regions are applicable to numerous other cases.

Within this framework, the essay emphasizes several analytic issues that arise repeatedly in conjunction with efforts to manage resources and maintain environmental quality at the international level. First, what constitutes an efficient pattern of exploitation for various resources and what institutional arrangements are most likely to facilitate the achievement of this goal? Efficiency refers initially to the equalization of marginal revenue and marginal cost, a condition that permits the maximization of profits or rents. But in this analysis it will also encompass certain criteria of social welfare like Pareto optimality. Second, what constitutes a just distribution of resources or of the proceeds from their exploitation among the actors in an international region and how can such a pattern of distribution be realized? This question suggests an analysis of the distributive consequences of adopting different systems of property rights and institutional arrangements. Third, what are the probable consequences of different patterns of resource exploitation in the region for non-economic values such as the conservation of living species and the preservation of the physical habitat? This query prompts an examination of feasible trade-offs between economic goals — like efficiency — and various non-economic values as well as an assessment of the likely consequences of different institutional arrangements for such trade-offs.[2]

These concerns lead naturally to an emphasis on the analysis of alternative regimes for international resource regions. A regime is a system of governing arrangements, together with a collection of institutions (formal or informal) for the implementation of these arrangements, in a given social structure or region. In this connection, it is helpful to begin by characterizing the existing regime in a particular region and assessing its consequences in terms of certain well-defined criteria of evaluation. But it is also important to think systematically about alternative regimes for specific regions and about the probable consequences of each of these alternatives. This is especially true with respect to a region like Beringia in which rapidly unfolding problems of resource management and environmental quality are raising fundamental questions about the adequacy of the existing regime. Accordingly, this essay devotes considerable attention to the analysis of alternative regimes for Beringia.

A. Beringia

The marine areas extending to the north and to the south of the Bering Strait together with the associated coastal littorals of the mainland of North America and eastern Siberia have come to be known during the past several decades, at least among scientists, as Beringia. The name was apparently first proposed during the 1930s by the Swedish botanist, Eric Hūlten. Since then, the name has been used quite extensively by biologists and other natural scientists, though it has not yet become familiar to students of international politics, economics, and law.[3]

There is of course no official delineation of the boundaries of Beringia. Moreover, it soon becomes apparent that different functional activities are not perfectly congruent with respect to their areal configuration. For example, commercially significant fisheries are not distributed areally in exactly the same way as geological structures containing extensive deposits of oil and natural gas. Nevertheless, the map on the following page (Figure I) gives a reasonable first approximation of the realm of Beringia. An inspection of this map makes it clear that the Bering Sea and the Chukchi Sea together form the core of the Beringian region. However, for some purposes it will be desirable to extend the region north to include the Beaufort Sea, the East Siberian Sea, and parts of the Arctic Ocean proper and south to encompass the Gulf of Alaska and certain other portions of the Northeastern Pacific Ocean.[4]

Beringia exhibits several striking biological and geological features that have important implications for the utilization of the natural resources of the region. Several of these deserve brief notice at the outset.[5] The Beringian seas have a high concentration of nutrients and support a large growth of phytoplankton and zooplankton. Though there are other seas, such as the North Sea, which are more productive than the Beringian seas in terms of some criteria, it is widely agreed that the Beringian seas are among the most biologically productive in the world.[6] Several distinguishable factors account for this productivity, including the shallowness of large portions of the marine area of Beringia, the large-scale upwellings of the Northeastern Pacific caused by the presence of the Aleutian chain, and the extensive upwellings within the Bering Sea and the Gulf of Alaska along the edge of the continental shelf. All this makes Beringia an important international region from the perspective of commercial fisheries, though it certainly does not mean that the renewable resources of the region are inexhaustible.[7]

Geologically, large segments of the marine area of Beringia are essentially a continental land mass. In this region, the continental shelves of eastern Asia and western North America are continuous, forming an undersea plain several hundred thousand square miles in extent.[8] At various times in the earth's history, this plain has emerged

13

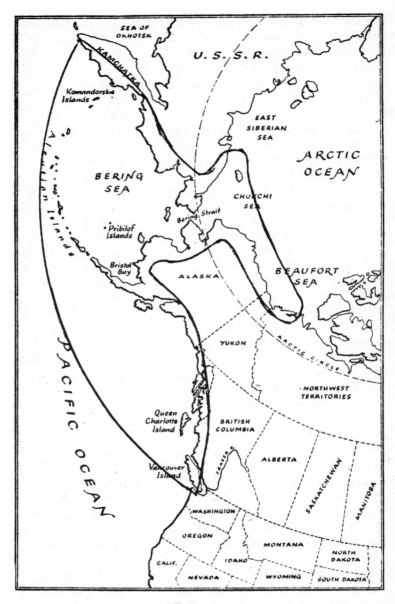

Figure I
The Beringian Region

from its shallow covering of sea water and become a 'land bridge' connecting the two great land masses of the western hemisphere. In fact, the term 'land bridge' is somewhat misleading, connoting as it does a narrow isthmus. At some times, the Bering Land Bridge was 1,000 miles wide at its narrowest point. Generations of land animals, as well as early man, evidently lived and died without ever leaving the land bridge.

The physical remnants of the Bering Land Bridge are the coastal littorals of Beringia and particularly the islands within the former land bridge area. The most important of these are Wrangel, St. Lawrence, St. Matthew, Nunivak, and the Pribilofs. Deep oceans lie both to the north and to the south of the Aleutian chain, and these islands were never actually part of the land bridge. However, they form an important part of contemporary Beringia with numerous implications for legal jurisdictions and economic activities in the region.

To appreciate fully the characteristic features of Beringia, it is necessary to discard the sharp conceptual distinction between 'land' and 'sea'. During the past 70 million or more years, much of Beringia has alternated between being a low-lying plain and a shallow sea. At present, most of Beringia's resources, geological, biotic, and human, are inextricably focused on the interface between land and sea. As Beringia comes more under the influence of modern technological society, this concept of the inseparability of land and sea will become increasingly central to thinking about the future of the region and the management of its resources.

Though it naturally has its own special features,[9] Beringia is a member of a class of specifiable international regions exhibiting certain common problems of resource management and characterized by the overlapping of two or more sovereign jurisdictions. Other members of this class having important parallels with Beringia include: 1) the North Sea, 2) the Baltic Sea, 3) the Mediterranean Sea, 4) the Caribbean Sea, 5) the Sea of Japan, 6) the East China — Yellow Seas, 7) the Arctic, and 8) Antarctica.

Accordingly, the analysis of problems of resource management and the maintenance of environmental quality in the Beringian region has potential relevance well beyond the confines of Beringia itself. Moreover, the fact that the problems of resource management are more severe in certain other regions (e.g. the North Sea) than they have so far become in Beringia provides an ample stream of evidence concerning the consequences that are likely to ensue in Beringia if more systematic efforts are not made to deal with the governance of Beringia in the near future. In a sense, Beringia currently offers a striking opportunity to come to grips with the international relations of resource management from a perspective that is largely preventative rather than restorative, but this opportunity will not last indefinitely.

B. Current International Status

For the most part, the Beringian region constitutes a microcosm of the major relationships included under the general rubric of the law of the sea. The four Geneva Conventions of 1958 are applicable to Beringia just as they are to other marine areas of the world. However, this general legal framework is indeterminate with regard to a number of central issues (e.g. the width of the territorial sea) and by no means uniformly adhered to by the major actors in Beringia. And in specific cases, such as the Convention on the Continental Shelf, the geological and biological characteristics of Beringia make it difficult to apply the relevant standards and criteria with any precision. Similarly, the outcome of the current law of the sea conference, whatever its terms may be, will have significant implications for the governance of Beringia in the future.[10]

Beyond this, there now exists a complex web of functionally specific international agreements relating to the particular resource problems of the region. Virtually all of these involve issues arising from the harvest of fish and marine mammals in Beringia. These specific agreements are not insignificant, but it is widely agreed that they are entirely inadequate to deal with emerging problems of resource management in the region. Among other things, they are not comprehensive in their coverage, they are widely regarded as inequitable with respect to their distributive consequences, and they do not provide adequately for the conservation of several important renewable resources. Finally, there currently exist numerous claims and counterclaims of a unilateral nature which are relevant to the governance of Beringia. Some of these claims are in the form of official national legislation such as the Canadian Arctic Waters Pollution Prevention Act of 1970. Others are much more informal such as Soviet claims concerning jurisdiction over the Northern Sea Route. These unilateral claims add up to a substantial collection of unresolved jurisdictional issues which will require explicit consideration during the course of this study.

In general, then, it seems accurate to conclude that the existing international arrangements for Beringia involve large elements of inchoateness. In this connection, three specific points stand out in terms of the concerns of this study. To begin with, the central axis of

16

the emerging jurisdictional conflicts in the region is the growing clash of interests between coastal states and distant-water states.[11] Next, there seems little doubt that the prevailing governing arrangements for Beringia have begun to produce highly inefficient outcomes that work to the disadvantage of all relevant actors quite apart from questions involving the allocation of values among participants. Finally, there are no systematic efforts now under way to reformulate or restructure the regime for the Beringian region (in contrast to the global focus of the law of the sea conference) in order to improve the management of natural resources and the maintenance of environmental quality in the region.[12] Given the serious damage to common interests that has already occurred in such international regions as the Baltic Sea and the Mediterranean Sea and the even more serious damage that will almost certainly occur in the absence of restorative measures, it seems to me that there is a compelling case for a careful reconsideration of the governing arrangements for Beringia. This essay is intended as an initial step in this direction.

C. Changing Conditions

In earlier times, the inchoateness of the Beringian regime did not pose severe problems both because Beringia was undeveloped or only lightly developed in most respects and because the region was not a focus of conflicting human claims. Even in the case of commercial fisheries, the harvests were usually small enough relative to the supply so that the demands of all participants could be met without seriously depleting stocks.[13] And it may be that the issue of restructuring the international regime for Beringia would never have arisen except for the impingement of modern technological society on the region. However, a number of developments have occurred in recent years which make it clear that Beringia is now poised on the brink of a series of events that will determine irrevocably the region's role in the future of human utilization of the earth's resources. A few examples will serve to illustrate this point.

First, large reserves of oil and natural gas have been positively identified in Beringia. Development activities in this realm currently focus on onshore fields in such areas as the North Slope of Alaska and the Mackenzie Delta of Canada. However, speculative estimates indicate the presence of large reserves of oil and natural gas in offshore geological structures in the Gulf of Alaska, the Bering Sea, the Chukchi Sea, and the Beaufort Sea, and pressures are mounting rapidly to begin exploiting these resources on a large-scale basis.[14] These developments

17

raise important questions concerning the environmental impact of offshore production operations as well as the delineation of national jurisdictions on the continental shelves.

Second, the Beringian region is increasingly coming to the attention of those who are concerned with maritime commerce and navigation. The Northern Sea Route is now kept open for approximately 150 days a year and is utilized relatively heavily by the Soviet Union during the summer months. Tanker operations originating at Port Valdez are scheduled to reach major proportions before the end of this decade.[15] There has been considerable interest in the potential uses of the Northwest Passage for maritime commerce since the voyages of the *Manhattan* in 1969 and 1970. There are also possibilities of making use of ice-strengthened surface vessels and submarine tankers in trans-arctic navigation.

Third, while large portions of Beringia have been highly productive in terms of commercial fisheries for some time, many of the Beringian stocks are now being fished to capacity, and there is growing evidence that some of these stocks are being seriously depleted by uncoordinated fishing practices on the part of the fleets of the major states involved. Problems with the sockeye salmon runs in the Bristol Bay have been particularly dramatic and well-publicized since 1972,[16] but the issues involved extend to many species of pelagic, demersal, and sedentary fish as well.[17] Moreover, there is no doubt that the international fisheries of Beringia are currently managed on a highly inefficient basis so that it should be possible to alter existing arrangements in ways that would benefit all relevant participants.

Fourth, arctic and sub-arctic regions (like deserts) are environmentally fragile in certain important respects so that large-scale development for human use can cause extensive and irrevocable damage to the habitat unless it is carried out with great care. So, for example, it is widely believed that large oil spills in arctic waters will take considerably longer to decompose or disperse than similar spills in warmer waters, and large-scale disturbances of a layer of tundra over permafrost can take many decades to heal completely. Beyond this, unfolding developments in Beringia are now bringing into focus the fact that the exploitation of two or more resources (e.g. fish and oil) in the same region simultaneously may well generate serious conflicts and necessitate a careful examination of value trade-offs among the activities involved. In Beringia, efforts to exploit the resources of the outer continental shelf will certainly raise important issues of this type during the near future.[18]

18

D. The Problem Formulated

In contrast to Antarctica, then, Beringia is now beginning to feel the impact of a far-reaching upsurge of human interest along a number of dimensions.[19] These developments have proceeded far enough already to raise serious problems, but they have not yet gone so far as to damage the renewable resources of the region irreparably or to injure the quality of the Beringian environment irrevocably.[20] It is this combination of facts that seems to me to make the current inchoate governing arrangements of the region unacceptable for the future. The purpose of this essay is *not* to propose the removal of Beringia from the flow of human concerns and to advocate the transformation of the region into a permanent wilderness area. On the contrary, the central objective is to analyze institutional arrangements aimed at exploiting the vast natural resources of Beringia efficiently and distributing the proceeds fairly while minimizing the resultant damage to the quality of the region's environment.

After laying out a relatively detailed conceptual framework, I shall examine in some depth the evolving problems of resource management in Beringia. This will make it clear why the existing regime in the region is bound to produce unfortunate consequences under current conditions. Subsequently, I shall identify several alternative regimes or sets of institutional arrangements that could be introduced in Beringia during the foreseeable future. I shall explore the probable social (or group) consequences of each of these alternatives in some detail and assess their implications for the individual interests of the principal actors in the region. Finally, I shall conclude the essay with a discussion of a proposed regime for Beringia which strikes me as sensible in light of the preceding analysis.

Notes

1. For example, Terence Armstrong, a well-known student of the region, speaks of 'the rapidly rising level of exploitation of resources in the Arctic, the international legal problems this would pose, and the threat to the environment implicit in any large-scale exploitation' [*Polar Record*, 16 (1972), 100].
2. For an illuminating discussion of such trade-offs in the context of living species see Frank T. Bachmura, 'The Economics of Vanishing Species', *Natural Resources Journal*, 11 (1971), 674–692.
3. An important collection of essays on Beringia by natural scientists is David M. Hopkins ed., *The Bering Land Bridge*, (Standford 1967).
4. Though the Sea of Okhotsk contains important fisheries, it is generally treated as part of the Northwestern Pacific Ocean and is not included in the

Beringian region in this study.

5. For a fuller description of these features consult Center for Northern Studies, 'Toward a Responsible Regime for Beringia', (Wolcott, Vermont 1973).

6. There are several measures in terms of which it is possible to evaluate the biological productivity of oceanic water masses. Harry L. Rietze, for example, asserts that 'The concentration of nutrient materials in the subarctic Pacific is . . . greater than in any other oceanic water mass' ['Alaska Fisheries', Sidney Shapiro ed., *Our Changing Fisheries*, (Washington 1971), 260]. Other experts dispute this claim to primacy, but there is no doubt that large portions of the Beringian seas are extremely highly productive in biological terms.

7. In this connection, the following point is particularly noteworthy: 'With the advent of large, mobile distant water fishing fleets — essentially a development of the past 10 years — the threat of rapid depletion of fish stocks becomes real' (William M. Terry, 'International Facets', Shapiro, *op. cit.*, 160).

8. Thus, 'The extent of the Continental Shelf off Alaska is estimated by the U.S. Coast and Geodetic Survey to be 550,000 sq. miles, or about 65 percent of the total Continental Shelf off the United States' (Rietze, *op. cit.*, 259). Furthermore, this does not include the extensive area on the Soviet side of the so-called 'Convention Line'.

9. Many of these stem from the ecological characteristics of arctic and subarctic regions. The relevance of these factors is discussed in detail later on in this essay.

10. The first substantive session of the Third United Nations Law of the Sea Conference took place in Caracas during the summer of 1974; a second session convened in Geneva during the spring of 1975, and a third session is scheduled for New York in 1976. Any general legal developments emanating from this conference (even including a failure to reach specific agreements) will have considerable relevance for the future of the Beringian region.

11. For background information on this range of issues see John R. Stevenson and Bernard H. Oxman, 'The Preparations for the Law of the Sea Conference', *AJIL*, 68 (1974), 1–32.

12. To the best of my knowledge, this essay constitutes the first systematic effort to examine the issues involved in restructuring the governing arrangements for Beringia to deal with the rapidly emerging problems of resource management in the region.

13. In the 1930's, there was already some concern about the condition of the Beringian stocks of halibut and certain species of salmon. Even in these cases, however, the problem of stock depletions has taken on qualitatively new proportions in recent years.

14. The world energy 'crisis', which has emerged since the fall of 1973, has generated rapidly expanding pressures to begin exploiting these reserves of oil and natural gas even before the probable environmental consequences of such exploitation are fully explored.

15. The trans-Alaska pipeline is presently expected to come on line at a rate of approximately 1.2 million barrels of oil per day sometime during 1977. It is slated to reach a flow of about 2 million barrels per day toward the end of the decade. All this oil will be shipped by tanker from the tanker port at Valdez now under construction.

16. See, for example, 'Alaska Fishery May Close', *Polar Times*, 77 (1973), 4.

17. Note also the proposition that 'Because of the migratory nature of much of the North Pacific's natural resources — the fur seal, whale, sea lion, herring, halibut, etc. — sound management necessarily becomes a matter of

international cooperation and exploitation one of international competition'
[George Rogers, 'The North Pacific as an International Marine Region:
Patterns of Conflict and Cooperation', *Inter-Nord*, 8 (1966), 159].

18. A particularly interesting American development in this context is the recent
creation of four Outer Continental Shelf Offices within the Bureau of Land
Management of the Department of the Interior. One of these offices focuses
on the offshore provinces adjacent to Alaska and is located in Anchorage
(the others deal with the California coast, the Gulf of Mexico, and the
Atlantic coast).

19. For comparative material on the situation of Antarctica see Howard J.
Taubenfeld, 'A Treaty for Antarctica', *International Conciliation*, No. 531,
January 1961 and Edvard Hambro, 'Some Notes on the Future of the
Antarctic Treaty Collaboration', *AJIL*, 68 (1974), 217–226.

20. For a discussion that is highly relevant to this point see Robert B. Weeden
and David R. Klein, 'Wildlife and Oil: A Survey of Critical Issues in Alaska',
Polar Record, 15 (1971), 479–494.

CHAPTER II

CONCEPTUAL FRAMEWORK

The purpose of this chapter is to lay out the conceptual framework
employed in this study. For convenience, the discussion has been
organized around four central themes. In the first instance, I shall
develop the concept of an international resource region since I propose
to portray Beringia as a member of the set of such regions. Next, I
should like to introduce the principal actors with a stake in Beringia
together with their key interests. At this stage, I shall limit the discussion to a brief characterization of the *dramatis personnae* concerned
with problems of resource management in the region. The following
section of the chapter outlines the major substantive issues that arise
in the analysis of resource management in the North Pacific. It should
become apparent from this initial discussion that the international
relations of resource management in this geographical region are
relatively complex. The chapter concludes with a brief assessment of
the concept of a regime as a system of government for a specified area.
This will set the stage for the more systematic analysis of the probable
consequences of alternative regimes for Beringia which is a prominent
concern of later sections of this essay.

A. International Resource Regions

An international resource region is a geographical area demarcated in
terms of the functional issues associated with the management of natural
resources and the maintenance of environmental quality. All such
regions must exhibit the following distinctive characteristics. First, they

must constitute natural systems or meaningful managerial units from the perspective of efforts to manage resources and maintain environmental quality. Second, international resource regions must be affected by multiple sovereign jurisdictions or lie outside the sovereign jurisdiction of any given state. That is, a region of this type must not be subject to effective management on the part of a single state.

It is possible to identify a number of distinguishable bases of international resource regions.[1] In the first instance, there are numerous natural systems that cut across the jurisdictions of individual states but that are far from global in their extent. Thus, international fisheries commonly extend into several sovereign jurisdictions but most of them are confined to a relatively well-defined geographical region.[2] The salmon fisheries of the North Pacific constitute a clearcut case in point. Similarly, many types of marine pollution have a distinct regional configuration without being global in their implications.[3] In this connection, 'Regional problems result from physical, including biological, linkages between two or more nations, with little or no spillover to the world at large because of the particular combinations of relatively low persistency of pollutants and relatively limited scope of the natural systems involved in transporting them'.[4] In such cases regional coordination is important from a managerial point of view but there is no reason to transform these issues into global concerns.

Geographical regions may also exhibit special physical features that make regional coordination desirable without calling for global attention. So, for example, many international resource regions are essentially mediterraneans in the sense that they involve situations in which a number of surrounding states wish to utilize the resources of a marine area simultaneously. Here there are typically conflicts among alternative uses of the region's resources as well as problems of depletion when two or more of the relevant states wish to exploit the same resource in the region.[5] Beyond this, regions often display special climatic conditions or ecological characteristics that strongly suggest management on a regional basis. Where ecosystems cut across national boundaries, as in the Arctic, it is impossible to manage them effectively through uncoordinated national actions, though global management is often unnecessary.

In many cases, the socioeconomic bases of international resource regions are just as compelling as the physical bases. Efforts to exploit resources frequently generate important dependencies or interdependencies among states that are regional rather than global in scope. A few examples will make this proposition clear. It is common for the

23

fishermen of two or more states to be interested in exploiting the same stocks of fish. This is the case, for example, with Japanese and Soviet efforts to harvest various demersal fish in the eastern Bering Sea. Also, situations frequently arise in which the nationals of one state wish to exploit resources under the complete or partial jurisdiction of another state.[6] Thus, Japanese and Soveit fishermen have a strong interest in harvesting various species of crabs along the continental shelves adjacent to the United States in the eastern Bering Sea and the Gulf of Alaska. Beyond this, situations often arise in which one state seeks transit rights through areas under the jurisdiction of another state. Recent Canadian-American interactions concerning the potential use of the Northwest Passage as well as a pipeline for natural gas across Canada raise interesting questions along these lines. In all these cases, socioeconomic dependencies or interdependencies generate persuasive reasons to engage in joint or coordinated management programs on a regional basis. But they do not indicate a pressing need for global, as opposed to regional, forms of coordination.

All this suggests that there are often substantial gains to be achieved by transcending national perspectives in efforts to manage natural resources and to maintain environmental quality. Further, it seems reasonable to suppose that there will be cases in which transaction costs will not be prohibitive when coordinated management arrangements are regional in scope and limited to a relatively small number of actors. At the same time, transaction costs ordinarily rise steeply as the number of actors participating in a management scheme increases.[7] This is true both of the initial costs involved in negotiating the basic agreement and of the ongoing costs associated with the implementation and operation of the management system. The current global negotiations concerning the law of the sea illustrate this point with particular clarity.[8] Accordingly, there will almost always be powerful incentives to restrict the scope of international coordination mechanisms in the realms of resource management and environmental quality, even though there may be numerous cases in which the case for some coordination above the level of individual states is compelling. The conclusion to be drawn from this argument is that international resource regions are apt to become increasingly prominent during the near future not only because of the configuration of certain natural systems but also because of the impact of important socioeconomic forces.

My intention in this discussion is not to propose international resource regions as an exclusive alternative either to national management practices or to certain global arrangements relevant to resource management and environmental quality.[9] Instead, I wish to argue for a perspective in which the region is treated as the appropriate managerial unit for purposes of coping with some well-defined problems while other administrative levels are retained in other areas. Thus, many functional activities would remain subject to regulation and management on the part of individual states. Similarly, global rules and institutional arrangements would continue to be operative with respect to some issues. Nevertheless, special regional regimes would be introduced to deal with those functional activities in the realms of resource management and environmental quality for which the region emerges as the most appropriate managerial unit. In this context, the argument for regional arrangements in the realms of resource management and environmental quality is analytically parallel to the argument for customs unions in the realm of standard economic interactions. The essential idea is to supplement other administrative or managerial units rather than to replace them.

Even if the basic idea of working with international resource regions is accepted, there remains a serious demarcation problem in specific cases. A little reflection will make it clear that there are numerous possible boundary criteria in specific cases and that these criteria will often produce results that are not congruent. Even in the case of criteria involving purely physical features, incongruities are the rule rather than the exception. With respect to the Arctic, for example, the tree line and the 10°C isotherm for July identify areas that diverge considerably.[10] Beyond this, there is no reason to assume that the areal configurations of different resources will be identical. Thus, international fisheries typically exhibit different patterns of distribution than geological structures containing reserves of oil and natural gas. Moreover, there are cases in which political rigidities interfere with efforts to determine the most appropriate boundaries for an international resource region. This will occur when certain states refuse to participate in coordinated management systems or when self-interest prompts parties to attempt to distort the evidence concerning the areal configuration of relevant natural systems.

Under the circumstances, it is clear that it will generally be impossible to resolve the demarcation problem for international resource regions with precision. Fortunately, however, it is ordinarily unnecessary to achieve absolute precision concerning the outer boundaries of such a region in order to proceed with coordinated management practices. Widespread agreement on a core area is usually

25

sufficient to serve as a basis for the implementation of managerial arrangements. The precise scope of specific arrangements can then be determined on the basis of experience combined with *ad hoc* negotiations among the affected parties. This point takes on considerable importance in light of the fact that even when outer boundaries are difficult to agree upon, there is often substantial consensus concerning the nature of the core area of a given region.

The specific case of Beringia illustrates many of the preceding comments about the nature of international resource regions. It would be difficult indeed to obtain widespread consensus concerning the exact location of the outer boundaries of this region. And we will certainly want to be free to think in terms of somewhat different areal configurations in analyzing the management of the various resources of the region. Nevertheless, I think it is accurate to say that there is a high level of consensus concerning the core area of Beringia. Húlten thought of Beringia in terms of ' . . . the vast arctic lowland [in the land bridge area] that must have been exposed during the worldwide glacial epochs.'[11] Hopkins describes Beringia as including '. . . western Alaska, Northeastern Siberia, and the shallow parts of Bering and Chukchi Seas.'[12] Most other scientists working in this area would find these formulations acceptable. Though it will become clear as this essay progresses that there are good reasons for extending the domain of Beringia somewhat in dealing with specific resource problems, this agreement on the core area of Beringia gives us a reasonably solid base from which to embark on the analysis of the problems of resource management of this region.

It also seems desirable at this point to comment briefly on several distinctive features of Beringia as an international resource region. In the first instance, it is a resource rich but currently relatively undeveloped region situated in the midst of the developed world and dominated by the major industrialized states. This means that issues concerning economic development will dominate the managerial horizon in Beringia during the foreseeable future.[13] It also suggests that this region is likely to be an important battleground in the emerging conflict between those who wish to pursue traditional patterns of economic development and those increasingly concerned with such non-economic values as the preservation of wilderness areas and the minimization of various forms of pollution.

Next, Beringia is sparsely populated (though it is immensely rich in terms of several important natural resources), and the human population of the region is almost certain to remain limited despite rapid growth in the utilization of Beringia's resources. This indicates that policy-making affecting Beringia will continue to be highly sensitive to the activities of outsiders as it has been in the past. It also implies that non-economic values will be difficult to achieve in Beringia in the face of powerful pressures to pursue standard forms of economic development. This is so because many of the benefits of economic development (e.g. inexpensive oil) will accrue directly to outsiders while many of the costs (e.g. the destruction of wilderness areas) will have no direct impact on most outsiders.[14]

Another distinctive feature of Beringia as a region is that it is economically important primarily as a supplier of natural resources (i.e. raw materials and food products) for the markets of the industrialized states. Combined with the sparse population of the region this fact suggests that there is some danger that Beringia will be exploited and plundered by the major industrialized states without much concern for the quality of the region's environment. There are countervailing forces at work and there is nothing inevitable about such an outcome, but the intrinsic characteristics of the region suggest that potential problems along these lines should be borne in mind constantly.[15]

Finally, Beringia is characterized by the severity of its arctic and sub-arctic conditions. These conditions take such forms as sea ice, permafrost, extreme cold, and biological depauperization. Such conditions raise the costs of exploiting most natural resources and make much of Beringia inhospitable for large human populations. Even more important, however, they contribute to the characteristic ecological fragility of the region. This means that many of the concerns that have been expressed about the ecological destruction that could flow from large-scale economic development in Beringia are quite realistic.[16]

B. Actors and Interests

Since this study deals with resource management at the international level, it is hardly surprising that the most important actors to be considered are states or nation states. However, there are other types of actors that have major interests in Beringia and that cannot be ignored in any attempt to sort out the various problems of resource management in the region. These other actors include: states (in the American federal sense) and provinces, bureaucratic interests within federal and state governments, corporate actors and economic groups, organizations of native peoples, and private interest groups. Though the interests of these various actors sometimes overlap, they are seldom identical and they are frequently incompatible. Therefore, any

27

study of resource management must consider the complex interactions of these actors as they pursue their different goals and objectives. The purpose of this section is to introduce the most important of these actors in a preliminary way.

Four states currently dominate the scene with respect to interstate relations in the Beringian region. These are the United States, the Soviet Union, Japan, and Canada. No institutional arrangements for resource management in the region can succeed without taking into account the interests of these states. There are, in addition, several other states (e.g. the Republic of Korea, Taiwan, Poland, and East Germany) which have recently begun to play some role in the region, at least in the realm of commercial fishing. Their interests may become a factor of growing importance in efforts to manage the renewable resources of Beringia. Beyond this, a great number of states have a potential or indirect interest in the resources of Beringia since the region is a rich source of animal protein and hydrocarbons. But it is unlikely that such states will play an important role in developing arrangements for the management of the region's resources, unless the international system as a whole experiences dramatic and quite unforeseen transformations during the near future.

The United States is primarily a coastal state with respect to commercial fishing (with some notable exceptions like the tuna industry).[17] This is especially true of the Beringian region in which American fishing interests are focused predominantly in the Gulf of Alaska and the eastern Bering Sea. Moreover, though the American consumption of fish products continues to rise, commercial fishing is a particularly inefficient and unhealthy industry in the United States. Therefore, fishing is a somewhat marginal American concern at the federal level, despite the fact that fishing interests are relatively vocal and influential in several regions of the country including Alaska.[18] With respect to hydrocarbons, on the other hand, the story is notably different. The United States is the world's largest consumer of fossil fuels; problems associated with the supply of energy have come to occupy a central place in American politics in the wake of developments in the Middle East since the fall of 1973, and the major oil interests are highly influential at all levels of government in the United States. Therefore, there is every reason to believe that the United States will endeavor to play a central role in the development and management of the major reserves of oil and natural gas which are now being identified in the Beringian region. In the realm of transportation, the United States has in recent history been one of the leading advocates of freedom of navigation and relatively unrestricted use of territorial waters and straits as well as the high seas. As this orientation has emanated primarily from a desire on the part of the military to maintain maximum freedom of transit in the world's waterways rather than from any powerful concern with maritime commerce, there is good reason to believe that the United States will continue to be a supporter of maximum freedom of navigation in the foreseeable future.[19] With respect to the Beringian region, this means, for example, that the United States is strongly opposed to the so-called 'sector principle' and in favor of keeping the Arctic as free of national claims as possible.[20] Finally, it is important to note that the United States is becoming increasingly sensitive to environmental issues at the international level. This is not to say that the maintenance of environmental quality will take precedence over freedom of navigation in the American hierarchy of values when the two interests clash.[21] But there is good reason to conclude that this growing concern with the environment will have a real impact on such matters as the management of the resources of the outer continental shelves in Beringia.

The Soviet Union has experienced a dramatic expansion of its maritime interests in the post-World War II period. From a position of relative insignificance, the country has risen to a prominent place in the areas of naval power, commercial fishing, and maritime commerce.[22] Accordingly, it is not surprising that the overall Soviet position on the use of the oceans has begun to shift substantially from the somewhat protectionistic or nationalistic posture of earlier days to the orientation of a major maritime power with emphases on such things as freedom of transit and access to common property resources. Under the circumstances, there is little doubt that the American and Soviet positions on the use of the oceans are becoming more compatible, though this does not mean that the two countries see eye to eye on all issues of resource management in Beringia, as we shall see later on in this study. In the North Pacific, the Soviet position on commercial fishing is an ambivalent one. While the Soviets have recently become a major factor in the high-seas fisheries of the eastern Bering Sea and the Gulf of Alaska, they are also anxious to protect the coastal fisheries of eastern Asia from the inroads of the Japanese and, increasingly, the Koreans. The resultant crosspressures make the Soviet posture on the management of the renewable resources of Beringia a tortuous one. With respect to hydrocarbons, the Soviet position in the Beringian region is much less sensitive than that of the United States. The Soviets have obvious potential jurisdictional claims in the area and they have engaged in a certain amount of exploration in such places as the Chukchi Sea. However, the Soviet Union is currently self-sufficient with respect to oil; it contains a substantial portion of the known world reserves of oil and natural gas, and it has been reliably reported that major new strikes are being made in areas of north-western Asia under Soviet jurisdiction (e.g. the Yamal Peninsula).[23] Thus, while the Soviets will undoubtedly be interested in the hydrocarbons of Beringia for political reasons, their economic interest in these resources is not nearly so pressing as that of the United States. In the areas of transportation and maritime commerce, Soviet interests appear to be evolving rather rapidly at the present time. Not only has the Soviet Union become a major factor in international maritime commerce, but such commerce has also begun to play a critical role in the economic development of Soviet Asia.[24] An interesting barometer of Soviet attitudes toward these issues in recent years has been the evolution of Soviet thinking about the role of the Northern Sea Route.[25] With respect to environmental concerns, it is undoubtedly accurate to say that these issues have not yet reached the political prominence in the Soviet Union that they have recently attained in the United States. But the Soviet record on environmental questions is by no means uniformly negative (this seems especially true in the Arctic), and there is evidence that such concerns are now beginning to surface more and more influentially in Soviet politics.

Japanese interests in the resources of the Beringian region are focused overwhelmingly in the area of commercial fisheries. Since World War II, Japanese activities in the region have expanded dramatically so that Japan is now the leading exploiter of many of the Beringian stocks of renewable resources.[26] Moreover, since fish products constitute a particularly important source of protein in Japanese diets and since the high seas fisheries closer to the home islands are now deteriorating quite sharply, the significance of the Beringian fisheries to Japan is difficult to overestimate.[27] Japan is a classic example of a state with predominantly distant-water rather than coastal interests in the realm of commercial fishing. This inevitably brings Japan into conflict with both the United States and the Soviet Union in the Beringian region. Beyond this, Japan has an extreme need for oil and natural gas since it produces virtually no fossil fuels within its own domain. There is no way for Japan to obtain direct jurisdiction over any of the hydrocarbons of Beringia, but the Japanese have expressed a general interest in purchasing oil and natural gas from this region and they can be expected to show an interest in cooperative ventures in which they would help finance the extraction of these resources.[28] It is not surprising, therefore, that American oil executives have already begun to think of Japan as a potential consumer of Alaskan oil when it begins to come on line in large quantities.[29] The Japanese also have a major stake in maritime commerce at the international level. But they have little interest in freedom of transit for security reasons, and they have not yet expressed any serious interest in commercial transportation in the Beringian region (e.g. involving the Northern Sea Route).[30] The Japanese have less concern about jurisdiction in the Arctic than any of the other major states involved in Beringia. And they have yet to express any great concern for the issues involved in the maintenance of environmental quality at the international level, though this may change in the near future. Finally, the Japanese have extensive interests in direct investment in resource-based industries (e.g. timber and minerals) in Canada, western Alaska, and eastern Siberia as well as in the marine portions of Beringia.[31] Should these interests expand the Japanese may come to play a central role in resource management in the Beringian region well beyond the realm of commercial fisheries.

Canadian interests in the resources of Beringia are relatively straightforward. In general, the Canadian position in recent years has been characterized by a substantial growth of concern about national sovereignty and jurisdiction in contrast to the more internationalist orientation of Canada in earlier times.[32] With respect to commercial fishing, Canada is even more fundamentally a coastal state than the United States. Thus, the primary concern of the Canadians in this area focuses on the actual or potential inroads of the Japanese and others in the commercial fisheries of the Pacific Northwest (e.g. the halibut off the coast of British Columbia). Since the major oil strikes on the North Slope of Alaska in 1968, the Canadians have become highly interested in the prospects of locating commercially significant reserves of hydrocarbons in the Canadian Far North. In fact, evidence is now mounting that the Canadian Arctic contains unusually rich deposits of oil and natural gas, though many of these deposits will probably fall outside the Beringian region.[33] While such resources will contribute greatly to the economic strength of Canada, the prospect of them has already sharply heightened Canadian sensitivities where Canadian sovereignty in the Far North is concerned. The main issue here centers on fear of American encroachment either in the form of various types of economic control or in the form of jurisdictional claims in the Arctic. Under the circumstances, Canada has recently embarked on a series of moves aimed at securing Canadian sovereignty in the Far

North, a development that has so far been received rather sympathetically by the Soviet Union and somewhat skeptically by the United States. Related to these developments is the striking growth of Canadian concern about certain international aspects of environmental quality in arctic and subarctic areas. Thus, growing indications of probable economic development in the Far North have induced the Canadians to take such unilateral steps as the promulgation of the Arctic Waters Pollution Prevention Act of 1970.[34] While steps of this kind are not difficult to justify from various points of view, they contain the seeds of potentially serious friction between Canada and the United States.[35]

The interests of South Korea, Taiwan, Poland, and East Germany in Beringia are limited at this time entirely to the realm of high seas fishing.[36] Among these states, only South Korea has so far mounted large enough operations to require consideration in efforts to manage the fish stocks of Beringia.[37] However, the activities of these new entrants in the Beringian fisheries are of potentially great importance. By and large, these activities are not covered by the various regional agreements concerning fisheries which now exist in Beringia. And the expansion of these operations could decisively disrupt the rather delicate balance currently maintained under the terms of such agreements as the International North Pacific Fisheries Convention.[38] In short, the interests of these states point to a serious deficiency in the existing governing arrangements for Beringia.

With respect to the role of states (in the American sense) or provinces as actors in the Beringian region, interest currently focuses overwhelmingly on the role of the State of Alaska. This is due primarily to the fact that other states or provinces with autonomous interests in the region have not yet surfaced in any dramatic fashion. In the Japanese case, such units are not of great importance, and the geographical separation between the home islands and Beringia tends to preclude extensive development along these lines. Soviet resource policies in maritime areas are effectively controlled by the central government, and local authorities in Siberia do not appear to play any autonomous role in planning for the management of the marine portions of Beringia. The Canadian case, by contrast, is at least potentially more interesting. British Columbia has independent provincial interests relating to the regulation of fisheries and the utilization of the resources of the continental shelf. But Canadian fisheries policy is largely under federal control, and the autonomous interests of British Columbia have not yet surfaced in a politically effective fashion. Beyond this, the Yukon and the Northwest Territories (though they are not formally provinces) have extensive interests in the development of the energy resources of the Canadian Far North. However, the population of these territories is so sparse that it may prove impossible for them to achieve any effective political influence vis-à-vis the federal government in the area of resource management.[39]

The case of Alaska, on the other hand, is relatively dramatic. Though Alaska was largely under the jurisdiction of the federal government in earlier times (some would say it has been treated essentially as a colony of the lower forty-eight),[40] relations between the State of Alaska and the federal government with respect to resource management are changing quite rapidly at the present time. The principal sources of contention in this area involve: 1) the locus of governmental authority to deal with various problems of resource management and; 2) the distribution of benefits from such sources as lease sales and royalties. For example, in recent years extensive litigation between the State of Alaska and the federal government has occurred concerning jurisdiction over the waters of the Lower Cook Inlet.[41] It is highly likely that there will be litigation in the near future arising from disputes about jurisdiction over the Beaufort Sea fringe adjacent to Prudoe Bay.[42] And it is possible that efforts to extend the jurisdiction of the State over activities in the Bristol Bay will generate serious contention in the future.[43] Similarly, a major battle is now in the offing between the federal government and the state government concerning resource management on the outer continental shelves and the apportionment of governmental revenue derived from the utilization of these resources. The federal government currently enjoys a strong position in this area under the terms of the governing legislation as interpreted by the Supreme Court in the spring of 1975.[44] However, the climate of political opinion on the key issues at stake appears to be changing considerably, and this may well lead to significant policy changes during the near future, at least in the area of revenue sharing.[45] Beyond this, there are serious federal-state disagreements in the area of fisheries management where current American policies are particularly complex and inefficient[46] as well as in the area of pollution control where there is little reason to suppose that the interests of the state government and the federal government are entirely congruent. In summary, then, it would be a serious mistake to ignore the emerging conflicts between the federal government and the State of Alaska in examining the problems of resource management in Beringia, though it is difficult to predict at this time how these issues are likely to be resolved during the next twenty-five years.

Though we often speak of states and nation-states as coordinated entities at the level of international relations, this vantage point tends to obscure the impact of various bureaucratic interests that are by no means identical with the 'national interests' of the states concerned. Several examples should serve to underscore the relevance of bureaucratic actors and interests within governments regarding the problems of resource management in the Beringian region. In the first instance, military bureaucracies have interests that are pertinent to Beringia in the American, Soviet, and Canadian cases. So, for example, the United States Navy is adamantly committed to a maximalist position with respect to freedom of transit through all waters other than 'internal' waters.[47] The American Navy also has a major stake in the development of hydrocarbons in Beringia emanating from the fact that it currently possesses jurisdiction over United States Naval Petroleum Reserve No. 4,[48] which many believe contains reserves of oil and natural gas as large as those of the Prudhoe Bay fields.[49] For its part, the Soviet military has a long history of extreme sensitivity about jurisdiction in Arctic regions, as evidenced in several noteworthy incidents (e.g. the Vilkitski Strait incident of 1967).[50] This may possibly cause problems for rational resource management in the Arctic in the near future.[51] Similarly, relations between the Soviet Navy and the Soviet fishing fleets are close (involving such things as the training of naval personnel in fishing operations).[52] A situation such as this may make the Soviet Union hesitant about various types of regulatory schemes for fishing operations. In the Canadian case, the military has recently begun to take an active interest in the development of the Canadian North. There is some evidence to suggest that economic development in the Far North will potentially provide a badly needed source of identity for the Canadian military.[53] However, this may produce complications when considering efforts to achieve international coordination of resource management in Beringia.

It is also important to note that different resources as well as environmental issues tend to fall under the jurisdiction of disparate bureaux within any given government. Not only are these bureaux apt to have interests of their own which are not identical with the 'national interest', but it is also common for such agencies to engage in elaborate forms of bureaucratic warfare in which the objective of each bureau is to maximize its own jurisdictional scope and, therefore, power.[54] An Some examples from the American case will serve to highlight the importance of this phenomenon. The following agencies are all relevant to the problems of resource management in Beringia.

Commercial fisheries are under the jurisdiction of the National Oceanic and Atmospheric Administration (NOAA) in the Department of Commerce. Oil and Natural Gas are regulated by the Bureau of Land management (BLM) in the Department of the Interior with continental shelf developments the special province of a subsidiary Outer Continental Shelf (OCS) Office. Environmental issues are the special concern of the Environmental Protection Agency (EPA) and the Council on Environmental Quality (CEQ). Problems of navigation and commerce are of particular concern to the Navy and the Maritime Administration (MARAD) in the Department of Commerce. The Bureau of Indian Affairs (BIA) and the National Parks Service (NPS) in the Department of the Interitor have interests that crosscut the concerns of the other bureaux. Additionally, most of these agencies have their regional counterparts in the government of the State of Alaska. Under the circumstances, it would hardly be surprising if outside observers come away with the feeling that the goal of rational resource management in the Beringian region is one of the early casualties in the conflicts that occur continuously in this labyrinth of bureaucratic organizations.[55]

Turning away from the arena of governmental actors *per se*, we need to take a brief look at the principal corporate actors that are relevant to the problems of resource management in Beringia. In fact, the distinction between governmental actors and corporate actors should not be overemphasized. In a socialist system such as the Soviet Union, the separation is rather between different segments of the bureaucracy. Relations between industry and government in Japan are so close that it is often difficult to identify the real locus of policy-making. Even in the United States, governmental intervention in the corporate world in the form of such things as regulation and *de jure* or *de facto* subsidies is sufficiently extensive to warrant emphasizing the links as well as the gaps between the two.

Two types of corporate actors are particularly prominent in the Beringian region: the major oil companies and the fishing interests. A number of the multinational oil giants have already taken an interest in the hydrocarbon resources of Beringia. The major stakes in the Prudhoe Bay fields are held by Atlantic-Richfield, British Petroleum (BP), and Exxon.[56] In the Canadian Far North, several of the multinationals (e.g. Imperial Oil is a subsidiary of Exxon) are in competition with a company called Panarctic Oil Ltd. in which the Canadian government has a 45% interest.[57] A variety of other companies (e.g. Union, Mobil, Socal) have interests in other parts of Alaska; and most of the major oil companies are at least potentially

35

interested in the oil and natural gas reserves of the outer continental shelves of Beringia.[58] By and large, the oil companies are interested in profit maximization. Under current conditions in the Western world, this is apt to entail a desire to push oil development vigorously in a wide range of areas and to keep environmental concerns within reasonable bounds. But it would be a mistake to assume that the oil companies will invariably wish to maximize production in the short run, especially if the Beringian reserves turn out to be truly extensive.[59] Moreover, the oil companies will inevitably exhibit an interest in selling on the international market (e.g. in Japan, which is an obvious potential consumer of Beringian oil) rather than channeling production entirely into Canada and the United States.[60] This is likely to generate substantial conflicts between the companies and the governments of the United States and Canada which are preoccupied with the idea of energy independence. As indicated above, Canada is already moving in the direction of extending governmental control over the hydrocarbon reserves of the Canadian Far North,[61] and it will be interesting to observe how the United States reacts to this situation as Prudhoe Bay production comes on line and serious development begins to occur in other parts of Beringia.[62]

The corporate situation in the area of fishing interests presents a striking contrast with the case of hydrocarbons. Above all, there are no giant multinational corporations in this area. In the case of the United States, the fishing interests with stakes in the Beringian region are relatively small corporations; many of them are controlled from the lower forty-eight states (though certain fishing interests are politically influential in Alaska), and they have relatively little political power at the federal level.[63] Most of these corporations are somewhat backward technologically, rate poorly in terms of various measures of productivity, and are not very profitable. There is considerable controversy over the extent to which the American fishing industry has been harmed by governmental actions such as the Merchant Marine Act of 1920 (the Jones Act), which has the effect of forcing American fishermen to utilize expensive American-built ships.[64] However, it is difficult to escape the conclusion that the most important determinants of the inefficiency of the American fishing industry lie in the basic organization of the fisheries themselves.[65] In broad terms, this picture seems relatively accurate for the Canadian case as well.[66] Though Canadian fishermen are not hampered by an analogue of the Jones Act, they are also unable to match the efficiency of the Japanese and the Soviets in the waters of Beringia. The Japanese fishing industry, on the other hand, offers a real contrast with the cases of the United States and Canada. Japanese high-seas fishing is dominated by large capital companies such as Taiyo Gyogyo, Nippon Suisan, Nichiro Fisheries, and Kyokuyo Hogei.[67] These companies rely heavily on modern technology, achieve substantial economies of scale, and enjoy considerable influence in governmental circles.[68] For its part, the government operates an extensive licensing system, which serves to minimize competition among the Japanese high-seas fishing fleets. Even so, fishing is a relatively low-wage industry in Japan, and it is reportedly becoming more and more difficult to attract workers to this industry.[69] Finally, Soviet fishing operations (except for a few local, coastal activities) are fully controlled by the central government through the Ministry of Fisheries. The high-seas fisheries of Beringia are administered by Dalryba, the bureau within the Ministry responsible for all Far Eastern fisheries.[70] Soviet state fisheries are highly modernized, but their development is responsive to a number of factors outside the realm of calculations concerning economic efficiency.[71]

Beringia is also the homeland of several groups of native peoples whose concerns deserve discussion in this survey of actors and interests relevant to the problems of resource management in Beringia. The native peoples of Soviet Beringia (mostly Kamchadel, Koryak, and Chukchi) lack independent organization and have yet to emerge as autonomous actors in this area.[72] Much the same is currently true of the Eskimos of the Canadian Far North and the Indians of British Columbia, though there are now some indications of emerging native claims in Northern Canada as well as some growth of sensitivity to native affairs on the part of the Canadian federal government.[73]

In the case of the United States, by contrast, dramatic developments are occurring with respect to the economic and political roles of the native peoples. The 1970 census recorded approximately 53,000 native peoples in Alaska (Eskimos, Aleuts, and Indians), and the growth rate of these populations is high.[74] These peoples have recently organized themselves into twelve Regional Corporations under the terms of the Alaska Native Claims Settlement Act of 1971.[75] They have substantial financial resources, and they are in the process of taking title to 40 million acres of land in Alaska as specified in the settlement.[76] Moreover, the leaders of these groups have exhibited considerable organizational skills, and they have obtained highly competent legal services. Accordingly, it is not surprising that the Regional Corporations, together with the Alaska Federation of Natives, are rapidly gaining political influence, though the 1971 legislation envisions them as purely

37

economic entities. While it is now clear that the Corporations will play a role of some importance with respect to resource management in Beringia (e.g. a number of the Corporations have signed exploration agreements with various major oil companies),[77] it remains to be seen exactly what the development priorities of the native leadership will be. On the one hand, there is a fascination with the material benefits of modern technological society which the native peoples have not previously enjoyed. At the same time, however, many of the native peoples are becoming increasingly sensitive to the sociocultural and environmental disruptions that are virtually certain to accompany economic development and the introduction of the material benefits of modern technological society. Consequently, the native peoples are now rather ambivalent about their interests, though it is clear that their effective influence is growing in the Beringian region. The future role of these groups constitutes one of the more fascinating elements in the overall picture of resource management in Beringia.

Finally, let me say a few words about private interest groups as actors relevant to the problems of resource management in Beringia. Broadly speaking, two sets of private interest groups deserve mention at this point. In the first instance, there is a wide range of groups whose principal interests can be classified under the heading of conservation.[78] Examples relevant to Beringia include the International Union for Conservation of Nature and Natural Resources (IUCN), the World Wildlife Fund, the National Wildlife Federation, the Wilderness Society, the Environmental Defense Fund, and the Sierra Club.[79] The specific programs and objectives of these organizations differ considerably, but as a group they are currently of growing significance. In specific terms, some of them have played noteworthy roles in the controversy over the trans-Alaska pipeline as well as in efforts to safeguard the Polar Bear and several endangered species of great whales.[80] More generally, the activities of such groups have undoubtedly contributed to the growing awareness of environmental problems which is now filtering into most segments of society, including governmental agencies.[81] Nevertheless, they have not yet achieved a high level of coordination among themselves, and as of yet they are hardly a match for actors like the multinational oil companies.

The other set of private interest groups that deserve mention at this point center on the concerns and needs of tourists. Beringia has recently experienced a rapid upsurge of tourist interest (tourists now go to such places as Barrow, Prudhoe Bay, and the Pribilof Islands), and it appears that this interest will continue to grow despite concomitant increases in costs.[82] This is a development of some significance not only because tourists have certain special needs, but also because they can generate serious dangers to floral and faunal conditions in ecologically delicate areas if their activities are not handled carefully. Accordingly, the growth of interest groups organized around the concerns of tourists is a matter that needs to be recognized and taken seriously in thinking about the problems of resource management in the Beringian region.

C. Substantive Issues

Having introduced the principal actors concerned with resource management in Beringia, I want to take a brief look at the substantive issues at stake. Any regime for the management of natural resources in Beringia will produce consequences in a number of distinguishable functional areas, in contrast to physically specifiable domains. Though there are significant interaction effects, I believe it is useful to think in terms of the following functional areas: fish and marine mammals, hydrocarbons, transportation and navigation, environmental quality, and security.

1. *Fish and Marine Mammals.* The issues in this area focus on the management of renewable resources that are of substantial interest to several sovereign states and that have been treated as common property resources in recent history.[83] In the case of Beringia, commercial fishing is highly developed south of the Bering Strait. There is extensive interest in various species of anadromous, pelagic, demersal, and sedentary fish as well as several species of marine mammals. The fisheries involve complex interactions between the interests of predominantly coastal states such as the United States and primarily distant-water states such as Japan. Important problems of conservation have come sharply into focus in recent years as some of the Beringian stocks have been fished extremely heavily. None of the relevant stocks are now harvested in an economically efficient fashion.[84] Conflicts concerning the distribution of the harvest are becoming more and more prominent in this region. The renewable resources of Beringia are currently exploited more heavily than any of the region's other resources, and it is in this area that the most complex problems of coordinated management presently occur.

2. *Hydrocarbons.* With respect to non-renewable resources, interest in the Beringian region focuses overwhelmingly on the prospects of identifying large reserves of oil and natural gas in the area. In contrast to the case of renewable resources, management problems in this area are now largely incipient rather than full-blown since little oil or natural

gas is actually being produced in Beringia at this time.[85] However, Prudhoe Bay oil is scheduled to come on line in 1977; there are numerous indications of the existence of massive reserves of oil and natural gas in the Beringian region, and it is certainly not premature to begin thinking about the international aspects of resource management in this functional area. A number of important questions come to mind immediately in this connection. How will jurisdictional conflicts among the United States, the Soviet Union, and Canada be settled in the case of offshore oil and natural gas? Will the exploitation of offshore oil and natural gas in Beringia generate conflicts with the highly developed commercial fisheries of the region? Are there reasons to believe that various forms of pollution emanating from offshore production are apt to be particularly common or unusually difficult to cope with in the Beringian region? Will governments tend to become more directly involved in the exploitation of hydrocarbons in this area as is currently happening with respect to offshore production in the North Sea?[86]

3. *Transportation and navigation.* Here we must think primarily in terms of what are coming to be described as flow resources, in contrast to renewable and non-renewable resources. Up to now, navigational issues affecting Beringia have focused more on the conerns of various navies than on the interests of groups involved in maritime commerce. Consequently, questions of access and transit rights have been the principal issues arising in this functional area. For example, there have been periodic disagreements between the United States and the Soviet Union over the rights of American warships (including Coast Guard vessels) in the Kara, Laptev, and East Siberian Seas. But this picture is now beginning to change. The production of oil in the Beringian region will raise important new issues in the realm of transportation.[87] The region is a growing focal point in air transport patterns between Europe, North America, and East Asia. There is also increasing interest in various forms of maritime transport involving arctic and sub-arctic routes. Therefore, it seems reasonable to conclude that new issues will arise in this functional area to join the traditional problems of access and transit rights. These issues will probably revolve around such problems as traffic regulation, ship-based pollution, and conflicts over other uses of the marine areas.

4. *Environmental quality.* This functional area is somewhat ill-defined and tends to cut across the other areas in complex ways. In general, what I have in mind here is a range of problems that arise as a consequence of large-scale human use of natural resources. In the specific case of

Beringia, a number of concrete problems along these lines are currently prominent and are likely to raise international questions in the foreseeable future. Thus, problems concerning the conservation of living species have been important in the region for some time (e.g. efforts to protect the fur seal and the sea otter go back to the late nineteenth century).[88] Similarly, a variety of actual or potential pollution problems are beginning to receive serious attention in the context of Beringia (e.g. relatively intensive studies have been conducted concerning the probable impact of oil terminal operations at Valdez on the waters of Port Valdez and Prince William Sound).[89] Beyond this, interest is now growing in the problems of preserving the physical habitat as well as various cultural values under the impact of large-scale economic development.[90] More generally, there is no doubt that it will be important to think more systematically in the near future about various value trade-offs in the realm of resource management in rapidly developing regions like Beringia. For example, the production of oil and natural gas on the outer continental shelves will conflict with some forms of commercial fishing and with efforts to preserve the natural habitat.[91] Under the circumstances, it will become necessary to make difficult choices among the values in question.

5. *Security.* The functional area of security does not pose problems of resource management in the same sense as the various issue areas introduced in the preceding paragraphs. Nevertheless, Beringia is a region in which the security interests of several great powers impinge directly upon each other. It encompasses the point of closest physical proximity of the United States and the Soviet Union.[92] Because the area is so sparsely populated states with major interests in the area periodically become concerned with perceived threats to their claims of sovereign jurisdiction in the region. Discoveries of oil and natural gas in the region will only serve to accentuate the existing problems emanating from the fact that Beringia and the Arctic are among the few areas of the world in which there remain major ambiguities in the delineation of national sovereignties.[93] Under the circumstances, it seems highly relevant to ask questions about the extent to which the security interests of the major actors in the region are likely to impinge on the prospects of achieving coordinated solutions for the region's major problems of resource management. Will security problems prove to be a lesser or greater obstacle to functional cooperation in Beringia than in other geographical regions of the world?

If we shift from functional areas to physically specifiable domains, it is possible to obtain an additional perspective on the substantive problems of resource management in Beringia. Consider first the notion of vertical domains, starting from the bottom and working up. To begin with, there are the resources of the seabed and the subsoil under the seabed. In the case of Beringia, the critical issues here center on the resources of the continental shelves.[94] This is partly due to the fact that a high proportion of the Beringian seabed is composed of continental shelves[95] and partly to the fact that the resources of these continental shelves (e.g. sedentary fish and hydrocarbons) are of great significance. In this connection, it is important to note that the continental shelves between western Alaska and eastern Siberia are continuous so that the usual criteria of demarcating the boundaries of national jurisdiction over continental shelves are not applicable.[96] Accordingly, the treatment of the outer continental shelves constitutes both an issue of importance and a source of potential conflict in the Beringian region.

Moving on, we come to the domain of the water column. The critical resource issues here focus on the management of stocks of fish and marine mammals and on the regulation of various forms of pollution. With respect to fisheries, the current difficulties stem from the inadequacies of decentralized management practices in combination with the common property status of the resource. In the case of pollution, there are special problems of biodegradation in arctic and sub-arctic waters and of oil spills associated with offshore drilling. The next vertical domain is the surface of the Beringian seas. The principal problems in this domain are those emanating from activities in the realm of transportation and navigation. Here we need to think about such problems as the establishment of traffic regulations, the control of various forms of pollution, and the minimization of gear conflicts between different types of fishing operations. Moreover, the sea's surface is a focal point of security concerns in Beringia in the sense that it remains the principal plane of naval operations even in the age of nuclear-powered submarines. Finally, there is the vertical domain composed of the superjacent airspace over the Beringian region. Here the principal issues have to do with the use of the airspace for transportation and with the special implications of aerial activities and air defense zones in the realm of security.[97] So far, the management problems in this domain seem considerably less pressing than those associated with the other vertical domains. But it is worth pointing out that air transport in Beringian airspace has been increasing at a relatively rapid rate during recent years.

Domains relevant to the problems of resource management can be delineated horizontally as well as vertically. In this context, the key issues center on the types of jurisdictional arrangements that prevail as we move outward from the land masses of the various states in the region and, therefore, on the problems of managing resources whose natural pattern of distribution cuts across several jurisdictional domains. The first two horizontal domains, internal waters and territorial seas, are often difficult to separate precisely. One of the central issues occuping policymakers in this area is the specification of baselines to serve as authoritative boundaries between internal waters (which can be subjected to unlimited sovereign jurisdiction by the coastal state), and territorial seas.[98] Coastal states interested in extending their unilateral jurisdiction over resources generally favor baselines that maximize the extent of internal waters as well as doctrines that allow for a relatively broad band of territorial seas. In the Beringian region, Canada is increasingly coming to represent interests of this type.[99] Distant-water states wishing to obtain maximum freedom of access to resources adjacent to various coastal states, on the other hand, have every reason to favor restrictive delineations of internal waters and territorial seas. Japan is currently the preeminent occupant of this role in Beringia. Both the United States and the Soviet Union, by contrast, are somewhat cross-pressured in these terms. While the United States has traditionally favored restrictive delineations of internal waters and territorial seas, American fishing interests in Alaska have strong incentives to advocate the expansion of coastal state jurisdiction, and the government of the State of Alaska has good reasons to take an expansive view of the concepts of internal waters and terretorial seas because of the jurisdictional provisions of the Submerged Lands Act of 1953.[100] For its part, the Soviet Union has traditionally behaved like a coastal state anxious to extend its unilateral jurisdiction in the domains of internal waters and territorial seas.[101] But the Soviets how find themselves with a set of interests that give them powerful incentives to downplay their traditional views and to advocate restrictive delineations of these domains.

Proceeding horizontally beyond the band of territorial seas, we come to the central focus of current jurisdictional controversies with respect to horizontal domains. In short, there is an expanding thicket of claims and counterclaims concerning such concepts as contiguous zones, special fishing zones, 'economic zones', and patrimonial seas, all of which involve efforts on the part of coastal states to extend their unilateral jurisdiction over the resources of the oceans in areas adjacent to their territories.[102] The fundamental issue here involves the allocation of the resources of the oceans, and there are real dangers that the requirements of efficient resource management will be drastically subordinated to the short-run desires of individual actors to maximize their individual shares. There is presently a worldwide trend toward the expansion of coastal state jurisdiction in these domains.[103] But there is some reason to doubt whether this trend is likely to be as compelling in Beringia as it apparently is in other regions. Several of the most powerful actors in Beringia (e.g. Japan and the Soviet Union) have major interests that run counter to this trend, and the United States has traditionally adopted a conservative position with respect to the expansion of coastal state jurisdiction, though its concrete interests now leave it rather crosspressured in this realm.

Wherever the contiguous zones or economic zones ultimately end, the residual horizontal domain is composed of the high seas. During recent history, the resources of the high seas have been treated as common property resources without any significant entry restrictions.[104] For reasons examined in some detail in the next chapter such arrangements are apt to be viable only when the resources in question are not heavily utilized. In the case of Beringia, the most important problems in this realm currently involve the management of international fisheries. Whereas the utilization of these fisheries was once relatively light, the rapid expansion of high-seas fishing in the region since the 1950s has produced a situation characterized by heavy usage of these resources.[105]

D. Regimes and Their Evaluation

This study is concerned primarily with the problems of developing an international regime for the management of the natural resources of the Beringian region which is simultaneously acceptable to the principal actors involved and desirable in terms of certain well-defined normative criteria. In this conceptual chapter, my concern is not to examine the details of alternative regimes that may be desirable for Beringia; that task will become important later on in this study. Here I wish to concentrate on the antecedent tasks of clarifying the basic concept of an international regime and of setting forth a set of criteria to be borne in mind in the evaluation of alternative regimes.

At the most general level, a *regime* is a set of agreements among some specified group of actors spelling out: 1) a well-defined distribution of power and authority for the relevant social structure or geographical region, 2) a system of rights and liability rules for the members of the social structure, and 3) a collection of behavioral prescriptions or rules which indicate actions the members are expected to take under various circumstances. In short, a regime is a system of government, though it need not involve the existence of a written constitution or the presence of any formal institutional arrangements. Every social structure will have a regime of some sort at all times, whether the consequences of the regime are generally regarded as desirable or undesirable. Since the interests of the participating actors typically differ considerably, there will be many situations in which the consequences of a given regime are evaluated favorably by some participants and unfavorably by others.[106]

With respect to the distribution of power and authority, regimes can vary along a continuum from extreme centralization to extreme decentralization. Note also that it is logically possible for power and authority to vary independently. It is undoubtedly common to think in terms of regimes in which both power and authority are centralized or in which both are decentralized. Some have hypothesized that stability requires a high degree of congruence between these two elements of regimes. In principle, however, there is no reason why a regime cannot combine centralized authority with decentralized power or *vice versa*. In fact, I would argue that possibilities along these lines are well worth reexamining in the context of the present study of resource management at the international level rather than simply discarding them at the outset on *a priori* grounds.

Rights and liability rules constitute a '. . . set of economic and social relations defining the position of each individual [actor] with respect to the utilization of scarce resources.'[107] Regimes for social structures or regions may vary greatly with respect to the structure of rights and liability rules they exhibit. And these variations will generally have substantial implications for such things as the handling of externalities, the locus of efficient solutions in the use of specific resources, and, above all, the distribution of values among the members of a social structure.[108] So, for example, the expansion of coastal state jurisdiction in marine regions would be highly favorable to the relevant coastal states in distributive terms. Similarly, it is typically more difficult to achieve economic efficiency in common property systems than in social structures in which private property arrangements are dominant.

Regimes may also vary greatly with respect to the content of the behavioral prescriptions they encompass. The only requirement is that there be some agreement among the relevant actors about the nature and content of the pertinent behavioral prescriptions. Therefore, regimes may range from the null case in which the only behavioral prescription is that each member is to behave in whatever way he desires under all conditions to highly structured cases in which there are numerous behavioral prescriptions demanding specific actions under well-defined conditions. It is also pertinent to note that behavioral prescriptions may and often do change substantially even in the absence of any real alterations in the distribution of power and authority in the social structure. Most regimes have specific provisions for the modification or transformation of behavioral prescriptions, whether these provisions take the form of highly articulated legislative procedures or more *ad hoc* procedures involving bargaining and coercive diplomacy.[109] Whether or not it is desirable to say that there has been a change of regime when existing behavioral prescriptions are altered significantly strikes me as a relatively unimportant issue.[110] The main point is to avoid thinking of regimes as rigid and unchanging structures whose existence is somehow separate from ongoing political and economic interactions within the relevant social structure.

It will sometimes be desirable to consider regime types falling at various points along the continua between the polar cases of centralization and decentralization with respect to power and authority. Moreover, there is a common tendency to conceptualize regimes as ideal types. There is no doubt that this practice is frequently helpful in the achievement of analytic clarity. But it is also important to bear in mind that real-world regimes are typically mixtures of several ideal types and that this certainly should not be construed as a criticism of real-world regimes. Similarly, actual regimes tend to evolve continuously in various ways. Once the principal features of a given regime are identified, it is tempting to codify the regime and to treat it as an unchanging structure if only for the sake of intellectual neatness and certitude. But regimes are responsive to a wide range of underlying sociopolitical and economic factors and they tend to shift continuously in the wake of changes in these underlying factors.

This discussion also leads to the following observations about efforts to design appropriate regimes for given social structures or regions. Such efforts will invariably pose the classic contractarian problem.[111] Under real-world conditions (as opposed to the ideal conditions assumed by writers like Rawls), there will seldom be a single regime type that is simultaneously optimal for all the actors in a given social structure or region.[112] Nevertheless, there are apt to be many cases in which some regime types are distinctly preferred to others by all concerned so that the relevant actors have a strong common interest in reaching some agreement with respect to the

46

choice of a regime.[113] Under the circumstances, the selection of a specific regime from the set of undominated regime types will typically become a matter of vigorous bargaining among the members of the social structure.[114]

In closing this section, I wish to articulate a series of criteria of evaluation for the assessment of regimes. I will make extensive use of these criteria later on in this study in examining the probable consequences of alternative regimes for Beringia. The criteria I propose to employ fall into three distinguishable clusters.

1. *Social (or group) consequences.* The issues here concern the consequences of any given regime for the members of a social structure or region taken as a group in contrast to the distribution of values among the members.[115] To what extent would a particular regime lead to the exploitation of the region's resources in an economically efficient fashion? Several formulations of the concept of efficiency are relevant in this context. When the production of standard economic goods is involved (e.g. in the fisheries), efficiency will refer to the equalization of marginal revenue and marginal costs, a condition that permits the maximization of profits or rents. In other situations, efficiency will refer to the maximization of social welfare. The most widely accepted standard in this realm is undoubtedly the notion of Pareto optimality.[116] Thus, a regime will be regarded as inefficient if it yields an outcome that could be improved upon for one or more of the actors in the region without damaging the interests of any of the others.

Efficiency is not the only relevant criterion in the area of social consequences. How extensively would the natural resources of the region be utilized if a given regime were introduced? The issues here concern the absolute level of use and the rate of use of various resources in contrast to the question of whether they are exploited in an economically efficient fashion.[117] In the case of renewable resources, the concept of maximum sustainable yield (MSY) constitutes a helpful yardstick since it is illuminating to enquire whether a given resource is being exploited beyond the level of maximum sustainable yield and, if so, whether such use is likely to lead to serious problems of depletion.[118] With respect to non-renewable resources, on the other hand, the major issues are the rate at which a given resource is depleted and the extent to which this rate conforms to various conceptions of what is socially desirable.[119]

What would be the consequences of a given regime for various values that are not reflected in ordinary market calculations? These

47

values include such things as collective goods, the regulation of externalities or social costs, intangibles not reflected in market prices, and political goals. In resource regions like Beringia, values of this kind typically manifest themselves in the form of issues like the provision of employment opportunities in depressed areas,[120] efforts to protect wilderness areas from the destructive consequences of economic development,[121] and the conservation of living species which are subject to heavy commercial exploitation.[122] Sensitivity to these concerns is apt to be a function of the content of such things as liability rules and behavioral prescriptions, and regimes may vary greatly with respect to these matters.

2. *Distributive implications.* Leaving aside issues relating to the aggregate production of values, there are important questions concerning the distribution of values among the actors with an interest in a given region. Though these questions are often deemphasized in economic analyses of regimes, they lie at the heart of the politics of governing arrangements.[123] What would be the impact of a given regime on the *actual* distribution of values among the relevant actors? That is, who would get what with respect to the principal values at stake; which actors would be particularly favored by the introduction of a given regime, and what specific mechanisms would produce these distributive results?[124]

The discussion of distribution raises inescapable normative issues over and above the empirical questions referred to in the preceding paragraph. To what extent would a given regime do justice to the distributive claims of the actors currently active in the region?[125] Often this is essentially a matter of dividing a finite pool of resources among competing claimants. For example, what are the relative merits of American and Japanese claims to the salmon of the Bering Sea? In other cases, however, distributive justice involves difficult value trade-offs. Thus, does the provision of employment opportunities in western Alaska justify certain sacrifices of economic efficiency with respect to the organization of the fishing industry? Should oil companies be made legally liable for all the negative effects of marine oil spills even if this drives up the price of oil on the open market?[126]

To what extent would a particular regime for a region like Beringia do justice to the actual or potential distributive claims of outsiders? There are in fact several distinguishable issues of this type. Does the regime include provisions for new entrants wishing to utilize the region's resources or does it have the effect of creating an exclusive club limited to the initial members? What are the probable consequences of the regime for outsiders who are consumers of the region's products in the sense that they purchase them in the relevant international markets?[127] Will the regime encourage helpful responses to the needs of the developing countries of the world? This last issue is especially important in the case of a region like Beringia which is rich in resources but dominated by the major industrialized states of the world.

3. *Feasibility.* A final cluster of criteria of evaluation focuses on the political feasibility of regimes. These criteria relate to the implementation and maintenance of regimes in contrast to their probable productive or distributive consequences. To what extent is a given regime likely to prove fundamentally acceptable to the principal actors involved? If a regime type is demonstrably unacceptable within the context of a particular region, there is little point in pursuing it in depth no matter how desirable it may seem from other points of view. Economic and political factors are by no means totally unalterable, and it would be a mistake to discard otherwise desirable regime types solely because their implementation would require certain changes along these lines. However, the pursuit of totally unacceptable regimes is little more than an exercise in the construction of intellectual utopias.[128]

How costly would it be to achieve compliance with the principal behavioral prescriptions of a given regime?[129] This is partly a matter of the extent to which the actions demanded by the relevant prescriptions are regarded as unusually onerous by the actors in question. But it is also a function of such things as the ease of violation without being detected, and probability of known violators being sanctioned, and the nature of the sanctions employed. There are wide variations in the extent to which actors comply with the behavioral prescriptions of different regimes, and a regime that looks attractive on paper may be less desirable than a regime whose prescriptions are intrinsically weaker but likely to be complied with at a much higher level.

To what extent will a given regime prove stable? I use the term 'stability' to mean nothing more than the capacity of a regime to survive over time. The analysis of stability in this sense requires the formulation of some standard in terms of which to judge when qualitative changes from one regime type to another occur in a given social structure or region.[130] But there is no doubt that regimes commonly vary greatly with respect to stability. Note also that stability *per se* is not an unadulterated good. If a given regime is widely regarded as producing desirable outcomes, its continued existence will generally be viewed favorably by the relevant participants. But there are many cases in which stability itself is achieved only at a considerable cost in terms of other valued outcomes. Here it becomes relevant to enquire whether gains with respect to such things as order stemming from the presence of stability are sufficient to offset losses in terms of other values.

Notes

1. For parallel discussions of the concept 'region' in other fields consult John Friedmann, 'The Concept of a Planning Region – The Evolution of an Idea in the United States', John Friedmann and William Alonso eds., *Regional Development and Planning,* (Cambridge 1964), 498–518; Harry W. Richardson, *Regional Economics,* (New York 1969), 223–246, and Jerome Rothenberg, 'Local Decentralization and the Theory of Optimal Goverment', Matthew Edel and Jerome Rothenberg eds., *Readings in Urban Economics,* (Cambridge 1972), 545–568.
2. J. A. Gulland, *The Management of Marine Fisheries,* (Seattle 1974).
3. Oscar Schachter and Daniel Serwer, 'Marine Pollution Problems and Remedies', *AJIL,* 65 (1971), 84–111.
4. Clifford S. Russell and Hans H. Landsberg, 'International Environmental Problems – A Taxonomy', Robert Dorfman and Nancy S. Dorfman eds., *Economics of the Environment,* (New York 1972), 50.
5. See, for example, Leonard B. Dworsky, George R. Franies, and Charles F. Swezey, 'Management of the International Great Lakes', *Natural Resources Journal,* 14 (1974), 103–138.
6. At the present time, there are many cases in which the jurisdictional status of a given area is not entirely clear. For example, recent years have witnessed a proliferation of nationally proclaimed contiguous fisheries zones, but such zones have not yet been clearly recognized in any international convention.
7. E. J. Mishan, 'The Postwar Literature on Externalities: An Interpretative Essay', *Journal of Economic Literature,* IX (1971), 21–24 and Warren J. Samuels, 'The Coase Theorem and the Study of Law and Economics', *Natural Resources Journal,* 14 (1974), 18–20.
8. For relevant background see John R. Stevenson and Bernard H. Oxman, 'The Third United Nations Conference on the Law of the Sea: The 1974 Caracas Session', *AJIL,* 69 (1975), 1–30.
9. For a discussion that adopts a different perspective on some of the same issues see Ernst B. Haas, 'Is There a Hole in the Whole? Knowledge, Technology, Interdependence, and the Construction of International Regimes', *International Organization,* 29 (1975), 827–876.
10. R. Thorén, *Picture Atlas of the Arctic,* (New York 1969).
11. David M. Hopkins ed., *The Bering Land Bridge,* (Stanford 1967), 3.
12. *Ibid.,* vii.
13. For relevant discussions consult George W. Rogers ed., *Change in Alaska,* (College and Seattle 1970), esp. parts IV and V.
14. As an editorial writer in the *Marine Pollution Bulletin* puts it, '. . . there is [a] greater temptation to regard sparsely populated areas as fair game for any kind of wanton and destructive exploitation for the short-term

advantage', [*Marine Pollution Bulletin*, 1 (May 1970), 65].

15. For a well written, though somewhat one-sided, presentation of these concerns see Tom Brown, *Oil on Ice*, (San Francisco 1971).
16. Robert F. Scott, 'Ecology and the Environmental Crisis', Rogers ed., *op. cit.*, 121–131.
17. Lewis M. Alexander, 'National Jurisdiction and the Use of the Sea', *Natural Resources Journal*, 8 (1968), 373–400.
18. Consult, *inter alia*, Arlon Tussing, 'The Place of Trade with Japan and Japanese Investment in Alaska's Economic Development', Arlon R. Tussing *et. al.*, *Alaska-Japan Economic Relations*, Institute of Social, Economic, and Government Research, University of Alaska (1968), 1–86.
19. John R. Stevenson and Bernard H. Oxman, 'The Preparations for the Law of the Sea Conference', *AJIL*, 68, (1974), 1–32.
20. Gordon W. Smith, 'Sovereignty in the North: The Canadian Aspect of an International Problem', R. St. J. Macdonald ed., *The Arctic Frontier*, (Toronto 1966), 194–255.
21. So, for example, the United States has lodged vigorous protests against the Canadian Arctic Waters Pollution Prevention Act of 1970 largely on grounds of freedom of navigation. See H. L. Dickstein, 'International Law and the Environment', George Keeton and Georg Schwarzenberger eds., *Yearbook of World Affairs 1972*, (New York 1972), 245–266.
22. William E. Butler, *The Soviet Union and the Law of the Sea*, (Baltimore 1971).
23. 'Oil Reported Beneath Arctic', *Polar Times*, 65 (December 1967), 28.
24. Terence Armstrong, 'International Transport Routes in the Arctic', *Polar Record*, 16, No. 102 (1972), 375–382.
25. Consult the reports appearing regularly in the *Polar Record* for a record of Soviet activities with respect to the Northern Sea Route.
26. Hiroshi Kasahara and William Burke, *North Pacific Fisheries Management*, RfF Program of International Studies of Fishery Arrangements, Paper No. 2, (Washington 1973).
27. *Ibid.* and Georg Borgstrom, *Japan's World Success in Fishing*, (London 1964).
28. See, for example, 'Siberian Gas-Development Pact Revealed', *Oil and Gas Journal*, 72 (2 December 1974), 47.
29. See 'Slope Oil to Create West Coast Surplus', *Oil and Gas Journal*, 72 (23 December 1974), 12–13. The emergence of such interests would almost certainly generate conflicts with the government of the United States, which is interested in regulating the marketing of oil in order to achieve energy independence for the United States.
30. For a preliminary indication that this may change see Robert Trumbull, 'Japan Seeks Use of Arctic Route', *New York Times*, 12 June 1967 [reprinted in *Polar Times*, 64, (June 1967), 30].
31. See the essays in Tussing *et. al.*, *op. cit.*
32. Allan Gotlieb and Charles Dalfen, 'National Jurisdiction and International Responsibility: New Canadian Approaches to International Law', *AJIL*, 67 (1973), 229–258.
33. R. A. Rudkin, 'Petroleum Potential of Arctic Canada', *Oil and Gas Journal*, 72 (11 March 1974), 147–151.
34. Arctic Waters Pollution Prevention Act of 1970, Revised Statutes of Canada, RSC Ch. 2, 1st. Supplement, c. 47, 1969–1970. The Act actually came into force on 8 February 1972.
35. Gotlieb and Dalfen, *op. cit.*
36. Gulland, *op. cit.* and Kasahara and Burke, *op. cit.* Data on fishing

operations in Beringia is published regularly in the 'Monthly Report', of the Northwest Fisheries Center, National Marine Fisheries Service, National Oceanic and Atmospheric Administration, United States Department of Commerce.

37. Kasahara and Burke, *op. cit.*, 24–26.
38. International Convention for the High Seas Fisheries of the North Pacific Ocean, signed at Tokyo on 9 May 1952 by representatives of the United States, Canada, and Japan (TIAS 2786, 4 UST 380).
39. In fact, resource policies for these territories currently appear to emanate primarily from interactions between the Department of Indian Affairs and Northern Development (DIAND) and the Department of Energy, Mines and Resource in the Canadian federal government.
40. Until recently, well over 90% of the land area of Alaska was under the direct jurisdiction of some agency of the federal government.
41. The jurisdictional claims of Alaska were upheld by the Federal District Court for Alaska and by the Federal Circuit Court of Appeals. Acting on an appeal by the Bureau of Land Management of the Department of the Interior (representing the federal government), however, the Supreme Court overturned these rulings on 23 June 1975 and affirmed the jurisdiction of the federal government over the Lower Cook Inlet (U.S. Supreme Court No. 73–1888).
42. See Howard M. Wilson, 'Pending Burst of Leasing Spells Big Alaskan Search', *Oil and Gas Journal*, 72 (2 December 1974), 27.
43. Presumably, the outcome of the Lower Cook Inlet case has damaged the position of the State with respect to jurisdictional claims in the Bristol Bay. This is true because the historic bay argument employed unsuccessfully by the State in the dispute over the Lower Cook Inlet would also figure in any argument over the Bristol Bay. However, it is important to note that the climate of political opinion concerning these matters now appears to be changing substantially so that the results of past litigation cannot be taken as a certain guide to the probable outcomes of future controversies.
44. The relevant legislation is the Outer Continental Shelf Lands Act, 7 August 1953, (PL 212; 67 Stat. 462). Federal jurisdiction over the outer continental shelf was reaffirmed by the Supreme Court in March 1975 when it ruled against the jurisdictional claims advanced in this area by the State of Maine.
45. See 'Sharing of OCS Revenue Becoming Key Issue', *Oil and Gas Journal*, 73 (14 April 1975), 42–43 and 'Changes Seen Likely in U.S.-Shelf Leasing', *Oil and Gas Journal*, 73 (7 April 1975), 64.
46. The states exercise jurisdiction out to the limit of territorial waters, while the federal government exercises jurisdiction in the contiguous fisheries zone stretching from three to twelve miles. Needless to say, the fish themselves do not conform to these arbitrary boundaries.
47. Stevenson and Oxman, 'The Preparations . . . ', *op. cit.*
48. However, a debate is now arising concerning the appropriate method of exploiting the hydrocarbon reserves of this area. See 'Ford Seeks Private Leasing of NPR 4', *Oil and Gas Journal*, 73 (10 February 1975), 28.
49. See Bob Potterfield, 'Pet-4: Alaska's Next Oil Bonanza', *Alaska Construction and Oil*, 15 (December 1974), 10–13, 16, 18–20 and Bob Potterfield, 'Pet-4 – Still Looking for the Big Strike', *Alaska Construction and Oil*, 16 (April 1975), 66–67, 70, 72, 74, 76.
50. Donat Pharand, 'Soviet Union Warns United States Against Use of Northeast Passage', *AJIL*, 62 (1968), 927–935.

51. William E. Butler, 'The Legal Regime of Russian Territorial Waters', *AJIL*, 62 (1968), 51–77 and S. M. Olenicoff, 'Territorial Waters in the Arctic: the Soviet Position', RAND, R-907-ARPA, July 1972.
52. Terence Armstrong, 'Soviet Sea Fisheries Since the Second World War', *Polar Record*, 13, No. 83 (May 1966), 155–186.
53. On the role of the Canadian military in the development of the Far North see Colin S. Gray, *Canadian Defense Priorities: A Question of Relevance*, (Toronto 1972), 184–193.
54. An effort to develop this point of view theoretically is William A. Niskanen, Jr., *Bureaucracy and Representative Government*, (Chicago 1971).
55. Many observers have commented on the bureaucratic struggle precipitated by the passage of the Alaska Native Claims Settlement Act of 1971 in these terms.
56. 'Alaska: Alyeska Isn't the Whole Story', *Oil and Gas Journal*, 72 (25 November 1974), 78, 80, 83–85, 86, 88, 90, 94, 96.
57. Richard Rohmer, *The Arctic Imperative*, (Toronto 1973), 71–84 and Rudkin, *op. cit.*
58. Bill Schultz, 'After Prudhoe Bay? The Outer Continental Shelf', *Alaska Construction and Oil*, 15 (January 1974), 48–52 and Howard M. Wilson, 'Alaska Report', *Oil and Gas Journal*, 73 (2 June 1975), 73–112.
59. The analysis of these issues is made complex by the mixture of private market incentives and public regulation affecting the behavior of the industry. Thus, 'The petroleum industry operates within the framework of two distinct systems. The first of these is the competitive system where economics and technology largely govern the actions of any firm seeking to maximize its profits. Options available to any firm, however, are constrained by a system of public policies superimposed over the competitive system. It is these two systems working together that make analysis of the petroleum industry extremely complex' [Harry R. Johnson, 'Petroleum in Perspective' *Natural Resources Journal*, 11 (1971), 146].
60. Howard M. Wilson, 'Prudhoe Oil Will Bring Profound Change to West Coast Crude Flow Patterns', *Oil and Gas Journal*, 72 (18 March 1974), 96–100.
61. Michael Crommelin, 'Norway, the North Sea, and Canada', *Northern Perspectives*, II (1974), 5.
62. For background information consult Michael Crommelin, 'Offshore Oil and Gas Rights: A Comparative Study', *Natural Resources Journal*, 14 (1974), 457–500.
63. Lawrence W. Van Meir, 'Economics in Fisheries', Sidney Shapiro ed., *Our Changing Fisheries*, (Washington 1971), 120–133.
64. Merchant Marine Act of 1920, 5 June 1920, (PL 261; 41 Stat. 988).
65. On this point consult the essays in A. D. Scott ed., *Economics of Fisheries Management: A Symposium*, Institute of Animal Resource Ecology, University of British Columbia (1970).
66. Tussing, *op. cit.*, 48.
67. Philip E. Chitwood, 'Japanese, Soviet, and South Korean Fisheries Off Alaska', Fish and Wildlife Service, United States Department of the Interior, Circular 310, (Washington 1969), 2.
68. Borgstrom, *op. cit.*
69. Kasahara and Burke, *op. cit.*, 15. In addition, the Japanese fishing industry is currently experiencing an economic recession.
70. Ole A. Mathisen and Donald E. Bevan, 'Some International Aspects of Soviet Fisheries', *Mershon Center Pamphlet Series No. 7*, Ohio State University (1968), 14–18.

71. Armstrong, 'Soviet Fisheries Since the Second World War', *op. cit.*
72. See Terence Armstrong, 'The Administration of Northern Peoples: The USSR', Macdonald ed., *op. cit.*, 57–88.
73. Rohmer, *op. cit.*, 189–195.
74. These are divided roughly as follows: ½ Eskimo, $3/8$ Indian, and $1/8$ Aleut. The native peoples make up approximately one-sixth of the population of Alaska.
75. The Alaska Native Claims Settlement Act, 18 December 1971, (PL 92–203; 85 Stat. 688).
76. The terms of this legislation are discussed in some detail in Stewart French, 'Alaska Native Claims Settlement Act', Arctic Development and the Environment Program, Arctic Institute of North America, (Montreal and Washington 1972).
77. 'Alaska: Alyeska Isn't the Whole Story', *op. cit.*, 94.
78. The term 'conservation' encompasses a variety of concerns in this context. Such groups range from organizations concerned with safety and rational planning in the realm of resource utilization to organizations whose goal is to prevent the exploitation of certain resources altogether.
79. This list is merely illustrative; there are numerous other organizations of a similar type with interests in Beringia.
80. See, for example, Brown, *op. cit.* and Christian Vibe, 'Can the Polar Bear Survive?' *Polar Times*, 71 (December 1970), 12–13.
81. See Bryan Cooper, *Alaska — The Last Frontier*, (London 1972), 206–227.
82. For some relevant figures consult Stephen M. Brent and Robert M. Goldberg, editors-in-chief, *The Alaska Survey and Report: 1970–1971*, (Anchorage 1970), 189–193.
83. H. Scott Gordon, 'The Economic Theory of a Common Property Resource: the Fishery', *Journal of Political Economy*, LXII (1954), 124–142.
84. A partial exception to this generalization is the international management system for the northern fur seal. Consult George W. Rogers and Don C. Foote, 'The North Pacific Fur Seal Industry, the Record of International Management', *Inter-Nord*, 10 (1968), 151–154.
85. The only oil and natural gas fields currently in the production phase in Beringia are those on the Kenai Peninsula and in the adjacent waters of the Upper Cook Inlet [George W. Rogers, 'Off-Shore Oil and Gas Developments in Alaska: Impacts and Conflicts', *Polar Record*, 17, No. 108 (1974), 255–275].
86. Consult, *inter alia*, Irvin L. White, Don E. Kash, Michael A. Chartock, Michael D. Devine, and R. Leon Leonard, *North Sea Oil and Gas*, (Norman, Oklahoma 1973); 'New U.K. Bill Would Toughen Shelf Controls', *Oil and Gas Journal*, 73 (14 April 1975), 30–31, and 'U.K. Rethinking North Sea Tax Policies', *Oil and Gas Journal*, 73 (20 January 1975), 42.
87. Armstrong, 'International Transport . . .', *op. cit.*
88. Rogers and Foote, *op. cit.*
89. D. W. Hood, W. E. Shiels, and E. J. Kelley eds., *Environmental Studies of Port Valdez*, (Fairbanks 1973).
90. See, for example, the discussions in Rogers ed., *Change in Alaska, op. cit.* and Cooper, *op. cit.*
91. Betzi Woodman, 'OCS Hearings Generate Profound Statements', *Alaska Construction and Oil*, 16 (March 1975), 16–18 and Nancy Munro, 'OCS Development — What it Means', *Alaska Seas and Coasts*, 3 (15 April 1975), 1–4.
92. The distance from Cape Prince of Wales to Cape Dezhnev across the Bering Strait is 50 miles; Big Diomede Island (under Soviet jurisdiction) and Little

Diomede Island (under American jurisdiction) are only 2.5 miles apart [Thorên, *op. cit.*, 1].
93. Smith, 'Sovereignty in the North . . . ', *op. cit.*
94. That is, deepsea mining does not appear to be an important prospect in Beringia. On the issues raised by deepsea mining in contrast to offshore production of hydrocarbons see Ross D. Eckert, 'Exploitation of Deep Ocean Minerals: Regulatory Mechanisms and United States Policy', *Journal of Law and Economics*, 17 (1974), 143–177.
95. The continental shelves between western Alaska and eastern Siberia are continuous throughout the Chukchi Sea as well as a large portion of the Bering Sea. The resultant undersea plain covers several hundred thousand square miles.
96. There are also 'adjacent state' problems in demarcating the boundaries of American and Canadian jurisdiction over the Beringian shelves [Donat Pharand, *The Law of the Sea of the Arctic with Special Reference to Canada*, (Ottawa 1973), 309–318].
97. On the idea of air defense zones see George S. Robinson, 'Military Requirements for International Airspace: Evolving Claims to Exclusive Use of a *Res Communis* Natural Resource', *Natural Resources Journal*, 11 (1971), 162–176.
98. On jurisdiction in the territorial seas see the provisions of the 1958 Geneva Convention on the Territorial Sea and the Contiguous Zone [Convention on the Territorial Sea and the Contiguous Zone, signed at Geneva on 29 April 1958, entered into force on 10 September 1964 (TIAS 5639; 15 UST 1606]. For a helpful commentary consult Philip C. Jessup, 'The United Nations Conference on the Law of the Sea', *Essays on International Law from the Columbia Law Review*, (New York 1965), 197–231.
99. Pharand, *The Law of the Sea* . . . , *op. cit.*, Part II.
100. The Submerged Lands Act, 22 May 1953 (PL 31; 67 Stat. 29). Under the terms of this legislation, both internal waters and territorial seas fall under the jurisdiction of the governments of the various states.
101. Butler, 'The Legal Regime . . . ', *op. cit.*
102. For a discussion of the various proposals that have been advanced in this area see Stevenson and Oxman, 'The Third United Nations Conference . . . ', *op. cit.*
103. *Ibid.* and Edward Miles, *Organizational Arrangements to Facilitate Global Management of Fisheries*, RfF Program of International Studies of Fishery Arrangements, Paper No. 4, (Washington 1974).
104. Francis T. Christy, Jr. and Anthony Scott, *The Commonwealth in Ocean Fisheries*, (Baltimore 1965), Ch. 1.
105. Eugene H. Buck, 'Alaska and the Law of the Sea — National Patterns and Trends of Fishery Development in the North Pacific', Arctic Environmental Information and Data Center, (University of Alaska 1973).
106. My use of the concept 'regime' is somewhat similar to that of Cooper [Richard N. Cooper, 'Prolegomena to the Choice of an International Monetary System', *International Organization*, 29 (1975), 63–97]. On the other hand, this usage of the concept seems to differ considerably from that of Haas [Ernst B. Haas, 'On Systems and International Regimes', *World Politics*, XXVII (1975), 147–174].
107. Eirik Furubotn and Svetozar Pejovich, 'Property Rights and Economic Theory: A Survey of Recent Literature', *Journal of Economic Literature*, X (1972), 1139.
108. Alan Randall, 'Coase Externality Theory in a Policy Context', *Natural Resources Journal*, 14 (1974), 35–54.

109. Such provisions bear some resemblance to what Hart calls 'secondary rules' [H.L.A. Hart, *The Concept of Law*, (Oxford 1961), Ch. V].

110. Nevertheless, this has been a major preoccupation in the literature on political 'systems', See, for example, David Easton, *A Systems Analysis of Political Life*, (New York 1965).

111. For a widely-read, recent analysis of contractarian problems see John Rawls, *A Theory of Justice*, (Cambridge 1971).

112. Real-world conditions virtually never approach Rawls' conception of a 'veil of ignorance' (*ibid.*, 136–142).

113. These are the classic conditions underlying mixed-motive or bargaining situations [see Thomas C. Schelling, *The Strategy of Conflict*, (Cambridge 1960), esp. Ch. 1].

114. For a suggestive discussion along these lines see James Buchanan and Gordon Tullock, *The Calculus of Consent*, (Ann Arbor 1962), esp. Ch. 6.

115. For a general analysis of resource management developed largely from this perspective consult Anthony Scott, *Natural Resources: the Economics of Conservation*, (Toronto 1973).

116. For a survey of social welfare criteria consult Jerome Rothenberg, *The Measurement of Social Welfare*, (Englewood Cliffs 1961).

117. The concept of economic efficiency in itself says nothing about absolute level or rate of use. It merely suggests utilization at the level at which marginal revenue equals marginal costs. And of course in cases where economic efficiency is not achieved, this criterion tells us nothing about the level or rate of use of a given resource.

118. Frank T. Bachmura, 'The Economics of Vanishing Species', *Natural Resources Journal*, 11 (1971), 674–692.

119. On the question of whether it is meaningful to speak of a socially desirable rate of use for resources see Scott, *Natural Resources . . .*, *op. cit.*, 107 *et. seq.*

120. See Tussing, *op. cit.*, esp. 41.

121. John V. Krutilla, 'Conservation Reconsidered', *American Economic Review*, LVII (1967), 777–786.

122. Bachmura, *op. cit.*

123. A classic example of the tendency of economists to deemphasize distributive questions is Ronald H. Coase, 'The Problem of Social Cost', *Journal of Law and Economics*, 3 (1960), 1–44.

124. It is now widely accepted among social scientists that no regime is neutral with respect to its distributive consequences.

125. The discussion of such issues of course requires the identification of normative standards in terms of which to judge the justice or fairness of actual distributive outcomes. For an important recent effort to develop such standards see Rawls, *op. cit.*

126. In a regulated market (such as has existed in the United States in recent years), there is the further question of deciding how much profit to allow the companies to obtain.

127. For example, a regime will ordinarily influence the absolute level of the harvest in international fisheries and this will, in turn, affect the price of fish on the world market.

128. I do not mean to deny that efforts to construct relevant utopias are useful in some circumstances [see Saul H. Mendlovitz ed., *On the Creation of a Just World Order*, (New York 1975)].

129. On problems of compliance see Oran R. Young, 'Compliance and Politics', mimeographed, (Austin 1974).

130. Oran R. Young, 'A Systemic Approach to International Politics', *Research*

Monograph No. 33, (Princeton University 1968).

CHAPTER III

EVOLVING PROBLEMS OF RESOURCE MANAGEMENT

This chapter examines the principal natural resources of the Beringian region in some detail, assesses the current level of utilization of these resources, and identifies the resultant problems of resource management emerging at the international level. This discussion will highlight a number of defects in the existing regime for Beringia, but its purpose is not to propose or even to identify new institutional arrangements for dealing with these defects. Such considerations will become an important focus of attention in later chapters. The objective here is to provide extensive background material concerning the problems of resource management in Beringia which will serve as a solid foundation for the organizationl and legal arguments advanced in subsequent chapters.

At the outset, several comments of an introductory nature seem appropriate. The various functional areas of interest in the realm of resource management in Beringia are not perfectly congruent with respect to geographical scope. That is, the geographical domain that seems most appropriate or rational from the point of view of resource management varies somewhat from one functional area to another. However, it would be a mistake to overemphasize the ambiguities generated by these fluctuations in the boundaries of the Beringian region. The core of the region is the same in each case: the marine areas to the north and south of the Bering Strait together with the associated coastal littorals. The divergances are not extreme, and the geographical overlap among the functional areas is considerably more striking than the incongruities. And the several functional areas are tied together by strong and growing interdependencies. For example, there are substantial interaction effects between the utilization of renewable and non-renewable resources in Beringia and between maritime commerce and the management of commercial fisheries. It is also important to emphasize the fact that Beringia is still a *relatively* undeveloped region from the point of view of resource utilization. Only in the area of commercial fishing are the region's resources now being subjected to heavy use. With respect to virtually all other natural resources, the region is just now reaching the threshold of rapid development. At the same time, there are compelling reasons to believe that this situation will change dramatically over the next several decades. Thus, it seems certain that Beringia's natural resources will be exploited more and more extensively during the foreseeable future. Consequently, resource management in the region is presently fraught both with opportunities and with dangers. There are opportunities in Beringia to develop viable institutions for resource management at the international level. But the speed with which usage of the region's resources is likely to increase could easily outpace developments in the realm of effective managerial arrangements.

A. Fish and Marine Mammals

The most complex resource management problems in Beringia are those associated with the commercial fisheries (including the harvest of marine mammals). The management of renewable resources involves several problems that are inherently more complex than those associated with the management of other resources. Moreover, commercial fishing has reached a far more advanced state in Beringia than the activities involved in the exploitation of other resources. Even so, many of the relevant problems in this area have emerged only recently and have yet to be fully understood by various actors in the region. This is largely due to the fact that the management problems of a heavily utilized fishery are qualitatively different than those of a lightly utilized fishery.

Geographically, the region of prime interest with respect to commercial fishing in Beringia runs from the Bering Strait south to approximately 47–48°N latitude and from the west coast to North America westward to the east coast of the Kamchatka Peninsula.[1] Therefore, it encompasses the North Pacific Ocean but does not extend to the Sea of Okhotsk or to the Arctic Ocean. Within this context, it will often be helpful to distinguish between the northeastern

Pacific and the northwestern Pacific. The northeastern Pacific includes the area to the east of 175°W longitude and encompasses the major commercial fishing grounds of the eastern Bering Sea, the Gulf of Alaska, and the Pacific coast of southeastern Alaska and Canada (sometimes called the transition area). The northwestern Pacific, by contrast, covers the area to the west of 175°W longitude and takes in the major fishing grounds of the western Bering Sea (as far west as the coast of Siberia and the Kamchatka Peninsula).[2] The demarcation point at 175°W longitude has some biological significance in terms of the population dynamics of highly migratory species of fish (though it is actually based on an inaccurate conception of the migratory patterns of salmon). But this point has attained considerable prominence in recent years because of its incorporation as an 'abstention line' in the International North Pacific Fisheries Convention of 1952, which governs certain commercial fishing operations of Japan, Canada, and the United States.[3] These geographical considerations are displayed graphically on the map on the following page (Figure II).

Before proceeding to the principal issues of this section, it seems appropriate to say a few words about the omission of the Arctic Ocean proper and the Chukchi Sea from the geographical scope of this functional area. It is generally agreed that the Arctic Ocean is currently insignificant from the perspective of commercial fishing and that its potential is not great in this area.[4] The case of the Chukchi Sea, on the other hand, is more complex. Fishing has occurred here in the past, and there is in fact some commercial fishing in the Chukchi Sea at this time (e.g. a fishing cooperative has operated successfully in Kotzbue for a number of years). But the Chukchi stocks are sparser than those in other parts of Beringia; individual fish tend to be small in size, and the fact that the sea is covered with sea ice during a large part of the year makes it relatively inhospitable from the point of view of commercial fishing.[5] It is therefore quite unlikely that the Chukchi Sea will become an important focus for commercial fishing, though it will undoubtedly continue to support small fishing operations as well as local harvesting on the part of native peoples.[6]

In modern times, fish stocks have been treated as *common property* resources under international law.[7] This means both that such resources (or portions of them) are not subject to exclusive appropriation on the part of any actor and that there are no entry barriers restricting the right of any individual actor to harvest these resources. The migratory habits of some fish (e.g. pelagic species like tuna, herring, and saury) would make it difficult for individual actors to subject these

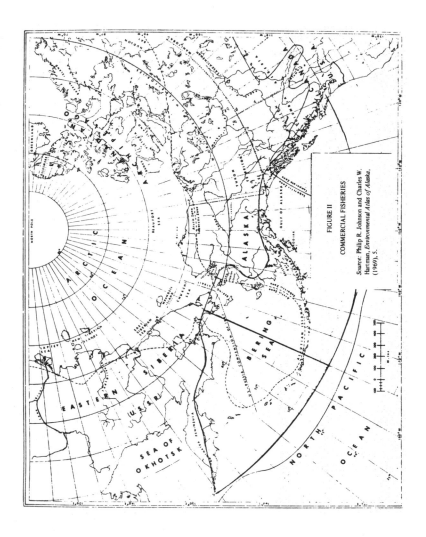

FIGURE II

COMMERCIAL FISHERIES

Source: Philip R. Johnson and Charles W. Hartman, *Environmental Atlas of Alaska,* (1969), 5.

resources to exclusive appropriation even if desired. But the fundamental premise underlying this conception of the fisheries was originally the notion that fish are so numerous that every actor can harvest as large a quantity as desired without interfering with the activities of others or depleting the natural stocks of fish. In earlier times, this premise was substantially correct with respect to many marine fisheries. That is, the ratio of human predation to the natural or standing stocks of most species of fish was sufficiently low so that it was feasible to conceptualize many fisheries as unlimited resources without any serious crowding among users. Under the circumstances, experts periodically debated whether human predation was a major factor in the population dynamics of important fish stocks,[8] and management problems in most commercial fisheries were minimal, confined to occasional issues concerning congestion or gear conflicts in particularly desirable fishing grounds.

More recently, however, the emergence of several new factors affecting commercial fisheries has radically altered the consequences of a common property regime for such resources in many parts of the world. Aggregate world demand for fish and fish products has risen rapidly and promises to continue to rise steadily during the foreseeable future.[9] Next, the amount of effort devoted to fishing by various actors has risen dramatically in recent years. Spurred by the growing world demand for fish and the absence of entry barriers in the fisheries, influential actors have expanded their fishing operations at an extraordinary pace in numerous geographical regions. At the same time, improved harvesting technology has created a situation in which individual ships are capable of remaining in the fishing grounds for substantially longer periods of time and landing fish in a highly efficient fashion. On the other side, the fact that fish are a natural resource means that supply functions in this area are relatively inelastic. Over the short run at least, supply becomes entirely inelastic beyond a certain point.[10] In the case of Beringia, the impact of these developments can be dated with considerable accuracy from the rapid growth of high-seas fishing in the region on the part of Japan starting in 1952 and on the part of the Soviet Union starting in 1959.[11]

The results of this situation are relatively straightforward, though their implications are extremely serious.[12] The following formulation of Christy and Scott captures the essence of the problem clearly:

> The individual user of a common property resource is usually in physical competition with all others in his attempt to get a large

share of the product for himself. It is unreasonable to expect an individual producer to willingly and one-sidedly restrain his effort; anything that he leaves will be taken by other producers. Furthermore, in the fishery there is no limit on the number that can participate so that as long as there is any profit to be gained, additional producers will enter the industry until all true profit (or rent) is dissipated. With such conditions, with demand increasing, and without controls, it is inevitable that the fishery will not only become depleted but also that the exploitation of the fishery will become economically inefficient in its use of labor and capital.[13]

Moreover, the large natural fluctuations of fish stocks regularly accentuate these problems, since harvesters tend to expand their efforts to reap the profits attainable during good years in the fisheries with the result that they have excess capacity during lean years. Consequently, 'It is not only possible but normal for excess capacity to develop quickly and to persist over long periods of time, accentuated by the traditional immobility of labor in the fisheries and the related ability to maintain capital equipment at little or no real cost.'[14]

Figure III portrays this situation for a given fishery in succinct graphical form.[15] The x axis of this figure represents different levels of effort while the y axis is a measure of total yield both in quantity and in revenue. The curve TC is an aggregate cost curve (based on the simplifying assumption of linear costs), and the curve TR/TY is a sustainable yield curve reflecting the fact that catch per unit of effort (cpue) will eventually decline due to both stock depletion and crowding in the fishery. In the absence of controls, equilibrium will occur at the intersection of the curves where the total revenue of the fleet is just sufficient to cover the total costs and there is no true profit or economic rent.[16]

This analysis yields several important conclusions. Common property arrangements without controls will tend to produce stock depletions in the sense that the equilibrium point will typically occur at a level of yield distinctly below the level of 'maximum sustainable yield' for the stock in question.[17] They will also be economically inefficient in the sense that they generate situations in which *total* benefits and costs, rather than *marginal* benefits and costs, are equal. Under the circumstances, a reduction in effort would actually lead to an increase in yield from the fishery as well as creating some economic profit or rent.[18] Even in an era of rising prices for fish and fish products, the result will typically be an unprofitable industry in

Figure III
Consequences of Common Property

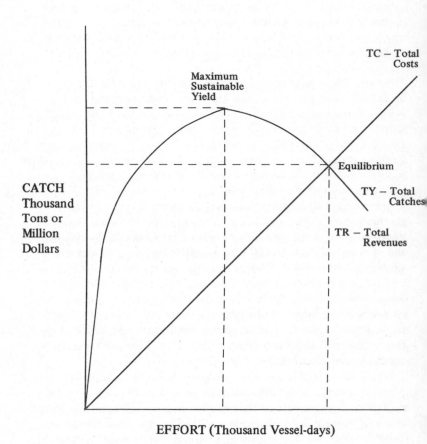

EFFORT (Thousand Vessel-days)

Source: Francis T. Christy, Jr., 'Alternative Arrangements for Marine
Fisheries: An Overview', *RFF Program of International Studies of
Fishery Arrangements*, (Washington 1973), 10.

which wages are low and over-capitalization occurs in the form of idle equipment. Furthermore, all these problems are apt to be severely aggravated by the large natural fluctuations in fish stocks mentioned previously. Optimistic decisions called forth by good years in the fisheries often generate circumstances in which fishermen sustain losses over the long run and actual yields fall farther below maximum sustainable yields than they would at the intersection of the curves TC and TR/TY. Therefore, it seems perfectly accurate to conclude that 'The basic theory of a high sea fishery, whether exploited by a single nation or more than one nation, suggests a bleak economic existence, to say the least.'[19]

Several additional problems contribute to the difficulties of managing commercial fisheries, especially at the international level. There are significant interdependencies among species of fish and among fishing operations, which become increasingly prominent as a fishery is utilized more and more heavily.[20] In the case of Beringia, for example, fur seals and pollock are linked in a predator-prey relationship, and there are serious potential conflicts between trawling operations for demersal fish and the harvesting of crabs. Next, there are interdependencies among international regions in an era of modern, distant-water technology and heavy usage of the fisheries.[21] To illustrate, efforts to regulate the fisheries of a given region through the imposition of quotas or entry restrictions may merely increase the strain on the stocks of another region as excess fishing capacity shifts to new grounds. Similarly, the intrusion of various political and security objectives frequently makes it difficult to prevent stock depletions and to achieve economic efficiency in marine fisheries. In Beringia, there is reason to believe that the rapid expansion of Soviet high-seas fishing activities during the 1960s was due in part to the pursuit of security objectives, and the willingness of many policymakers in Alaska to place the maintenance of high levels of employment above the achievement of efficiency or even the prevention of stock depletions is well known.[22] Finally, the management of international fisheries is complicated by substantial differences among states with respect to their economic systems. Thus, 'the objectives of international fishery management must be modified to accommodate different national objectives which in turn are based on different systems of social and economic organization, different alternatives for dealing with structural unemployment, and different degrees of dependence on fishing exports to meet current foreign exchange requirements.'[23]

Though the absence of coordinated management will typically

damage the interests of all relevant actors, it is generally impossible to design managerial arrangements that produce optimal results for everyone at once. Nevertheless, several critical issues arise in all efforts to manage commercial fisheries effectively, whether they are exploited by fishermen from one state or several.[24] Above all, effective management requires some method of restricting entry,[25] since unregulated or decentralized equilibrium ordinarily leads to stock depletions and economic inefficiency under conditions of heavy usage.[26] Therefore, 'The historic concept of freedom of the seas is clearly incompatible with any program of rational exploitation of marine resources.'[27] The imposition of entry restrictions logically implies the development of some criterion to determine desirable levels of harvesting for fish stocks. Since this issue has generated considerable controversy involving relatively technical arguments, a discussion of desirable levels of harvesting is reserved for an appendix to this chapter where it can be perused by those who are interested. But note that the introduction of entry restrictions also implies some method of apportioning the yield from a fishery. The method may be implicit in the sense that the harvest simply goes to those participants who are most efficient or arrive on the scene first until some overall quota for the stock is reached. But this procedure typically leads to highly inefficient results in the forms of extreme overcapitalization in fishing equipment and idleness of workers during most of the year. It is also likely to raise serious questions in the realm of equity. Alternatively, it is possible to deal with the allocation of the harvest explicitly through efforts on the part of the relevant actors to negotiate individual quotas or to set up some distributive mechanism (e.g. a market in entry rights).[28] This process is apt to be affected by significant bargaining impediments and it may well require the creation of an enforcement mechanism to be effective. But the case for some such approach to the management of the heavily used fish stocks of an international region like Beringia is compelling.

These problems of managing commercial fisheries lend themselves to interpretation in terms of several theoretical perspectives. It is clear that there will be a strong tendency toward overinvestment in decentralized or unregulated fisheries and that this will lead to stock depletion and the dissipation of economic rent under conditions of heavy usage. At the same time, institutional arrangements for the coordinated management of a fish stock (whether it is exploited by the nationals of one state or numerous states) constitute a collective good in the sense that all members of the user group will benefit from such arrangements if they are supplied at all.[29] Consequently, there are apt to be 'free-rider' incentives with respect to the management of fish stocks with each user hoping to benefit from the regulatory efforts of others.[30] This means that we should expect a tendency toward under-investment in coordinated arrangements for the management of fish stocks. Since the user group is small in the case of Beringia (at least if the users are conceptualized at the level of states), it is reasonable to hope that some of the collective good of managerial arrangements will be supplied through a bargaining process.[31] The fact that such arrangements could probably be made self-supporting in financial terms bolsters this hope, though the previously mentioned political and economic differences among the relevant actors might make it difficult to achieve results that approach economic efficiency.[32] Nevertheless, conceptualizing the management of commercial fisheries as a problem concerning the supply of collective goods makes it clear that the issues involved are complex ones.

The problem of developing managerial arrangements for the fisheries of an international region like Beringia can also be interpreted as an N-person, nonzero-sum, cooperative game.[33] It is possible to articulate such an interpretation at either of two levels: taking the relevant states as the players or taking the corporate or bureaucratic organizations actually engaged in fishing as the players. In either case, the problem exhibits the typical pattern of mixed motives that characterizes nonzero-sum games.[34] On the one hand, the players have a common interest in maximizing their collective gains from the relevant stocks. This means they should normally share an interest in avoiding long-term stock depletions and that they would often be favourable to measures aimed at increasing economic efficiency (provided there is some way of making transfers with respect to profits). On the other hand, each player will be interested in instituting managerial arrangements that will produce distributive results asymmetrically beneficial to itself. Thus, '. . . no single set of decisions as to what fish to harvest, what level of fishing effort to maintain, and what types of gear to employ will be optimal for all four nations [the United States, the Soviet Union, Japan, and Canada — OY]. Even if costs and preference patterns were identical, there would remain the question of the division of the catch.'[35] Under the circumstances, the problem of developing effective arrangements for the management of the fisheries of Beringia emerges as a classic N-person, bargaining situation.[36] This perspective also confirms the complexity of the problem in view of the fact that there are currently large gaps in our knowledge of bargaining and our ability to cope successfully with bargaining situations (especially when there are more than two players). But it does suggest a variety of interesting analytic perspectives on the problem since there exists a substantial theoretical literature on the phenomenon of bargaining.[37]

The remaining task of this section is to set forth briefly a current stock assessment for the commercial fisheries of the Beringian region. In fact, it is not easy to make assessments of this kind with precision. There are serious problems with existing models of population dynamics with respect to fisheries, at least at the applied level.[38] Though the major variables affecting the condition of fish stocks (e.g. recruitment, natural losses, non-human consumption, human landings) are relatively well known, there are major problems in attaching meaningful weights to these variables and in specifying their relationships to each other with precision.[39] Moreover, fish stocks commonly constitute highly volatile ecological systems in the sense that 'large and frequent shifts in parameters are inevitable in the ecological setting of the sea.'[40] Interdependencies among stocks and species add further complexities to the task of modelling population dynamics in many cases.

Beyond this, significant data problems afflict all efforts to arrive at sound, up-to-date stock assessments for specific geographical regions.[41] It is inherently more difficult to obtain accurate information on marine populations than on terrestrial populations. Lags of 2–4 years in collating and processing data occur with respect to some Beringian stocks, a serious problem in the case of fisheries that are both heavily exploited and subject to large natural fluctuations (e.g. pollock). Important gaps in the relevant data are also prevalent. This is particularly true for certain time periods and the activities of some actors (e.g. the Soviet Union), and it is a major problem in the case of incidental catches that are not recorded. There are difficulties stemming from non-homogeneity in the data available on many Beringian stocks. Data sets are frequently based on divergent criteria such as numbers of fish, live weight, and dressed weight.[42] Finally, individual actors sometimes have powerful incentives not to report certain data on fish harvests or to distort such data. These incentives stem directly from the collective-goods and bargaining aspects of the problem of managing the fisheries.[43] It may be difficult to correct for this factor, but it seems important at least to note its existence.

All stock assessments for the Beringian region must therefore be treated as tentative and subject to relatively rapid change. Nevertheless, it still seems possible to arrive at some useful conclusions about these matters. For example, there is widespread agreement that stocks of salmon, halibut, fur seals, whales, and many demersal fish are currently fully utilized in Beringia and that some of these stocks are almost certainly overutilized. At the same time, there is evidence to suggest that stocks of saury, some demersals, and some sedentary fish in the region are not fully utilized at present, though it is probable that many (if not most) of these stocks are rapidly approaching full utilization under the impact of the continued expansion of high seas fishing in Beringia.[44] In this connection, a brief survey of the principal species of fish and marine mammals in Beringia should help to make the evolving problems of resource management in this functional area more concrete.[45]

1. *Anadromous fish.* The principal anadromous fish of commercial interest in Beringia is salmon. Five distinct species of Pacific salmon are commercially significant (pink, coho, chinook, chum, and sockeye), and a distinction is generally drawn between North American and Asian stocks of these fish.[46] Though all five species have been fished commercially over a long period of time, primary emphasis has fallen on sockeye and pink salmon in the northeastern Pacific and on sockeye, pink, and chum salmon in the northwestern Pacific. Salmon spawn in fresh water but they are highly migratory, swimming up to 2000 miles into the high seas during their oceanic phase. This makes the problem of managing salmon stocks a complex one that almost certainly cannot be solved effectively in the absence of coordination at the international level.[47] At this time, some efforts to regulate Beringian salmon stocks are carried out under the terms of the International North Pacific Fisheries Convention involving the United States, Canada, and Japan and the Soviet-Japanese Northwest Pacific Fisheries Convention of 1956.[48] But there are no comprehensive managerial arrangements for the salmon stocks of the region as a whole.

Though there is general agreement that the salmon stocks of Beringia are fully utilized, the question of whether they are experiencing serious depletion is more controversial.[49] There is no doubt that the harvest of some major stocks has exhibited a long-term decline going back as far as the 1930s.[50] Specific problems with salmon stocks, such as the collapse of the valuable sockeye runs in the Bristol Bay during the 1970s, have reached disastrous proportions in the region.[51] The existing international agreements relating to the management of salmon stocks are not particularly effective, since some of them are based on misconceptions concerning migratory patterns, and they do not contain comprehensive provisions for the restriction of entry at the international level.[52] Nevertheless, there is considerable controversy concerning the weight to attach to human predation, in contrast to natural factors, in explaining both short-run and long-run fluctuations in the vitality of salmon stocks.[53] This has encouraged the politicization of debates concerning such issues as the significance of Japanese harvesting of North American salmon west of the provisional 'abstention line' at 175°W longitude and made it difficult to assess conflicting claims about the state of the Beringian salmon stocks objectively.[54] What does seem clear, however, is that the salmon stocks of this region are very much in need of coordinated management at the international level and that the growing demand for fish in the next decade will accentuate this need.

2. *Pelagic fish.* Pelagic fish are migratory oceanic fish that spend much of their time in the upper levels of the water column. Some range extremely widely (e.g. tuna) while others remain closer to shore and have a more limited range (e.g. herring). In contrast to anadromous fish, these fish do not spawn in fresh water. The principal pelagic fish of commercial significance in Beringia at this time is herring. The herring fishery rose to substantial proportions in the region at an early date largely along the coast of British Columbia and in southeastern Alaska.[55] More recently, Soviet and Japanese trawlers in the Bering Sea have exhibited a growing interest in this fishery. Certain provisions for the regulation of the Beringian herring stocks were included in the International North Pacific Fisheries Convention, but most of these provisions were dropped in 1959, 1961, and 1963. Accordingly, this species is not subject to effective international regulation in Beringia, though it is harvested in commercially significant quantities by several major actors.[56]

There is some disagreement concerning the current state of the Beringian herring stocks.[57] The stocks of the Gulf of Alaska and the transition area are regarded as seriously depleted. The herring stocks of the western Bering Sea were depleted during the 1960s, but Japan and the Soviet Union have taken steps since then to restore these stocks. Until recently, herring stocks in the remainder of the Bering Sea were thought to be somewhat underutilized. However, the most important recent development in this fishery is the growth of Japanese and Soviet harvesting in the eastern Bering Sea. Evidence is now mounting that the stocks in this area are fully utilized and some signs of depletion are emerging.[58] All this leads to a somewhat mixed picture coupled with the general conclusion that there are almost certainly no significant underutilized stocks of herring in Beringia at

70

this time. Finally, the rapid decline of the herring fishery off British Columbia during the 1960s probably played a role in precipitating the rising nationalism characteristic of Canadian fisheries policy in recent years.[59]

In concluding this discussion of pelagic fish, it is worth mentioning that Beringia is thought to have considerable stocks of saury.[60] Thus, 'Probably the resources in the Northeast Pacific are of the same magnitude as those in the Northwest Pacific, where some hundreds of thousands of tons have been taken annually.'[61] However, saury is not now harvested in commercially significant quantities in the Beringian region.

3. *Demersal fish.* The category of demersal fish covers a wide range of groundfish, bottom fish, rockfish, and flatfish. All demersal fish live in close proximity to the seabed of the continental shelves and are much less migratory than anadromous or pelagic fish.[62] Among other things, this means that demersals pose somewhat different managerial problems at the international level, since the idea of coastal state regulation is more plausible with respect to demersals than with respect to other species of fish.[63] Nevertheless, the demersal fish of Beringia currently constitute an internationally shared resource in the sense that nationals of several states harvest them actively.

Traditionally, commercial operations involving demersal fish in Beringia centered on the harvest of halibut (together with some Pacific cod and blackcod). The halibut fishery arose at an early date in both the Gulf of Alaska and the transition area. At that time it was largely a preserve of American and Canadian coastal fishermen.[64] More recently, Soviet and Japanese trawlers have taken substantial quantities of halibut as an incidental catch in their pursuit of other species of demersal fish.[65] Efforts to manage the halibut stocks of the region have been made under the terms of the International Pacific Halibut Convention as well as the International North Pacific Fisheries Convention. But neither convention applies to Soviet activities, and the Japanese do not belong to the halibut convention. Moreover, it is virtually impossible to regulate the harvest of halibut separately from the harvest of other demersal fish in view of the fact that trawling operations for other demersals will inevitably pick up a substantial quantity of halibut as an incidental catch. There is general agreement that the halibut stocks of Beringia are currently fully utilized, and there is little doubt that serious depletion has occurred in such areas as the eastern Bering Sea.[66]

Beyond this, the rise of Japanese and Soviet high seas trawling in

71

the Bering Sea and the Gulf of Alaska during the 1960s and 1970s has produced a dramatic upsurge in the harvest of other demersal fish, including a variety of species often regarded as 'trash' fish in North American circles. Perhaps the most striking case in point is pollock (now the largest single species fishery resource in the region),[67] but other species of growing interest include Pacific cod, Pacific hake, blackcod (or sablefish), rockfishes such as Pacific Ocean perch, and various flatfishes other than halibut (e.g. turbot and yellowfin,rock, and flathead sole).[68] The harvest of these demersals is overwhelmingly dominated by Japan and the Soviet Union and has reached significant proportions only during the last 10–15 years. At present, the harvest of these species in Beringia is largely unregulated, a fact that has several important implications.[69] It highlights broader problems of resource management since some of these species exhibit interdependencies with other commercially significant species (e.g. the typical diet of fur seals includes pollock).[70] Even more important, this arrangement has led to severe depletions in some of these fisheries resulting from the Soviet and Japanese practice of expanding the harvest of a given species extremely rapidly until there is a (temporary?) collapse of the relevant stocks and then moving on to repeat the pattern with another species. In general terms, few would disagree with the proposition that Beringia is capable of sustaining extremely large harvests of these demersals, but there is widespread concern that the present pattern of exploitation will prove destructive to the long-term viability of these fisheries.[71]

4. *Sedentary fish.* The term sedentary fish refers to the living resources of the seabed. As such, it encompasses crabs, shrimp and prawns, and molluscs in the Beringian region. In most cases, there are distinct Asian and North American stocks of these species, and they are relatively easy to control from coastal locations since they live in shallow waters and are not highly migratory. Nevertheless, the exploitation of the major species of sedentary fish in Beringia is of interest to fishermen from a number of states. With a few exceptions (e.g. king crabs), the harvest of these species commercially in the region is a recent development.[72] Estimates of the potential harvest of many of these species run remarkably high, though there are some exceptions (e.g. king crabs are probably fully utilized throughout the region and the shrimp stocks of the eastern Bering Sea are severely depleted). Also, some of these species exhibit important interdependencies with other species (e.g. the tanner crab population of a given area is, in part, a function of the king crab population).[73] There

is, however, real concern that future harvests of these fish will expand too rapidly and in an unregulated fashion so that dramatic collapses in specific stocks will occur from time to time.[74]

Given the sedentary nature of these species, international disputes concerning these fisheries have typically taken a different course than disputes about other species. The pattern here involves a vigorous expansion of jurisdictional (and distributive) claims on the part of the relevant coastal states.[75] The United States has pushed hard in recent years to obtain a series of bilateral agreements in which Alaskan stocks of species such as king crabs have been progressively denied to Japanese and Soviet fishermen. And the Soviets have taken similar steps with respect to Japanese harvests of Asian stocks of sedentary fish.[76] There is no general or comprehensive system of management for sedentary fish in the Beringian region, and there is little evidence of concern for the achievement of economic efficiency in these fisheries. But major shifts in jurisdictional arrangements, which carry far-reaching distributive implications, have emerged in this area from a series of bilateral agreements negotiated during the last ten years.

5. *Marine Mammals.* The circumstances affecting most marine mammals in Beringia are different than those affecting most species of fish. There is a considerable tradition of institutionalized protection for marine mammals. The Fur Seal Convention, for example, goes back to 1911 and the sea otter has been effectively protected since then.[77] There is a relatively high degree of political sensitivity concerning problems of conservation (if not economic efficiency) in this realm. Thus, the United States promulgated a highly restrictive Marine Mammals Protection Act in 1972,[78] and other states have exhibited growing concern with the protection of marine mammals in recent years. Moreover, with the striking exception of whales, there are no commercial harvests of marine mammals that remotely compare with the large fisheries in terms of economic importance. Accordingly, the political impact of restrictive arrangements relating to most marine mammals is not as great as the parallel impact of coordinated managerial arrangements for commercial fisheries.

Presently, the major commercial operation involving marine mammals is the Japanese and Soviet harvest of whales.[79] The problems here are much the same as those encountered earlier in the Antarctic. There is international machinery for the management of the relevant stocks, but it has not been notably successful in preventing sock depletions.[80] Thus,

By 1963, the North Pacific catch exceeded that of the Antarctic. The pattern of excessive harvest of the Antarctic and North Atlantic fisheries was soon duplicated on the much smaller stocks of the North Pacific. The fishery shifted from blue whales to fin whales to sei whales as each species became progressively overfished. Meanwhile, the sperm whale fishery continued to expand, and the harvest of this species rose to a world-wide high of 29,000 in 1964.[81]

Efforts to manage the North Pacific stocks of whales on a species-by-species basis are now being pursued quite vigorously.[82] But there is no doubt that this fishery constitutes the one area where there are currently serious threats to the continued viability of stocks of marine mammals in the Beringian region.

The only other commercially significant operation involving marine mammals in Beringia at this time is the annual harvest of fur seals. The fur seal harvest is conducted on a strictly regulated basis under the terms of the Fur Seal Convention of 1911 (as reformulated in 1957).[83] It is widely regarded as a model of coordinated resource management at the international level, and it includes an explicit agreement concerning the apportionment of the harvest as well as the limitation of the total annual harvest. Nevertheless, the seal herds of the Pribilof Islands have recently declined somewhat so that it has been necessary to reduce annual harvest from 40–50,000 to 25–30,000. It has been widely suggested that the explanation of this decline lies in the upsurge of high seas fishing in the area.[84] If this should prove to be correct, it would constitute another important indication of the interdependencies among the living resources of Beringia.

There is no commercial harvest of walrus, sea lions, or other species of seal in Beringia at present, though these mammals are exploited to some extent by native peoples resident in the region. The walrus population is now regarded as quite viable, and there is some indication of Soviet interest in initiating a limited commercial harvest of walrus.[85] There is little likelihood of a commercial harvest of sea lions or various other species of seals during the foreseeable future. Although there is considerable concern about the viability of Polar Bear stocks, there is no commercial harvest of this species at present.[86] Polar Bear stocks are not large, and private hunting evidently made serious inroads on these stocks during the recent past.[87] However, a five-nation international agreement designed to protect Polar Bears was negotiated during the fall of 1973; international sensitivity concerning the future of this species is rising rapidly, and the prognosis for Polar

Bears seems quite favorable at this time.[88]

B. Hydrocarbons

Without doubt, the critical managerial issues associated with non-renewable resources in Beringia center on the prospects of identifying and exploiting large reserves of oil and natural gas. Current production of hydrocarbons in the region is small. But there is compelling evidence to indicate that Beringia contains large reserves of oil and natural gas, and these reserves may well turn out to be massive. Given the growing pressure on existing world reserves of hydrocarbons together with the political complications surrounding these resources, there is every reason to assume that the development of the hydrocarbon potential of Beringia will proceed rapidly in the near future.[89] This will not only alter the economic status of the region dramatically, it will also generate serious managerial problems as pressures for expanded hydrocarbon production come into conflict with other values such as the desire to preserve the physical habitat.

The geographical scope of Beringia in this case differs somewhat from the case of commercial fishing. The Gulf of Alaska and the Bering Sea remain important centers of attention. Beyond this, however, interest shifts to the north rather than to the south as in the case of fisheries. Specifically, it is necessary to consider the hydrocarbon potential of the Chukchi Sea and the Beaufort Sea. In addition, this survey encompasses the coastal littorals of northeastern Siberia, Alaska, and the Mackenzie Delta area of Canada, though it does not cover the hydrocarbon potential of the interior of these land masses. The resultant delineation of the Beringian region with respect to oil and natural gas is summarized in the map on the following page (Figure IV).

The management problems associated with the actual production of hydrocarbons are inherently less complex than those of the marine fisheries,[90] though the economic value of Beringian oil and natural gas may eventually match or exceed that of the region's fish.[91] In part, this is attributable to the fact that common property (or 'common pool') problems are not difficult to avoid with respect to hydrocarbons located on government-owned lands or on the outer continental shelves.[92] Historically, the tendency of oil to occur in relatively large underground reservoirs sometimes led to unfortunate consequences when discoveries took place on small, privately-owned tracts of land. Thus,

Once a reservoir was discovered, tract owners around the discovery

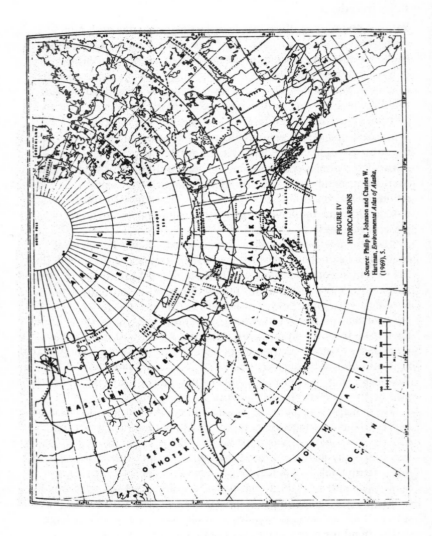

FIGURE IV

HYDROCARBONS

Source: Philip R. Johnson and Charles W.
Hartman, *Environmental Atlas of Alaska,*
(1969), 5.

well had to drill wells of their own to protect their own interest. Wells drilled close to boundaries required adjoining owners to drill offsetting wells. Far more wells were thus drilled than were necessary for effective and economical drainage of the reservoir. There were numerous side effects. The motivating gas pressures were rapidly exhausted, leaving large amounts of the oil unrecoverable. Oil production often ran ahead of the facilities for handling and moving it, running into open pools, fouling streams, and creating fire hazards.[93]

Over time, however, the resultant economic inefficiencies and environmental problems have been largely suppressed in most countries either through direct government management or through systematic government regulation in such forms as pro rating, spacing requirements, and unitization provisions.[94]

There is no reason to expect serious 'common pool' problems to arise in connection with the exploitation of hydrocarbons in a region like Beringia. Most of the relevant lands are under the control of various governments, and the offshore provinces of Beringia are under the direct jurisdiction of the respective federal governments. Under the circumstances, there is no doubt that government regulations will require wide spacing of production wells and unitization agreements whenever there is reason to believe that a single reservoir may cut across the boundaries of separately leased tracts.[95] Since the continental shelves in Beringia are continuous in many areas, it is of course possible that hydrocarbon reservoirs will be discovered which cut across international jurisdictional boundaries. In such cases, serious international conflicts are possible, and there is some danger of over-investment and excessively rapid production of the oil in question. However, it seems highly likely that the various actors in Beringia would respond to such situations by following the North Sea precedent of negotiating unitization agreements at the international level.[96]

All this suggests that debates concerning Beringian hydrocarbons will focus on the demarcation of jurisdictional boundaries rather than the development of coordinated managerial arrangements.[97] (There may be serious international conflicts concerning the location of such boundaries. More shall be said about potential Soviet-American boundary disputes in the next chapter.)[98] Also, given the special features of hydrocarbon production on the outer continental shelves,[99] there will almost certainly be growing pressures on non-socialist states like the United States and Canada to increase governmental involvement in the exploitation of Beringian hydrocarbons.[100] For example, there are already pressures mounting in the United States to make important changes in the existing system of bonus-bid leasing to private corporations when it comes to tapping the offshore oil and natural gas reserves of Beringia.[101] Nevertheless, none of these issues concerning the production of oil and natural gas produce the complexities from the perspective of the international relations of resource management which constitute a central feature of the marine fisheries.

Another part of the explanation of the difference between hydrocarbons and marine fisheries with respect to the complexities of the managerial problems they generate lies in the fundamental distinction between non-renewable and renewable resources. In the case of non-renewable resources, such as oil and natural gas, it is not necessary to worry about the continuing biological viability of stocks, the complexities of population dynamics, and the ecological volatility of living systems. To be sure, there are important questions concerning the optimal rate of depletion of finite and exhaustible resources. It may be difficult for firms to decide whether to exploit such resources rapidly in the short run at the expense of long-run production or *vice versa*.[102] Moreover, it is possible to argue that the decisions of private firms in this area will not yield socially optimal results.[103] However, while these value trade-offs may be difficult to make, the systemic complexities affecting such choices are not as great as in the case of living systems. Once jurisdictional boundaries are clearly demarcated, decisions in this realm should not have direct international ramifications.[104]

The achievement of economic efficiency with respect to hydrocarbons, on the other hand, poses extremely complex problems. It is important to note, however, that these problems stem primarily from the nature of the particular markets rather than from defects in the managerial arrangements dealing with the actual production of oil and natural gas. The international market for oil is substantially affected by political factors that outweigh any desire to achieve economic efficiency. Similarly, the domestic market for hydrocarbons in leading countries like the United States has long been governmentally regulated in the interests of pursuing objectives that transcend the goal of achieving economic efficiency in the hydrocarbon market itself.[105] Consequently, prices in these markets fluctuate unpredictably in response to political decisions, and it is difficult to make production decisions in such a way as to attain economic efficiency. This limits the value of economic efficiency as a criterion for analysis when thinking about the exploitation of the hydrocarbon reserves of a resource region like Beringia.

For reasons outlined in the preceding paragraphs, there is nothing in the actual production of hydrocarbons, even on the outer continental shelves, that suggests a pressing need for coordinated management at the international level in a region like Beringia. Nevertheless, the exploitation of these resources is virtually certain to produce side effects that will generate international, as well as national, issues of considerable political significance. Quite apart from the problems of demarcating jurisdictional boundaries, large-scale production of oil and natural gas in the region will yield negative externalities that take the form of collective goods for important groups of recipients and that do not respect national boundaries.[106] Two considerations are of particular importance here. First, the exploitation of oil and natural gas always involves a certain amount of pollution (broadly defined) both in the actual process of extraction and in conjunction with the transportation of hydrocarbons from the area of production to the markets. Second, large-scale production of hydrocarbons in Beringia will conflict with the utilization of other resources to some degree and exact some toll in terms of damage to non-economic values (e.g. the preservation of wilderness areas). Though detailed knowledge about these conflicts is extremely limited at present, it is not unrealistic to be concerned about such things as the impact of extensive developments in offshore oil and natural gas production on the marine fisheries of Beringia.[107]

In thinking about Beringia, it is relevant to add a brief discussion of the special problems associated with offshore hydrocarbon production, since this is where the region's greatest potential reserves lie. Presently, less than 20% of the world's hydrocarbons come from offshore production. However, it is widely expected that this proportion will increase to as much as 40–50% during the foreseeable future,[108] and Beringian reserves are quite likely to contribute significantly to this upsurge. Therefore, it is important to note that the dangers of producing large negative externalities are substantially greater in the case of offshore production than in the case of onshore production.[109] Special problems involving sea ice, currents, earthquakes, and tsunamis only serve to heighten these dangers in many parts of Beringia. The seriousness of these problems in absolute terms is a subject of some controversy, and technological advances may alter the picture with respect to some of them during the near future.[110] The present state of knowledge is insufficient to permit confident conclusions about the dangers of offshore production in Beringia. This would ordinarily suggest the desirability (at least in social terms) of moving cautiously in initiating the offshore production of oil and natural gas in the region. Yet the growing problems of the industrialized states in the international oil market coupled with the content of existing liability rules have set in motion powerful pressures to initiate large-scale offshore production that may prove irresistible.[111]

Let me turn now to a brief survey of the actual oil and natural gas reserves of Beringia. As with the assessment of fish stocks, there are fundamental problems in arriving at such estimates.[112] It is impossible to be sure just how much oil or natural gas a given geological structure will yield until actual production takes place. Once serious drilling has begun, there is some hard evidence on which to base estimates, though even then the extent of an oil or natural gas field is extremely difficult to judge. Furthermore, only part of the oil in each reservoir is actually recoverable, and the proportion that is eventually extracted is influenced by a number of factors such as the rate of production and the incidence of technological advances.[113] Prior to serious drilling, estimates of recoverable reserves are fundamentally speculative and subject to extreme fluctuations. Several different procedures are used in estimating potential reserves. All start with efforts to identify geological structures and sedimentary basins or provinces of the type that are known to have yielded hydrocarbons in other areas. But some rely heavily on various types of geophysical (largely seismic) evidence while others rely primarily on inductive inferences from other cases. When the results of several estimating techniques produce similar projections for a given area, it is undoubtedly reasonable to feel more confident than when major divergences occur. Even so, speculative estimates are typically formulated in terms of ranges and coupled with caveats that they may be off by a factor of two or more.[114] These points should be borne clearly in mind in the following discussion, since operations are still at a preliminary stage with respect to the bulk of the potential oil and natural gas reserves of Beringia.[115]

1. *Production.* At present, the only significant commercial production of oil and natural gas in Beringia is on the Kenai Peninsula and in the adjacent waters of the upper Cook Inlet south of Anchorage.[116] The Richfield Company (now part of Atlantic-Richfield) first identified oil with certainty in this area in 1957, and commercial production began in 1960. There are now fifteen production platforms in the Cook Inlet together with a number of oil and natural gas fields on the Kenai Peninsula operated by several major oil companies. From an initial production of 500,000 barrels of oil in 1960, the yield in this

area rose to 74.9 million barrels in 1969. However, 1969 was the peak year for the area; production is expected to average 60–70 million barrels a year during the 1970s with a further decline to something in the neighborhood of 20 million barrels by 1985. Consequently, this area is one of limited, though significant, production.[117] Its long-run potential is not great, but there may be some additional fields of short-run significance in other parts of the upper Cook Inlet. In addition, offshore production in the Cook Inlet has been a source of experience with production in the presence of sea ice, heavy currents, and tides, though conditions in some parts of the Gulf of Alaska and the Beaufort Sea would be considerably more severe.[118]

The only other production site in Beringia at this time is at the South Barrow Gas Field in Naval Petroleum Reserve No. 4.[119] Though this field has been producing steadily since 1949, 'Current PET-4 production is limited to natural gas for government agencies located at Barrow and the privately-owned Barrow Utilities, Inc., which serves village homeowners through an aging, low-pressure, above ground distribution system . . . '[120] None of this gas is exported, and the operation indicates nothing about the overall oil and natural gas potential of NPR 4. But it is the oldest continuous operation involving the production of hydrocarbons in Beringia.

2. *Development stage.* The development stage differs from the production stage in that no oil or natural gas is actually flowing to markets; it is distinguished from the exploration stage by the facts that production wells (in contrast to exploration wells) have been drilled or are being drilled and that the necessary infrastructure to handle commercial quantities of oil and/or natural gas is being developed. The principal area in Beringia which is currently in the development stage is the Prudhoe Bay region of the North Slope of Alaska.[121] A major oil strike in this region occurred in June 1968, after a number of years of relatively fruitless exploration. The major lease sale occurred in September 1969,[122] and commercial production has since been awaiting the construction of a pipeline across Alaska to transport crude oil to a tanker terminal at Port Valdez. There is general agreement that the Prudhoe Bay area contains something of the order of 10 billion barrels (bbl) of oil and 26 trillion cubic feet (Tcf) of natural gas. It therefore constitutes a large portion of known American reserves at this time (approximately 25%)[123] and it may expand in size as new discoveries are made. Since the passage of legislation for a crude oil pipeline across Alaska in the fall of 1973, the pace of development in the Prudhoe Bay area has quickened. It is

currently estimated that the pipeline will come on line at a rate of 600,000 barrels of crude oil a day (b/d) in mid-1977 and that it may reach its capacity of 2 million b/d by sometime in 1979.[124] Beyond this, considerable pressure has already arisen to construct a second pipeline to carry natural gas from the Prudhoe Bay fields (to be followed perhaps by another oil pipeline to carry oil from NPR 4 and other parts of the North Slope). At present, there are competing proposals to construct a gas line parallel to the crude oil line (the so-called El Paso proposal) and to route a gas line into Canada and on down the Mackenzie River valley (the Arctic Gas proposal). The debate concerning the relative merits of these proposals has recently become vigorous.[125]

3. *Exploration stage.* This stage does not encompass the development of production wells. But it does include the drilling of exploration wells and it ordinarily involves serious moves toward leasing arrangements for purposes of eventual production.[126] This means that estimates of hydrocarbon reserves in areas in the exploration stage are less solidly founded than in the case of the areas discussed above, but they are not purely speculative estimates. There are several separate areas in the exploration stage within the Beringian region.

There is a widespread belief that Naval Petroleum Reserve No. 4 contains large reserves of oil and natural gas.[127] NPR 4 is a large tract of land on the Alaskan North Slope containing approximately 37,000 sq. miles or 24 million acres.[128] It was established by the federal government in 1923 and is currently under the jurisdiction of the United States Navy. The premise underlying the creation of this and other such reserves (e.g. at Elk Hills, California) is that the federal government should control major reserves of hydrocarbons which could be utilized during wartime or other national emergencies. Accordingly, there has never been any large-scale commercial development of oil or natural gas in NPR 4, though the Navy carried out exploratory work in the area during the 1940s and 1950s.[129] At the same time, many current estimates suggest that NPR 4 contains as much oil and natural gas as the Prudhoe Bay area and some commentators believe that it may in fact contain larger reserves. It is hardly surprising then, that pressures are now growing to exploit the hydrocarbon reserves of NPR 4. These pressures have already induced the Navy to obtain the services of a civilian operator to undertake an expanded exploration program in the area.[130] Congress is now debating whether NPR 4 should be transferred from the jurisdiction of the Navy to that of the Department of the Interior so that lease sales to private corporations can be held. The prospects are very good for a debate in the near future concerning the idea of constructing another pipeline across Alaska to handle the flow of oil from NPR 4.[131] In short, issues concerning these reserves seem certain to gain increasing prominence.

Given recent developments in the Prudhoe Bay area and the possibility of large reserves in NPR 4, it is not surprising that there is considerable interest in the possibilities of exploiting hydrocarbons in the remaining segments of the Alaskan North Slope.[132] While earlier explorations to the south of Prudhoe Bay failed to locate commercially significant reserves, there is no doubt that the 'Oil and gas potential of the Alaskan North Slope outside the Prudhoe Bay field is going to be probed much more thoroughly in the next few years.'[133] Some of this area is already accessible to various oil companies under lease arrangements with the State government, and further exploration has already begun on these lands. Another large segment of the North Slope is under federal control in the form of the Arctic National Wildlife Refuge, which encompasses approximately 8.9 million acres to the east of Prudhoe Bay.[134] Predictably, a controversy has emerged concerning whether or not to permit exploration for oil and gas in this area. Finally, some sections of the northern part of Alaska are in the process of being transferred to the control of several native corporations.[135] This will change the legal arrangements governing exploration for oil and gas on these lands, but it is unlikely to slow the quest for such resources since funds from lease sales and royalties could constitute an important source of financial strength for these corporations. In this connection, several native corporations have already negotiated exploration agreements with major oil companies, and exploration wells are already being drilled by Standard Oil of California (under an agreement with the NANA Corporation) in the Selawik basin near Kotzbue.[136]

Another area in the exploration stage is the Mackenzie Delta-Beaufort Basin sector of the Canadian Arctic.[137] Serious exploration began in this area shortly after the Prudhoe Bay strike and has since been carried on vigorously by several firms (the leader is Imperial Oil, Ltd., a Canadian subsidiary of Exxon). Extensive and relatively successful exploratory drilling has been carried out in this area. For example, '. . . near the eastern side of the Mackenzie Delta, Imperial Oil brought in a well in 1970 and made another oil and gas discovery in the delta in 1971.'[138] Though proven reserves in this area are mostly natural gas and do not begin to compare with those of Prudhoe Bay, the overall potential of the area is widely believed to be large (one recent responsible estimate suggests 12 bbl of oil and 100 Tcf of natural gas).[139] There is every reason to think that commercial production will occur in this area within the next ten years. However, such developments are likely to generate serious debates concerning such matters as the most appropriate method of transporting natural gas (and perhaps oil) from the Mackenzie Delta[140] and the extent to which American-based or American-dominated companies should be allowed to play a role in the exploitation of these reserves.[141]

Finally, let me refer briefly to two areas that are peripheral to the Beringian region as delimited in this study but in which extensive exploratory efforts are taking place. One of these areas encompasses the Canadian Arctic Islands. Evidence of significant reserves of oil and natural gas has already been uncovered on Banks, King Christian, Ellesmere, and Melville Islands (largely by Panarctic Oil, Ltd.). And speculative estimates of reserves in the Arctic Islands indicate the presence of as much as 46 bbl of oil and 357 Tcf of natural gas.[142] The other area lies in western Siberia, especially on the Yamal Peninsula which juts into the Kara Sea.[143] Reserves in this area may be massive. For example, one source suggests that 'It is expected that this west Siberian region will become the country's [i.e. the Soviet Union's] biggest single producer of both oil and gas in five to ten years' time, and will meet about one-third of the country's demand for both fuels.'[144]

4. *Speculative estimates.* In this stage, emphasis is placed on various types of geophysical surveys in contrast to exploration wells. Extensive geophysical surveying has led to the conclusion that major hydrocarbon reserves probably exist in several parts of Beringia. Estimates of the magnitude of such reserves are even less certain than those discussed in the preceding paragraphs, and it is particularly difficult to make confident predictions about the probable course of development in these areas. Nevertheless, such cases are of special importance from the point of view of the international relations of resource management in Beringia not only because the associated transportation problems would often be less severe than in areas like Prudhoe Bay but also because they would all involve major offshore operations. The exploitation of these reserves may raise serious international questions concerning such things as jurisdictional boundaries, the control of marine pollution, and interference with the exploitation or maintenance of other resources.

Several parts of the Gulf of Alaska are now viewed as areas of great potential for the production of oil and natural gas partly because estimates of reserves are high and partly because transportation problems in the area would be minimal.[145] Seismic exploration in the Gulf began in the 1960s,[146] and responsible estimates of the area's reserves now run in the range of 7–20 bbl of oil, with some experts suggesting that the figure could go even higher.[147] Consequently, pressures to hold a lease sale in the Gulf have mounted steadily, even though the Council on Environmental Quality has designated the area a high-danger zone. The Department of the Interior has scheduled a first lease sale in the northeastern Gulf for December 1975 (with others to come later), and preparations for exploratory work in this area are now moving into high gear.[148] Though the present lease schedule for the Gulf may not be met, there is little doubt that serious exploration will take place in this area during the near future. Current estimates suggest that oil production in the Gulf may well reach a level of 200,000 b/d by the early 1980s and 1 million b/d by 1990.[149]

It is generally believed that the lower Cook Inlet contains commercially significant quantities of oil and natural gas.[150] A recent estimate puts the reserves of the whole Cook Inlet area at 2.5 billion barrels of oil and 18.4 Tcf of natural gas.[151] It seems reasonable to assume that a large portion of these reserves lie in the lower Cook Inlet in view of the declining production in the upper Inlet. The State of Alaska scheduled a series of lease sales in this area that were to have started in 1975.[152] However, the recent Supreme Court decision affirming federal jurisdiction over the waters of the lower Cook Inlet will necessitate a cancellation of these plans and a transfer of planning for lease sales to the Department of the Interior.[153] Serious exploration is now beginning in the lower Inlet, and Interior will undoubtedly experience mounting pressures to go ahead with lease sales in this area. On the other hand, the Council on Environmental Quality has designated the lower Cook Inlet a high-danger zone for offshore production, and a federal Environmental Impact Statement has not yet been drafted for the area. Under the circumstances, developments in this area may unfold somewhat more slowly than in the Gulf of Alaska, but hydrocarbon production in the lower Cook Inlet is probable during the 1980s.

Next, the Beaufort Sea off the North Slope of Alaska and off the Mackenzie River delta is viewed as an unusually rich area for oil and natural gas.[154] Plans are now developing to hold lease sales in the area during this near future.[155] The State of Alaska has scheduled a sale for 1976 in the Beaufort fringe area adjacent to Prudhoe Bay, and the federal government has scheduled a sale for late 1977 in the Beaufort Sea.[156] One recent estimate sets the recoverable potential of this area at 2.7 bbl of oil and 13.5 Tcf of natural gas.[157] Offshore drilling should be feasible in large portions of the Beaufort Sea since the continental shelf extends as far as 60 miles seaward in this area, and the water over these shelves is unusually shallow. On the other hand, the fact that the Beaufort Sea is covered with sea ice during most of the year will pose major problems in developing production wells for sustained use. Transportation problems would be considerably greater here than in areas like the Gulf of Alaska. There are also unresolved issues concerning the exact boundaries of Canadian and American jurisdiction on the continental shelves of the Beaufort Sea.[158] For these reasons, the Gulf of Alaska is likely to move more rapidly toward production than the Beaufort Sea. Even so, there is a high probability of serious developments in the Beaufort Sea during the next ten years.

There are sedimentary basins and geological structures that look promising as sources of oil and natural gas in several different parts of the Bering Sea. There are promising structures north of the Aleutian chain in what is called the St. George province. The southeastern portion of the Bristol Bay is referred to by numerous sources as a rich area for hydrocarbons;[159] an exploration well has actually been drilled at Cold Bay.[160] There are indications of commercially significant quantities of hydrocarbons in Norton Sound, especially in the area off the Yukon River delta.[161] Evidence is mounting that there is a highly promising geological structure located to the south of St. Lawrence Island.[162] Additionally, evidence has surfaced concerning a promising basin on the outer continental shelf off the eastern coast of the Kamchatka Peninsula. A responsible recent estimate of reserves in the Bering Sea to the east of the 'convention line' alone gives figures of 27.4 bbl of oil and 200 Tcf of natural gas,[163] and to grasp the full potential of the Bering Sea it is necessary to consider possible reserves on the western or Soviet side of the 'convention line'. Many of these areas are attractive from the point of view of transportation, and pressures are now mounting to hold lease sales in the Bering Sea. In fact, Interior has tentatively scheduled three sales in the Bering Sea during 1977 and 1978,[164] and numerous commentators have suggested the possibility of production from some of the basins during the 1980s. It is worth noting, however, that some of these areas will be affected by the absence of jurisdictional boundaries between the United States and the Soviet Union with respect to the resources of the continental shelf in the Bering Sea (the geological structure south of St. Lawrence Island is a case in point).[165] This ambiguity may constitute a serious impediment to further development for the immediate future in the areas affected.

Finally, there are indications of the existence of major hydrocarbon reserves in the Chukchi Sea as well as the Bering Sea, though the natural conditions of this area are more severe and the problems of transportation would be greater.[166] Specifically, there is a promising basin on the outer continental shelf between Point Hope to the south and Icy Cape to the north (the so-called Hope basin) which has been estimated to contain 6.6 bbl of oil and 33 Tcf of natural gas.[167] Beyond this, Soviet sources have hinted at the existence of hydrocarbon reserves off the northeastern coast of the Chukotsk Peninsula. Though it is unclear what the estimates of the reserves of this area are, it is probable that the area is geologically a continuation of the basin in the eastern Chukchi Sea. The fact that these areas are particularly inhospitable to the development of production and transportation facilities and that they are not adjacent to other promising areas (in contrast to a case like the Beaufort Sea) suggests that commercial production will occur at a later date in these areas than in many of the other offshore provinces of Beringia. Nevertheless, Interior has tentatively scheduled a lease sale for the Hope basin during late 1978,[168] and interest in the possible exploitation of Chukchi Sea oil is growing.

Let me conclude this section with a brief overview of current estimates of the hydrocarbon potential of the Beringian region. A recent United States Geological Survey estimate places the offshore reserves of Alaska alone at 30–600 bbl of oil and 170–340 Tcf of natural gas.[169] This means that Alaska ' . . . is rated . . . potentially the most prolific of the [American] offshore provinces in the first breakdown of this type revealed by the USGS.'[170] Next, reputable private estimates released in March 1974 yield the following figures for potential reserves north of 60°N latitude (Table I). The region covered by these estimates does not coincide with Beringia since it omits parts of the Bering Sea and all of the Gulf of Alaska and since large areas of Canada and the Soviet Union north of 60°N are not included in Beringia. Nevertheless, the figures give some idea of the order of magnitude of the reserves of oil and natural gas under consideration in this study. Beyond this, the State of Alaska released the following speculative estimates of recoverable reserves of oil and natural gas in Alaska during January 1974 (Table II).

TABLE I
HYDROCARBON RESERVES NORTH OF 60°N LATITUDE

	Oil in bbl	Gas in Tcf
Soviet Union	200	1,600
Alaska	40	300
Canadian North		
1) Mackenzie Delta	12	100
2) Arctic Islands	46	357

Source: R.A. Rudkin, 'Petroleum Potential of Arctic Canada', *Oil and Gas Journal*, 72(10), 11 March 1974, 147–151.

TABLE II
ESTIMATED SPECULATIVE RECOVERABLE RESOURCES OF OIL AND NATURAL GAS IN ALASKA

		Oil in bbl	Gas in Tcf
Offshore Provinces			
1. Beaufort		2.7	13.5
2. Chukchi		6.6	33.0
3. Hope		1.8	13.0
4. Bering Sea		27.4	200.0
5. Kodiak Island		2.4	17.5
6. Gulf of Alaska*		8.8	64.2
	Total	49.7	341.2
Onshore Provinces			
1. North Slope		15.5	41.8
2. Kotzbue*		.7	5.0
3. Koyukuk		3.4	9.3
4. Bethel		1.3	3.5
5. Bristol		.9	6.8
6. Yukon Kandik		1.7	11.4
7. Copper River		.2	1.2
8. Cook Inlet*		2.5	18.4
9. Other		.2	1.1
	Total	26.4	98.5

*Includes Onshore and Offshore Areas

Source: Robert M. Klein, William M. Lyle, Patrick L. Dobey, and Kristina M. O'Connor, 'Estimated Speculative Recoverable Resources of Oil and Natural Gas in Alaska', *Alaska Open File Report No. 44*, State of Alaska (Department of Natural Resources, Division of Geological and Geophysical Surveys), January 1974.

Again, the area covered is not identical with the Beringian region since it includes several onshore areas in Alaska that are not part of Beringia and it excludes Beringian reserves under Canadian and Soviet jurisdiction. But these figures also suggest clearly the presence of large reserves of hydrocarbons in the Beringian region. In short, what emerges from this survey is the conclusion that developments relating to oil and natural gas will loom large in the future resource management problems of Beringia, even allowing for substantial errors attributable to the speculative nature of current estimates in this functional area.

C. Navigation and Transportation

Discussions of resource management tend to focus on problems associated with renewable and non-renewable resources. However, it is important in a region like Beringia to consider the use of flow resources as well. In other words, it is possible to utilize the physical habitat (e.g. air and waterways) as a medium for the movement of persons and goods. At present, the most significant activities of this type in Beringia fall into the category of marine transportation,[171] but we must also take a look at air transporation in the region. In addition, there is a central distinction between commercial and military trans-portation in the analysis of flow resources. In the case of Beringia, both types of transportation are of considerable importance, though there is little doubt that commercial transportation in the region is likely to grow rapidly in significance relative to military transportation during the near future.[172]

The analysis of flow resources requires a geographical specification of the Beringian region somewhat more extensive than in the cases of commercial fishing and hydrocarbons, though there are various issues in this realm which are primarily of regional rather than global significance. In this context, Beringia starts in the North Pacific at, say, 47–48°N latitude and runs north to include a large segment of the Arctic Ocean. South of the Bering Strait, the region encompasses the Gulf of Alaska and the entire Bering Sea, but it still excludes the Sea of Okhotsk. North of the Bering Strait, the situation is actually somewhat more complex. To the east, the region includes the Beaufort Sea and the complex of waterways forming the western end of the Northwest Passage. To the west, the region extends to the East Siberian Sea and the eastern section of the Northern Sea Route. The northcentral portion of the region is composed of the Chukchi Sea and a major segment of the Arctic Ocean proper. In addition, the coastal littorals are once again included within the region since port facilities and air terminals constitute important elements in any pattern of marine or air transportation. For purposes of comparison, the region as delineated for this functional areas is exhibited on the map on the next page (Figure V).

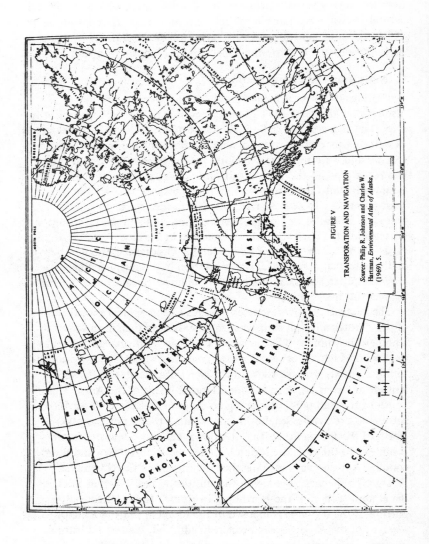

FIGURE V

TRANSPORATION AND NAVIGATION

Source: Philip R. Johnson and Charles W. Hartman, *Environmental Atlas of Alaska*, (1969), 5.

Beringia has a number of distinctive features that are relevant to transportation in the area. First, it is composed of two large marine areas (i.e. the North Pacific and the Arctic Ocean) connected by a relatively narrow and rather shallow passageway (i.e. the Bering Strait).[173] In addition, there are only a few channels through the Aleutian chain navigable by ships of commercial proportions.[174] Second, waters in large parts of this region (particularly in the northern segments) are unusually shallow due to the extensiveness of the continental shelves in the region.[175] In some instances, this poses barriers to passage on the part of large ships (e.g. large, modern oil tankers) and it introduces serious problems relating to the development of terminal facilities.[176] Third, a large portion of the region is covered with sea ice during the winter months, a factor that poses problems (though not necessarily insuperable barriers) for marine transportation. The pack ice is, of course, semi-permanent in large parts of the Arctic Ocean. But the winter sea ice extends far south into the Bering Sea during an average winter, as indicated by the map on the following page (Figure VI), so that navigation on the part of ships that are not ice-reinforced is possible for only a few months during the year.[177] Fourth, the human population of Beringia is extremely sparse, and there are few significant port facilities (aside from fishing operations) in the region at this time.[178] This situation will soon change as terminal facilities at places like Port Valdez become operational.[179] But this factor does indicate that the use of Beringia's flow resources is apt to focus on the shipment of natural resources like oil, natural gas, and other minerals.

The international issues arising in conjunction with the management of the air and sea as flow resources differ from those of renewable and non-renewable resources. Thus, flow resources do not generate the complex biological problems associated with the management of living resources. The conservation of stocks is not an issue here, though there are important problems of pollution which can affect the usability of flow resources. At the same time, flow resources are not finite and exhaustible in the same sense that non-renewable resources are. That is, it is ordinarily feasible to use flow resources over and over again without damaging their future usability.[180] Nevertheless, the utilization of flow resources in a marine region like Beringia raises issues that have important international implications.

The flow resources of the seas and the superjacent airspace have traditionally been conceptualized as common property resources. That

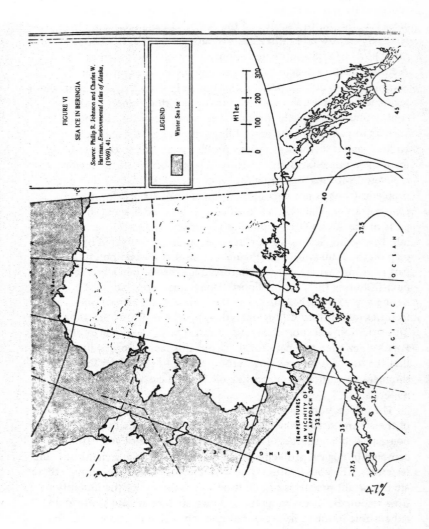

FIGURE VI
SEA ICE IN BERINGIA

Source: Philip R. Johnson and Charles W. Hartman, *Environmental Atlas of Alaska,* (1969), 41.

LEGEND

Winter Sea Ice

Miles

0   100   200   300

47%

is, they are widely regarded as accessible to all interested users and not subject to exclusive appropriation on the part of individuals. Under the circumstances, the familiar pattern of overinvestment or overuse often emerges in this realm just as it does in the fisheries.[181] In a sense, the problems are less severe in this area than they are in the fisheries since there is no direct analog to severe stock depletions. However, economic inefficiency and the production of negative externalities are both common with respect to flow resources. Economic inefficiency typically takes the form of excessive capitalization of fleets (e.g. the world's tanker fleet at present) or of costly delays caused by congestion in heavily used but unregulated waterways.[182] The most important negative externalities involve ship-based pollution and the noise and exhaust emanating from extensive air traffic.[183]

Though it may seem natural to think in terms of common-property arrangements for the flow resources of a region like Beringia, it is not always impossible to subject these resources to individual ownership. This is of course particularly true in the case of port facilities and air terminals. The history of marine transportation, for example, can be viewed in large part as a record of interactions between those who have wished to maximize the extent to which flow resources are conceptualized in common-property terms and those who have wished to establish individual rights in this realm and to expand national regulation of navigation and commerce in marine areas.[184] Numerous complexities have arisen in this realm concerning such matters as the extent to which coastal states are permitted to levy users' fees on marine commerce and the extent to which naval vessels and commercial vessels should be subjected to different rules. But the fact remains that the underlying issue has always been the confrontation between proponents of common-property arrangements and proponents of a regime of individual rights.

This discussion suggests that there would be a useful role for coordinated managerial arrangements at the international level in the realm of flow resources. Note, however, that the relevant institutions would constitute a collective good for the beneficiary group in question. This means that 'free-rider' incentives must be expected in this area and that there will be a tendency toward underinvestment in such arrangements.[185] Under the circumstances, there are two reasons to think in terms of regional, rather than global, institutions when dealing with the management of flow resources in Beringia. First, the natural systems involved in many of the problems are regional rather than global in scope. This is true, for example, with respect to most pollution problems. Second, efforts to supply collective goods are ordinarily more successful among small groups of participants than in large groups. Within small groups, the necessary agreements can be reached through bargaining processes without necessarily incurring prohibitive transactions costs.

Regardless of the specific institutional framework, it is possible to differentiate several international issues that arise again and again in efforts to manage the flow resources of seas and the superjacent airspace. In the first instance, there are numerous jurisdictional questions. Who has jurisdiction over ships at sea and planes in the air for what purposes? Who has the authority to promulgate rules concerning such matters in a decentralized polity like the international political system? Next, there are problems relating to various types of marine and air pollution. For example, what standards should be set in efforts to minimize these forms of pollution and how should these standards be enforced?[186] Similarly, issues often arise concerning the actual or impending congestion of flow resources. When usage is light, there are not likely to be any serious problems of congestion or crowding; usage by others in no way reduces the benefits to any given actor. But when heavy usage occurs, congestion may well become a major problem giving rise to a need for clearly formulated traffic regulations.[187] Finally, conflicts are apt to emerge between efforts to utilize flow resources efficiently and the exploitation of other resources within a specified geographical region. In the case of Beringia, it is not difficult to imagine conflicts of this kind involving such things as commercial fishing on the one hand and marine commerce on the other. Again, these problems will only become severe in situations characterized by heavy usage of a region's resources.[188] But it is clear that Beringia is now entering a period in which rather dramatic increases in the usage of the region's resources are highly probable.

Let me turn now to a more specific survey of the flow resources of Beringia. Beringia does not now constitute one of the world's principal commercial arteries. Nevertheless, the use of the region's waterways is by no means negligible at this time. Three of the major actors in Beringia (i.e. Japan, the Soviet Union, and the United States) are among the top ten powers of the world in the area of marine commerce.[189] A substantial increase in use of the sea and air is foreseeable as a consequence of rapid developments in the exploitation of the region's natural resources (especially in the realms of hydrocarbons and various minerals).[190]

1. *The North Pacific.* Though the flow resources of the North

Pacific are not heavily used at this time, a variety of actors already have significant interests in this realm. The bulk of Alaska's foodstuffs and consumers' durables is shipped to Alaska by sea from Seattle. Marine traffic using the great circle route between the United States and Japan passes through Beringian waters.[191] Commercial traffic entering or leaving the Northern Sea Route must go through the Bering Strait and make use of the Bering Sea and the North Pacific. During the summer months, there is regular barge traffic from the Pacific into the Arctic Ocean carrying supplies to such places as Prudhoe Bay. Furthermore, the North Pacific is of considerable interest to the navies of the Soviet Union and the United States. This is due, not only to a general desire to maintain freedom of access in all major waterways, but also to military concern about the vulnerability of Soviet and American land masses in this region to conventional military operations.

There is also reason to expect a substantial increase in marine commerce in the North Pacific during the next few years. Tanker traffic carrying Prudhoe Bay oil south from Port Valdez is scheduled to begin on a relatively large scale during 1977.[192] As the production of offshore oil gets underway in other parts of Beringia (e.g. the Gulf of Alaska), further dramatic increases in tanker traffic in the North Pacific will occur. Moreover, additional developments in the exploitation of Beringia's natural resources are likely to lead, during the next 20–30 years, to the extensive use of liquid natural gas (LNG) carriers and ore carriers on the marine highways of the region.[193]

By the same token, certain traditional uses of the flow resources of the North Pacific have declined during the twentieth century. For example, the region is no longer used by the great fleets of sailing ships that pursued whales in the Bering Sea during the second half of the nineteenth century and the early part of the twentieth century.[194] Similarly, the rapid decline of non-native populations in communities like Nome[195] coupled with the growing reliance on air freight has led to a dramatic reduction in the marine traffic of such places during the last 40–50 years. These points certainly do not suggest an overall reduction in the usage of the flow resources of the North Pacific, but they do indicate that qualitative changes have occurred over time in the patterns of this usage.

2. *The Northern Sea Route.* The Northern Sea Route is the name given to the Northeast Passage as it has been developed for marine transport during the twentieth century by the Soviet Union.[196] The route follows the coastline of the Soviet Union through the Barents Sea, the Kara Sea, the Laptev Sea, the East Siberian Sea, the Chukchi Sea,

down through the Bering Strait and into the North Pacific. The Northern Sea Route constitutes a northern maritime link between Europe and East Asia which is capable, in principle, of cutting up to 13 days off the time required to travel by sea between London and Yokohama.[197] The Route was first opened to commercial traffic by the Soviet Union during the 1920s and is now kept open for as many as 150 days a year, though this depends on the use of heavy ice-breaking equipment and is subject to variation from year to year as a function of weather conditions.[198]

The Northern Sea Route is of significance to intra-Soviet trade.[199] It is estimated that 200–400 freighters have sailed these waters every summer during recent years.[200] The majority of these do not traverse the whole Route. Instead, they carry supplies of various kinds to the growing Soviet communities of northern Siberia and timber and other raw materials to the markets of East Asia. There has never been any substantial volume of international traffic using the Northern Sea Route. Some years ago, the Japanese expressed an interest in using this Route, and it is easy to imagine the possibilities of shipping such things as North Sea oil to Japan via this Route.[201] However, there are serious impediments to such a development. Parts of the Sea Route are presently too shallow to accommodate large modern ships and, especially, tankers of the type that the Japanese have pioneered. More generally, there are serious international jurisdictional questions with respect to the Route. Various Soviet authorities have periodically advanced jurisdictional claims over the Sea Route on the grounds that it falls within Soviet 'internal waters'.[202] And it is true that the Soviet government expends considerable resources on keeping the Route ice free and maintaining it in usable condition. During 1967, the Soviet government offered to negotiate agreements with other governments regarding international use of the Northern Sea Route, but this offer was later withdrawn.[203] On the other hand, given the growing Soviet support of various policies resting on the concept of freedom of the seas, there is good reason to think that the Soviet government will become increasingly amenable to the idea that the Northern Sea Route should be viewed as an international waterway open to all nations under reasonable conditions.[204]

3. *The Northwest Passage.* The term 'Northwest Passage' refers to a series of straits and sounds in the Canadian Arctic archipelago, which make it possible, in principle, to travel by sea between the east and west coasts of North America.[205] Unlike the case of the Northern Sea Route, there is no history of actual commercial use of this seaway,

though the idea of eventual commercial use of the Northwest Passage has been publicized continuously over several centuries.[206] Recently, interest in opening up the Northwest Passage for commercial shipping has been rekindled by the voyages of the *Manhattan* during 1969 and 1970.[207] The *Manhattan* was a converted and ice-strengthened oil tanker (approximately 115,000 deadweight tons) commissioned by the Exxon Company to test the feasibility of transporting Alaskan oil through the Northwest Passage.[208] The ship made two trips through the Passage, one during the fall of 1969 and another under the even more severe conditions of the spring of 1970. Both trips were successful in the sense that they demonstrated the capacity of large tankers to traverse the Northwest Passage, though Exxon subsequently decided that it would be preferable (at least for the immediate future) to transport Prudhoe Bay oil via the pipeline to Valdez.[209]

Consequently, the commercial future of the Northwest Passage is highly uncertain at this time. It is possible that large increases in the production of oil in northern Beringia will make it more and more attractive to ship some Beringian oil to the east coast of North America by way of the Passage, but this would require solving difficult problems in the realm of terminal facilities.[210] It is also possible that portions of the Passage will play an important role in the economic development of Arctic Canada, though such prospects are quite uncertain and fall largely outside the geographical scope of Beringia in any case. Beyond this, it seems pertinent to note that there are potential questions concerning international jurisdiction in this case just as there are with respect to the Northern Sea Route. So, for example, under certain conceptions of archipelagoes, Canada could advance plausible claims to the effect that the Northwest Passage is part of Canadian internal waters and, therefore, entirely subject to the sovereign authority of Canada.[211] Alternatively, Canada could claim the passage as part of the Canadian territorial sea and seek to extend its jurisdiction over these waters for many purposes. It is not clear at this time exactly what will happen in this realm in the near future. But it is evident that the Canadian government is exhibiting growing sensitivity about issues relating to sovereignty in the Canadian Arctic,[212] and there is no doubt that jurisdictional issues concerning the Northwest Passage would have to be taken seriously if the Passage were to become commercially important.[213]

4. *Trans-arctic routes.* Recent years have witnessed a considerable growth of interest in the possibility of opening up direct commercial links between the Pacific and the Atlantic via trans-arctic routes.[214]

Enthusiasm for this prospect has been kindled by the passage of nuclear-powered submarines under the Arctic ice cap starting in 1958.[215] Though there are real technological difficulties associated with this idea, it is obviously attractive in terms of calculations of distances. Thus, '. . . the surface route from Tokyo to London totals 11,200 nautical miles; by the polar passage the distance shrinks to 6,500. Similarly, a vessel bound from Seattle to Oslo logs 9,300 miles, but an Arctic sub would travel only 6,100.'[216]

To date, this polar passage has not been used for commercial purposes. It is generally agreed, however, that it is now technologically feasible to construct vessels capable of carrying commercial cargoes over trans-arctic routes, though there are some unresolved issues relating to terminal facilities. The principal proposals in this area involve large, submarine freighters and reinforced, ice-breaking tankers of large proportions (i.e. 245,000 deadweight tons).[217] This means that the central issue in this realm is one of economic incentives rather than technological feasibility. In this connection, it is unclear whether the economic incentives will be sufficient to spur developments along these lines. Exxon's negative decision concerning the use of tankers in the Northwest Passage is certainly relevant here. But it would be a mistake to assume that undertakings of this type will not occur during the next 20–30 years, given their technological feasibility and the pace of change in maritime commerce in regions like Beringia.[218] Finally, it is important to note that important jurisdictional issues would also arise in conjunction with efforts to utilize the polar passage commercially. In this case, the problems would not center on national claims concerning 'internal waters'. Instead, they would emanate from the fact that the Arctic is presently a jurisdictional no-man's land which exhibits a complex mixture of the legal attributes of sea and land.[219] Accordingly, the expansion of commercial activities in this area would necessitate the clarification of some critical issues involving international jurisdiction.

5. *Air transport.* While marine transport is currently more extensive and commercially significant than air traffic in Beringia, air traffic in the region has been growing rapidly since the 1950s.[220] The increasing use of great circle routes has made the region a focal point in the growth of air links among Europe, North America, and East Asia[221] (see Figure VII). Thus, 'Eight [scheduled] airlines now operate over the Arctic Ocean. The pioneer was Scandanavian Airlines System in 1954: the route is from western Europe or Scandanavia to Anchorage, Alaska, and thence to Japan.'[222] Air traffic within the Beringian

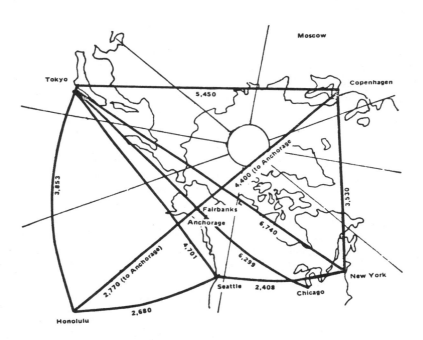

Figure VII

Source: Stephen M. Brent and Robert M. Goldberg, editors in chief,
The Alaska Survey and Report: 1970–1971, (Anchorage 1971),
211.

region has expanded rapidly during recent years, especially in response to developments in areas like Prudhoe Bay. There are no commercial flights between Alaska and Siberia across the Bering Sea or the Chukchi Sea at this time,[223] but the establishment of such links is likely to come soon with the subsidence of cold war attitudes and the growth of both commercial and touristic interests. There is no doubt that the rapid growth of air traffic in Beringia has played a crucial role in the emergence of Anchorage as a modern metropolitan center during the years since World War II.[224]

The international jurisdictional issues associated with these developments in air transport are not intrinsically complex. The general rule is that the status of airspace conforms to the status of the surface region directly below. So, for example, freedom of airspace obtains over all parts of the high seas, and state sovereignty extends over super-jacent airspace.[225] This general rule should be sufficient to resolve many of the international jurisdictional issues associated with air transport in Beringia. On the other hand, it is possible that agreements will be negotiated at the ongoing Law of the Sea Conference which will alter the status of airspace[226] and which will have significant implications for the growth of air traffic in Beringia. Moreover, there are already several specific problems in Beringia which are difficult to handle in terms of the general rule outlined earlier in this paragraph. One concerns the specification of air defense zones by the United States and the Soviet Union.[227] Given the sensitivity of both super-powers to the possibility of cross-polar air strikes, it is not surprising that the two states have advanced claims, based on security require-ments, to jurisdiction over airspace above adjacent marine areas in Beringia.[228] The other problem involves the airspace over the Arctic proper. Since jurisdiction with respect to the surface of the Arctic is currently inchoate, it follows that there are serious ambiguities concern-ing jurisdiction over the airspace of the Arctic. For this reason, it is pertinent to note that 'Up until the present time there does not seem to have been any particular effort to resolve these matters, even though use of Arctic and trans-Arctic air routes has increased greatly in recent years.'[229]

D. Environmental Quality

The environment is not just another resource defined on the same plane as renewable, non-renewable, and flow resources. Environmental concerns cut across each of the other functional areas and they often arise as a consequence of activities aimed at the utilization of other

100

resources. Nevertheless, it is frequently helpful to think of environmental conditions or goods, like clean air, unpolluted seas, and scenic areas, as exploitable resources.[230] Many of them are finite and subject to physical destruction (e.g. wilderness areas) so that it is important to regulate their use carefully. Others (e.g. stocks of wild animals) are subject to biological depletion or extinction and raise problems relating to the conservation of living species. The managerial problems of some environmental resources stem largely from direct use or exploitation for purposes of recreation, tourism, or private hunting.[231] Even more important in the context of this study, however, is that efforts to maximize profits from the commercial exploitation of natural resources frequently produce highly negative side effects for various environmental goods or conditions. In such cases, it is necessary (explicitly or implicitly) to make choices involving trade-offs between the maintenance of environmental quality and the minimization of costs involved in the production of resources like oil and natural gas.

There is some debate concerning the extent to which arctic and sub-arctic conditions, like those of Beringia, are unstable or delicate in ecological terms.[232] The concept of instability here refers to a '. . . state of inability to recover, the state in which perturbation leads to disintegration of the system', in contrast to a tendency to return to equilibrium following perturbations.[233] The term 'delicacy' refers to the probability of major deviations occuring in a given ecosystem. In fact, arctic and sub-arctic systems possess certain sources of stability which are not commonly present in other types of ecosystems. For example, 'One source of strength of arctic systems is their very large scale, which provides for the mending or, reestablishment, of regions of perturbation or distress.'[234]

At the same time, there are numerous sources of instability which make arctic and sub-arctic systems more susceptible to disintegration than other types of ecosystems. Such systems are slow-turnover systems in the sense that the growth cycles of plants and animals are unusually long. By way of illustration, this means that disturbances of the tundra take extremely long periods to mend and that serious depletions of the fish stocks of arctic lakes can be permanent or 'take many years to repair.'[235] Similarly, there is considerable evidence to suggest that rates of bacterial or biological degradation are slower at arctic and sub-arctic temperatures than they are in warmer regions. Consequently, oil spills may well constitute an unusually severe problem in Beringia, and human wastes of all kinds tend to remain in existence over protracted periods of time.[236] Moreover, arctic and sub-arctic environments are exceptionally vulnerable to air pollution, particularly in the form of temperature inversions which are popularly known as 'ice fogs'.[237] On balance, then, it seems accurate to conclude that:

> The apparent ruggedness is offset by slow regenerative processes in areas disturbed by man. The presence of the impermeable permafrost layer over much of the Arctic and the sub-Arctic prevents the dispersal of man's waste products and facilitates pollution of water and land. The air itself over centers of population is often exceptionally vulnerable to pollution.[238]

The underlying problems of managing environmental resources stem from several distinguishable sources. In the first instance, many environmental goods have traditionally been treated as common property resources. This is particularly true at the international level where such things as bird populations, stocks of wild animals, and the scenic wonders of marine areas commonly fall outside the exclusive jurisdiction of individual states.[239] Under the circumstances, the familiar problems associated with common property resources tend to afflict these environmental goods whenever they are subjected to heavy usage. Classic examples of overuse in this area are the destruction of the great buffalo herds in North America and the extinction of many species of birds.[240] But the problem is widespread, and it is not limited to situations involving the harvest of species having immediate commercial value.

Many of the most serious managerial problems in the realm of environmental quality stem from the fact that efforts to exploit other resources often have destructive side effects with respect to valuable environmental resources.[241] The production and transportation of hydrocarbons, for example, is responsible for extensive marine pollution and the destruction of wilderness areas in many parts of the world. Such negative externalities are typically not reflected in market interactions, given the content of existing systems of property rights and liability rules.[242] When the resultant problems are wholly confined to a single state, it is of course possible to think in terms of various form of government regulation aimed at the maintenance of environmental quality.[243] In marine regions like Beringia, however, the impact of such negative externalities commonly cuts across the boundaries of national jurisdictions, creating a need for some form of international regulation or management.

102

In this connection, it is pertinent to emphasize the fact that regimes or institutional arrangements designed to protect and manage various environmental resources will ordinarily exhibit many of the attributes of collective goods.[244] If they are supplied at all, the benefits will accrue to numerous beneficiaries and the costs (in terms of such things as increased oil prices) will also be borne by large groups. This means that the familiar problems of 'free-rider' incentives and underinvestment must be expected to arise in conjunction with the management of environmental resources.[245] Under the circumstances, it is not difficult to understand the problems that have plagued efforts to conserve various endangered species of great whales[246] or to construct effective institutions to cope with marine pollution.

There is no doubt that many problems relating to the management of environmental resources can only be solved through effective international coordination. Once again, however, there are two compelling reasons to focus many of the resultant activities at the level of resource regions rather than at the global level. In the first instance, the natural systems involved are often regional rather than global in scope.[247] So, for example,

.... there has come to be a greater recognition of the need for regional pollution control organs since it is apparent that, although pollution is a global problem, it is not uniformly global. Regional arrangements in the Baltic, the North Sea, Mediterranean, Caribbean and perhaps in the Arctic are now underway, and it is likely that these organs will have a decisive part to play in achieving day-to-day practical controls.[248]

In addition, the transactions costs of negotiating agreements for the supply of collective goods, such as institutions to manage environmental resources, are often prohibitive at the global level. There are many cases in which a small group of actors within a specified region can reach agreements through bargaining processes that would be unfeasible at the level of the whole international community.[249]

I turn now to a brief discussion of the most salient problems of environmental quality in the Beringian region. There are of course numerous issues relating to environmental resources that have some relevance to the region. Given the distinctive features of Beringia, however, it seems to me that the following distinguishable sets of environmental questions are likely to be particularly prominent in the region during the next 10—20 years.

1. *Conservation of species.* Two major problems relating to the
conservation of species are of great importance in Beringia. To begin
with, there is the problem of preventing the extinction or near
extinction of species.[250] This goal is now subscribed to, in principle,
on a widespread basis. It is formally incorporated in the 1958 Geneva
Convention on Fishing and Conservation of the Living Resources of
the High Seas. It constitutes a major objective of such specific
agreements as the International Whaling Convention and the new five-
nation agreement on the preservation of Polar Bears.[251] And there is
little doubt that popular sensitivity to the value of preserving species
is growing in many parts of the world.

Nevertheless, it is probable that the rate at which species are
becoming endangered is increasing, and the issues associated with the
preservation of species are somewhat more complex than they may at
first appear.[252] There is considerable controversy among biologists
concerning the question of what constitutes depletion of a species
beyond the point of recovery, and it is clear that this threshold will
vary significantly from species to species as a function of such factors
as length of life cycle and recruitment pattern.[253] Next, there may be
an important distinction with respect to some species between
absolute extinction and extinction from the point of view of
commercial significance. In the case of certain species of fish, for
example, some authorities believe that the gap between these two
thresholds is sufficiently large so that the tendency to stop harvesting
a species when it becomes commercially unprofitable to do so will
constitute an effective guarantee of the preservation of the species in
absolute terms.[254] But disagreements about this proposition are great
enough to make it a dubious premise on which to base major policy
choices.[255] Moreover, there is a real question whether it would not
be more appropriate to define the goal of preservation in terms of
biologically autonomous stocks rather than species. Recent botanical
experiences with strains of plants suggest the hypothesis that animal
stocks are not biologically identical even though they belong to the
same species. Therefore, the extinction of a given stock or sub-species
may lead to the loss of valuable biological qualities, even if it does not
endanger an entire species.[256] Thus, while the basic goal of preserving
species is now rather widely held, the remaining unresolved questions
in this area are of critical importance.[257]

Quite apart from the goal of preservation, there is the issue of
determining desirable levels at which to maintain various stocks of
fish, whales, and so forth. In fact, this is an issue of considerable

complexity, and there is no consensus at this time regarding its central normative aspects. It is much easier to agree that a given species should be preserved than to settle on an optimal level at which to maintain a stock.[258] Some argue that the idea of maximum sustainable yield constitutes a salient solution since it simultaneously allows for the maintenance of stocks in a healthy condition and permits individual stocks to make the maximum contribution of animal protein to human diets. But this goal has no particular economic significance. It hardly satisfies those who are opposed to all human predation on certain species. And it does not invalidate the opposing arguments that can be constructed to justify at least temporary depletion of specified stocks under certain conditions.[259] All this suggests the importance of the classic political question of who should have the authority to make binding decisions concerning matters of this kind. This is an issue that becomes particularly sensitive in cases where there are authentic biological disagreements with respect to the current condition of various stocks (e.g. sperm whales and Walrus in Beringia). Nevertheless, there are some cases in which it is generally agreed that common property arrangements have resulted in undesirable depletions of stocks, even in terms of weak social welfare criteria like Pareto optimality. Cases in point in Beringia are the fur seal and sea otter stocks during the late nineteenth and early twentieth centuries.[260] Under these conditions, there is a compelling argument for taking steps aimed at the regeneration of stocks even in the absence of final agreement on the question of optimal levels.

2. *Pollution control.* With respect to the management of non-renewable and flow resources, a central environmental concern in the Beringian region encompasses the control of pollution broadly defined.[261] Four distinct types of pollution are important in this region. To begin with, there is seabed-based pollution. The major issues here involve offshore oil seepages and spills of the type that occurred in the Santa Barbara Channel in 1968.[262] Given the severe conditions associated with arctic and sub-arctic waters and the slow rate of bio-degradation in the region, there is every reason to treat the dangers of this type of pollution seriously in such areas as the Gulf of Alaska, the Bering Sea, and the Beaufort Sea. While it is possible that technological advances will go far toward solving these problems during the foreseeable future, too little is known about them at this time to be confident of such an outcome.

Next, there is vessel-based pollution. Again, the critical problems of this kind in Beringia pertain to the exploitation of hydrocarbons,

105

though normal dumping of wastes from vessels at sea can become an environmental problem of considerable proportions in situations characterized by dense transportation networks.[263] In the case of hydrocarbons, vessel-based pollution can take the form of severe accidents (e.g. the Torrey Canyon disaster in 1967) or of the consequences of normal operations.[264] Though some research has been done on these issues, the potential problems are great enough to warrant much more attention in connection with the special features of Beringia. As Weeden and Klein have argued,

Little attention has been focused on the problems of massive oils spills in the tanker lanes between Alaska and the west coast of the United States, probably because the responsibilities for prevention and for assessing liability are scattered among many federal agencies, the oil industry, and the shipping industry. A simple calculation shows the very high probability that hugh volumes of crude oil will be spilled at sea. According to McCaull (1969), an average of one unit of oil is spilled at sea or in port through tanker mishaps for every 1000 units carried. At 2 million barrels a day, an average of 2000 barrels of crude oil would be spilled every day from ships loading at Valdez (the spills of course, would not be daily, but infrequent and massive).[265]

Beyond this, there is shore- and land-based pollution. One obvious source of such pollution is terminal operations involved in the transportation of oil or natural gas (the facilities under construction at the present time at Port Valdez are a case in point). Though this is an important source of pollution, extensive efforts are now being made to minimize the pollution potential of terminal operations.[266] Other forms of land-based pollution, however, are also relevant to the problems of resource management in Beringia. For example, construction operations can seriously disrupt the spawning beds of anadromous species of fish such as salmon, and effluents flowing into or dumped into major rivers can discharge into the sea with significant adverse effects on marine life.[267] In general, land-based activities are the largest source of pollutants in marine regions,[268] and the fact that pollution of this type tends to increase as a function of economic development suggests that land-based pollution will be a growing concern in Beringia.

Finally, there are some sources of pollution that do not fit neatly into any of these categories. Perhaps the most obvious case in point involves atmospheric pollution. In the Beringian region, for example, there is the possibility of radioactive wastes produced by underground nuclear tests. So far as is known, the last nuclear test in the region was the American Cannikin test on Amchitka, a 5 megaton explosion during November 1971.[269] But nuclear tests in Beringia could be resumed at any time in the future. Though the significance of the dangers associated with this form of pollution is a matter of some controversy, it would be a mistake to dismiss problems of this kind out of hand in this discussion of environmental resources.[270]

These several types of pollution pose certain common managerial problems. Above all, there are the issues involved in creating institutional mechanisms to prevent the occurrence of pollution and to restore the environment in the event that pollution does occur.[271] If the arguments set forth earlier in this section concerning the relative instability of arctic and sub-arctic ecosystems are correct, it follows that the prevention of pollution is a particularly important objective to be pursued in the Beringian region. As might be expected, there are also major jurisdictional issues that arise in conjunction with the control of pollution in a resource region like Beringia.[272] Is it possible to develop effective international rules to handle major problems in this realm? While a number of international conventions have been negotiated concerning such things as the prevention of the pollution of the sea by oil,[273] these conventions do not begin to constitute a comprehensive system of pollution control for marine regions and they are difficult to enforce.[274] Alternatively, is national jurisdiction desirable or feasible in dealing with the pollution problems of a region like Beringia? If so, how should such jurisdiction be divided among coastal states, flag states, and port states?[275] And what would constitute acceptable arrangements for such matters as the establishment of formal standards relating to marine pollution, inspection procedures applicable to vessels of foreign registry, detention of violators, and the meting out of penalities in cases of proven violations?[276] Beyond this, there are also important questions concerning the liability rules applicable to the kinds of pollution under discussion in this section. There are important normative issues involved in specifying the content of liability rules in this area.[277] A major drawback of the existing system lies in the confusing dispersion of liability among a number of public and private actors which often makes the legal responsibility for specific forms of pollution difficult to establish.[278] Accordingly, there is a clear need in Beringia (as in other resource regions) to reexamine existing liability rules in the interests of formulating a more effective and equitable system for the establishment of responsibility.

3. *Preservation of the habitat*. The habitat is the setting within which human activities take place. Though it is common to emphasize the physical setting in thinking about the human habitat, it is often helpful to extend this concept to include various aspects of the socio-cultural setting as well. Many features of the habitat have positive value for human individuals and groups, and these conditions or goods belong to the broader category of environmental resources.[279] With respect to the physical habitat, these resources encompass such things as wilderness areas, unscarred landscapes, and unique scenic attractions.[280] The sociocultural habitat, on the other hand, includes such resources as special life styles (e.g. the frontier spirit) and accumulated human heritages (e.g. the cultural heritage of the native peoples in Alaska).[281]

The preservation of the habitat is not a free good in most real-world situations. It is a goal to be pursued consciously and its achievement generally involves opportunity costs with respect to other goals (e.g. the production of cheap energy). In most parts of the world, a number of factors currently operate to favor the pursuit of traditional economic goals (e.g. maximizing the rate of growth of GNP per capita) when they conflict with efforts to preserve the habitat. Existing liability rules typically operate to encourage this result.[282] So, for example, firms involved in mining and the production of oil are not presently held responsible for many side effects of their operations which have destructive consequences for the habitat. Consumer demand for the preservation of the habitat is often relatively low since large numbers of people have not been taught (i.e. socialized) to place a high value on these resources in comparison with standard economic goods (e.g. consumers' durables).[283] It is not widely understood that ' . . . the supply of natural phenomena is virtually inelastic' and that this means that the long-run costs of destroying such things as scenic areas is apt to be extremely high.[284] And the preservation of the habitat will take the form of a collective good in many cases so that efforts to achieve this goal will often be affected by the familiar pattern of 'free-rider' incentives and underinvestment in collective goods. In short, ' . . . the central issue seems to be the problem of providing for the present and future the amenities associated with unspoiled natural environments, for which the market fails to make adequate provision.'[285]

With respect to resource regions like Beringia, it is especially pertinent to note that rapid economic development typically generates numerous threats to the preservation of the habitat, though it may seem highly desirable from other points of view.[286] Economic development radically alters previously wild and primitive areas and it displaces numerous pre-existing activities at the local level. It is often insensitive to aesthetic values (e.g. the preservation of scenic areas) because such values are frequently not incorporated in the cost-benefit calculations underlying the pursuit of economic efficiency. Moreover, economic development commonly leads to dramatic changes in pre-existing life styles and cultural patterns. Therefore, it is hardly surprising that those concerned with the preservation of the habitat in areas like Alaska have come to look upon rapid economic development as a fundamentally threatening force.[287]

Several of the distinctive features of Beringia also tend to exacerbate the difficulties associated with efforts to preserve the habitat of the region. First, the disruption or transformation of many features of the habitat of a resource region like Beringia is essentially an irreversible process. Choices that result in the extinction of species, the disfigurement of scenic areas, or the destruction of native cultures cannot be retracted at a later date.[288] Second, there are powerful short-run pressures to exploit the resources of Beringia rapidly which constantly threaten to overwhelm efforts to take into account the longer-run costs of such decisions in environmental terms. The impact of the energy crisis, and the resultant desire to achieve energy independence, on American decision making with respect to the offshore production of oil in Beringia constitutes a striking case in point.[289] Third, the sparse population of the region is a drawback from the point of view of mounting an effective defense of the Beringian habitat. While the raw materials and foodstuffs of the region are largely exported and benefit large numbers of consumers, the group *directly* affected by such things as the destruction of wilderness areas or the disfigurement of the Alaskan North Slope is small.[290] Consequently, those desiring rapid economic development in the region are likely to enjoy a political advantage over those primarily concerned with the preservation of the habitat at least with respect to policymaking at the federal level.[291]

The discussion of environmental resources in this section serves to highlight an issue that has been in the background throughout this chapter and that is destined to become increasingly prominent in Beringia in the next decade or so. This issue arises from the existence of extensive interdependencies among the various resources of a region like Beringia.[292] The fur seal population of the region, for example, is dependent upon the availability of various species of fish like pollock.[293]

Large-scale offshore production of oil in areas like the Gulf of Alaska will inevitably produce problems for the commercial fisheries of these areas (recent debates over activities in Kachemak Bay exemplify this point).[294] Efforts to minimize the production costs of Beringian oil are bound to raise serious problems in the realm of pollution control. And given the mobility of capital, equipment, and some forms of labor in the contemporary world, emerging interdependencies among different international resource regions cannot be ignored. All this means that policymakers concerned with the management of resources in a region like Beringia must constantly confront important value tradeoffs and make choices having profound distributive as well as productive implications. Furthermore, the need to cope with such issues will become more and more pressing during the near future as heavier usage of Beringia's resources accentuates and strengthens the interdependencies among these resources.

There is no way to resolve the critical normative issues underlying such value trade-offs in purely technical terms.[295] Consequently, questions concerning who makes important decisions of this kind and on the basis of what criteria become prominent in discussions of the management of resources in a region like Beringia. That is, the essential problems of politics emerge as central issues in this context. Not only do the multiple interdependencies among the region's resources necessitate complex choices among competing goals or objectives. It is also true that various public and private actors with extensive interests in the region have widely divergent value systems or utility functions so that it is impossible to make managerial choices or to devise managerial institutions that approach optimality for all interested parties at the same time.[296] Moreover, there are additional problems in this area arising from the fact that the policies advocated by some of the most powerful actors in Beringia are apt to produce results that are repugnant to many of the most articulate observers of the unfolding patterns of resource management in the region.[297] So, for example, many vocal observers would be severely distressed if large-scale offshore production of oil in Beringia were seriously to damage commercial fishing operations in the region, let alone cause severe damage to the more notable features of the region's physical habitat. When it is necessary for policymakers to cope with these problems of designing '. . . optimal systems involving multiple objectives incapable of expression in a common denominator', [298] there are seldom any solutions outside the push and pull of the political process. And the ultimate outcomes of this process will often deviate considerably from the requirements of many conceptions of fairness or justice.

E. Security

The functional area of security requires descussion here not because it raises special problems of resource management in its own right but because many observers believe that deepseated sensitivities about security constitute serious barriers to coordinated resource management at the international level. Specifically, it is common to hear the argument that proposed arrangements involving coordination between the United States and the Soviet Union are likely to prove unfeasible due to the impact of underlying politico-military conflicts between the two superpowers. The thesis of this section is that this argument is not persuasive, at least for the case of Beringia. While the complexities of resource management themselves may make it extremely difficult to work out coordinated arrangements at the international level to handle various resources, the central problems do not appear to stem from the intrusion of politico-military sensitivities.[299]

It is not difficult to understand why casual observers sometimes assume that security problems are of critical importance in the Beringian region. The region contains the points at which the United States and the Soviet Union are in closest physical proximity. In recent years, the public has been socialized to fear the possibility of cross-polar air strikes, especially those involving the use of nuclear weapons. Furthermore, the Arctic portions of Beringia are a source of considerable ambiguity with respect to the allocation of sovereign authority and the specification of jurisdictional rules governing a variety of human activities.[300] Consequently, it is not altogether impossible to imagine the occurrence of various incidents in this area which could escalate into more serious confrontations.

Beyond this, several more specific issues in the realm of security affairs are of some relevance to the future of Beringia. First, there is general agreement that the United States has installed antisubmarine warfare (ASW) devices on the seabeds of the Bering Sea and the Chukchi Sea, though the details of these emplacements remain secret. And there is every reason to conclude that the Soviet Union has roughly parallel ASW installations in the region. Second, both superpowers maintain extensive early warning surveillance systems, portions of which lie within the geographical confines of Beringia. In the American case, the outstanding example is the Distance Early Warning System (DEWLine) which stretches east-west along the 69th parallel from Cape Lisburne, Alaska and which is composed of a network of radar and communications stations serving as a forward line of surveillance for the North American Air Defense Command (NORAD).[301] It is clear that a similar system exists in the Soviet Union, though public information concerning the details of this system is more difficult to obtain.

Third, real sensitivities exist among naval authorities concerned with freedom of access for warships in various parts of Beringia. The United States and the Soviet Union have engaged in several disputes along these lines stemming primarily from Soviet claims concerning the boundaries of Soviet 'internal waters',[302] and there are possibilities of Canadian-American clashes in the future involving issues of this type in the Arctic. Fourth, somewhat similar problems exist with respect to sensitivities about contiguous air defense zones and alleged violations of Soviet or American airspace by military aircraft. So, for example, a potentially serious incident occurred during the Cuban missile crisis when an American U-2, on an air-sampling mission over the North Pole, strayed into Soviet airspace over the Chukotsk Peninsula on 27 October 1962.[303] Fifth, Beringia has been the scene of several underground nuclear tests during the years since the signing of the limited Test Ban Treaty in 1963.[304] None of these tests has produced any serious politico-military repercussions, but their occurrence does lend some military significance to the region quite apart from their environmental implications.

Sixth, it is possible to imagine Beringian supply routes becoming important during certain types of conventional warfare.[305] Large portions of the Lend Lease shipments from the United States to the Soviet Union during World War II reached their destination over Beringian supply routes. The Alcan Highway was constructed during the war as a supply route, the Northern Sea Route played a role in the shipment of Lend Lease materials, and cooperation reached the point of the United States loaning such things as icebreakers to the Soviet Union to facilitate supply operations.[306] Though this particular situation will not soon recur, it does illustrate the proposition that Beringian supply routes could play a role of some importance under conditions of conventional warfare. Seventh, there are those who believe that Beringia could become the scene of conventional military operations in the future. The battle of Attu, in the western Aleutians, during World War II is often cited as a precedent in this connection, and some observers suggest that conflicts over sovereignty in the Arctic may eventually become severe enough to precipitate conventional military clashes.[307] While such concerns seem rather unrealistic at present, perhaps they should not simply be dismissed out of hand.

It is incorrect, then, to argue that there are no politico-military issues of any significance affecting the Beringian region. But what is the relevance of these issues for the present study of resource management at the international level; are they likely to pose serious barriers to effective international cooperation? I can see no reason to reach pessimistic conclusions concerning the interference of politico-military sensitivities in the management of resources in Beringia. Though it seems unlikely that ASW devices and distance early warning systems will disappear or that nuclear testing will come to a complete halt, there is every reason to conclude that these phenomena are now widely accepted on a tacit basis and that they will not intrude on efforts to coordinate policies in the realm of resource management. Thus, a kind of compartmentalization has occurred so that it now seems quite feasible to work out cooperative arrangements in functional areas such as those related to resource management even though the politico-military sensitivities under discussion here are not likely to vanish.[308]

Beyond this, it is exceedingly difficult to construct realistic scenarios involving military confrontations affecting Beringia directly. Presumably, such scenarios would have to focus on Soviet-American or, less plausibly, Canadian-American clashes. But while there are indeed numerous potential conflicts involving the allocation of resources as well as jurisdictional boundaries in Beringia, it is hard, at this point in time, to imagine any of them leading to actual hostilities. Specific incidents involving such things as alleged violations of airspace or freedom of access for naval vessels are certainly imaginable. Nevertheless, the argument that such incidents could precipitate large-scale military confrontations does not seem persuasive. Such developments would require some form of escalation that is difficult to project realistically. Moreover, the United States and the Soviet Union are now moving closer together rather than farther apart with respect to their positions on such matters as freedom of navigation.[309]

Finally, it seems pertinent to note the role of various national military forces in the economic development of Beringia. The American military has played a central role in opening up Alaska during the last 30–40 years, and the economic importance of the military remains substantial in Alaska.[310] In the Soviet case, the military has been a highly important factor in the development of northern and eastern Siberia. And there appear to be close links between the Soviet navy and the high seas fishing fleet, which has grown dramatically since the 1950s in the North Pacific.[311] Similarly, the Canadian military appears to have acquired an interest in the possibility of carving out an important role for itself in the development of the Canadian Arctic.[312] These occurrences may be regarded as acceptable or objectionable from a variety of points of view; that is not a concern in this essay. The argument is that there is no compelling reason to conclude that these activities on the part of American, Soviet, and Canadian military forces are likely to constitute a serious barrier to effective international cooperation relating to the problems of resource management in Beringia. From a purely professional point of view, military decision makers are not necessarily opposed to internationalism. And the activities outlined above do not appear to pose any decisive institutional barriers to international coordination in the realm of resource management.

By way of conclusion, let me add that Beringia and/or the Arctic have been proposed from time to time as constituting an appropriate region in which to take preliminary steps toward disarmament. In the words of a specific proposal authored jointly by an American scientist and a Soviet scientist,

> The Arctic region may provide a useful area in which the initial stages of a disarmament agreement can be developed. This is because its military value is relatively less than that of many other regions.[313]

That is, disarmament seems attractive in this region for many of the same reasons that have led to some real successes in this realm in such cases as the Antarctic and the seabed.[314] There are various specific disarmament plans that could be adapted for application in Beringia and the Arctic, and serious negotiations concerning such issues have not yet begun. Nevertheless, the fact that these areas are often regarded as constituting an appropriate zone for the development of disarmament arrangements strikes me as further evidence for the proposition that politico-military sensitivities are not apt to pose insurmountable obstacles to the achievement of effective international coordination with respect to the problems of resource management in Beringia.[315]

114

CHAPTER III: APPENDIX

OPTIMAL HARVESTS IN MARINE FISHERIES

For reasons set forth in the body of this chapter unregulated common property arrangements (either at the international level or at the national level) will typically lead to the depletion of stocks of fish and marine mammals in the sense that the actual harvest of heavily used stocks will fall well below the level of maximum sustained yield. Also, such arrangements tend to stimulate substantial overinvestment in marine fisheries, a condition that produces economic inefficiency. To avoid these results it is necessary to introduce at least *de facto* entry restrictions for the fisheries in question. As suggested in the text, entry restrictions carry with them important implications concerning the distribution of the catch among the relevant participants. But the introduction of such restrictions also makes it necessary to think about the question of optimal levels for regulated harvests.

In fact, this issue has become a focus of considerable controversy.[316] Numerous thresholds have been advanced as candidates for the title of optimal level. Undoubtedly, the two most widely discussed thresholds of this kind are those that go under the headings of maximum sustained yield (MSY) and profit or rent maximization. The concept of maximum sustained yield suggests harvesting any given stock at the level that permits the greatest annual catch over the long run. It is, therefore, essentially a biological standard. Profit or rent maximization, by contrast, is an economic criterion which suggests harvesting any given stock up to the level at which marginal cost equals marginal revenue or at which the difference between total cost and total revenue for the fishery is maximized.[317] These two ideas are illustrated graphically for the hypothetical case outlined in Figure VIII.[318] This figure shows that the practical consequences of the two standards diverge substantially and that the criterion of profit or rent maximization will lead to smaller harvests than the criterion of maximum sustained yield (under a range of reasonable assumptions about economic characteristics of the fishery). Moreover, the figure makes it clear that these are not the only standards that could be utilized to determine optimal harvests in regulated fisheries. Thus, it would be possible, in principle, to aim for a level of harvest anywhere along the yield curve (i.e. TY/TR) to the left of its intersection with the cost curve (i.e. to the left of the point of equilibrium in the

115

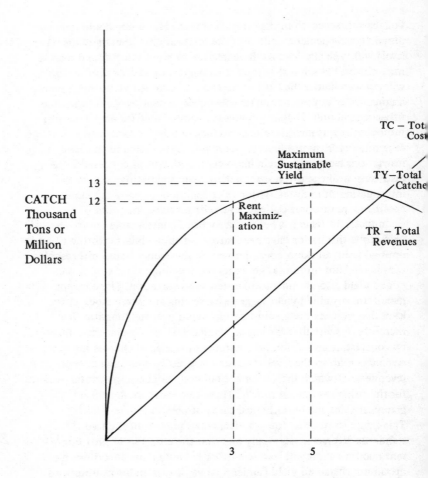

Figure VIII

Consequences of Common Property

Source: Francis T. Christy, Jr., 'Alternative Arrangements for Marine Fisheries: An Overview', *RFF Program of International Studies of Fishery Arrangements*, (Washington 1973), 10.

absence of regulation).

Underlying the dispute between advocates of MSY and profit or rent maximization as criteria for optimal harvests is a fundamental difference in perspectives. The idea of MSY is politically attractive in the sense that it represents that level of harvest at which the fisheries can make their maximum contribution to human consumption of animal protein (leaving aside the prospects for systematic aquaculture). In addition, MSY would often be preferable from the point of view of other political goals such as the maintenance of employment opportunities in the marine fisheries.[319] But the idea has no economic significance in any economic system in which cost-benefit calculations play a central role. That is, economic incentives (in the absence of systematic government intervention) will not induce fishermen to act in such a way as to produce the maximum sustained yield from a fishery. Consequently, the achievement of this objective would require the introduction of a system of government regulations and would ordinarily result in a shift of factors of production away from more 'profitable' enterprises (though not necessarily in the realm of food production).[320] Therefore, the conflict between the criteria of MSY and profit or rent maximization is, in part, a confrontation between political values and economic values which cannot be resolved in a technical or non-normative fashion.

There are also numerous arguments of a somewhat more technical nature concerning the relative merits of the two standards. So, for example, profit or rent maximization would typically require a greater reduction of present employment levels in the fisheries and a greater retirement of existing capital equipment as well;[321] this is a factor of some importance when the members of a highly immobile group are dependent upon fishing for their livelihood.[322] Profit or rent maximization is difficult to achieve in fisheries involving actors with different tastes, economic systems (e.g. capitalism vs. socialism), and types of *de facto* taxes or subsidies since the very meaning of the idea of maximizing the difference between total costs and total revenues becomes somewhat unclear and difficult to operationalize under such conditions.[323] Profit or rent maximization would presumably generate sharper controversies than MSY with respect to the allocation of overall profits or rents from a given fishery (whether this was done implicitly, through the allocation of catch quotas, or in some other fashion) because the total profits would be greater under a system utilizing the criterion of rent maximization. On the other hand, the achievement of MSY would necessitate the introduction of a relatively elaborate system of regulations. This might pose severe problems, given the international scope of the system required in a region like Beringia and the difficulties generated by the large natural fluctuations in fish stocks. Under the circumstances, neither profit or rent maximization nor MSY can serve as anything more than a target to aim for without expecting complete success.

If anything, the problems associated with these standards become more serious when the underlying characteristics of marine fisheries are taken into account. Thus, interdependencies among species of fish and marine mammals as well as among harvesting practices are great enough so that it is not entirely feasible to deal with the establishment of optimal harvest levels on a stock-by-stock basis, as though each stock were an isolated biological community.[324] Instead, it is important in this context to consider the major features of the whole system of living resources in a region. In addition, marine ecosystems are highly volatile which means that it is not adequate to compute optimal catch levels (whatever the criterion employed) on a once-and-for-all basis. On the contrary, it is necessary to make constant recomputations concerning the operational implications of any ideal criterion even after agreement is reached on a particular criterion in principle.[325] Even more important, the data problems characteristic of marine fisheries are such that it is commonly impossible to   make the relevant computations with sufficient speed and precision to utilize criteria such as profit or rent maximization and MSY rigorously.[326] In many cases, reasonable success would amount to an ability to recognize and to control serious stock depletions in contrast to an ability to apply specific analytic standards with pinpoint accuracy.

It is not surprising, then, to find experts now arguing that 'It is to be hoped that the late 1960s marked the end of the simplistic controversies over the relative merits of maximum sustained yield vs. maximum net economic yield as the objectives of fisheries management.'[327] But this still leaves the problem of specifying at least crude goals if we are to develop international (or national) managerial arrangements capable of avoiding the most serious negative consequences of unregulated common property arrangements in marine fisheries. All this suggests two final comments that seem applicable to the case of Beringia as well as to other international resource regions. In the first instance, it may often make sense to start by emphasizing efforts to identify really serious cases of stock depletion rather than laying down precise standards for optimal harvests. In cases where it is widely agreed that substantial depletion has occurred, it would then be possible to proceed on an *ad hoc* basis with plans to reduce the overall harvest of the stock in question in a manner viewed as equitable by all the participants. Current examples in Beringia would include the sockeye salmon in the Bristol Bay, pollock in the eastern Bering Sea, herring stocks in the Gulf of Alaska, and certain species of great whales throughout the region.[328]

In addition, specific plans adopted in individual cases under this arrangement would ordinarily result from hard bargaining involving political considerations rather than from precise calculations on the part of neutral experts. Such a process would not resemble the neat and efficient procedures many commentators associate with the concept of management. Outcomes would emerge from the bargaining process *ad hoc*, and it would be difficult in many cases to justify them as systematic applications of general rules or criteria.[329] Such a system would undoubtedly have real drawbacks. But it may currently be the most effective alternative to the existing unregulated common property arrangements in an international region like Beringia. Under the circumstances, there is a compelling case to be made for the proposition that a regionally coordinated management system (even with the drawbacks noted here) would produce results that would constitute a distinct improvement over those flowing from the continued operation of decentralized common property arrangements under any reasonable assumptions.

Notes

1. A problem in the analysis of the marine fisheries of the North Pacific stems from the fact that different data sets are not entirely compatible with respect to their geographical coverage. The delineation here follows that in Eugene H. Buck, 'National Patterns and Trends of Fishery Development in the North Pacific', *Alaska and the Law of the Sea*, Arctic Environmental Information and Data Center, (Anchorage 1973).
2. This delineation of Beringia overlaps to a considerable degree with what is described as the Northeast Pacific in J.A. Gulland compiler and editor, *The Fish Resources of the Ocean*, (Surrey, England 1971), 65–76.
3. Under the terms of this agreement, Japan and Canada refrain from fishing salmon in the eastern Bering Sea and Japan refrains from fishing salmon and halibut in the Gulf of Alaska and the transition area. The legal significance of these arrangements is discussed in greater detail in the next chapter.
4. J. A. Gulland, A. R. Tussing *et. al.*, 'Fish Stocks and Fisheries of Alaska and the Northeast Pacific Ocean', Arlon R. Tussing, Thomas A. Morehouse, and James D. Babb, Jr., eds., *Alaska Fisheries Policy*, (Fairbanks 1972), 75.
5. *Ibid.*, 93.
6. The Soviets have developed equipment capable of carrying on high seas fishing operations in the sea ice of the Bering Sea. It is possible that they

will attempt to emply the same techniques in the Chukchi Sea during the foreseeable future.

7. Francis T. Christy, Jr. and Anthony Scott, *The Common Wealth in Ocean Fisheries*, (Baltimore 1965). For a general review of the literature on property rights see Eirik Furubotn and Svetozar Pejovich, 'Property Rights and Economic Theory: A Survey of Recent Literature', *Journal of Economic Literature*, X (1972), 1137–1162.

8. Anthony Scott, 'The Fishery: The Objectives of Sole Ownership', *Journal of Political Economy*, LXIII (1955), 116–124.

9. James Crutchfield, 'The Marine Fisheries: A Problem in International Cooperation', *American Economic Review*, LIV (1965), 208.

10. *Loc. cit.*

11. Philip E. Chitwood, 'Japanese, Soviet, and South Korean Fisheries Off Alaska', Fish and Wildlife Service, United States Department of the Interior, Circular No. 310, (Washington 1969), 1.

12. Consult, *inter alia*, Christy and Scott, *op. cit.* and H. Scott Gordon, 'The Economic Theory of a Common Property Resource: the Fishery', *Journal of Political Economy*, LXII (1954), 124–142.

13. Christy and Scott, *op. cit.*, 7.

14. Crutchfield, *op. cit.*, 212.

15. This figure is from Francis T. Christy, Jr., 'Alternative Arrangements for Marine Fisheries: An Overview', *RfF Program of International Studies of Fishery Arrangements*, (Washington 1973), 10.

16. For a clear statement of this argument with applications to Beringia see Arlon R. Tussing, 'The Place of Trade with Japan and Japanese Investment in Alaska's Economic Development', Arlon R. Tussing *et. al., Alaska-Japan Economic Relations*, Institute of Social, Economic, and Government Research, (Fairbanks 1968), esp. 34–49.

17. This will occur under a range of reasonable assumptions about the shapes of the curves TC and TR/TY.

18. Christy, *op. cit.*, 14–16.

19. Crutchfield, *op. cit.*, 212.

20. John A. Knauss, 'Marine Science and the 1974 Law of the Sea Conference', *Science*, 184 (28 June 1974), 1340.

21. The extent of such interdependencies will be a function of the mobility of the relevant factors of production. While such mobility has traditionally been low in states with predominantly coastal fishing operations (e.g. the United States), it is relatively high in states emphasizing modern, high seas operations (e.g. Japan).

22. Tussing, *op. cit.*

23. James A. Crutchfield, 'Economic and Political Objectives in Fishery Management', Brian J. Rothschild ed., *World Fisheries Policy*, (Seattle 1972), 80.

24. These issues are clearly reviewed in Tussing, *op. cit.*

25. Gordon, *op. cit.*

26. There are of course other restrictions that have been used from time to time in efforts to regulate fisheries (e.g. gear restrictions, closed seasons, closed areas, and catch quotas). For a brief review of these techniques see Christy, *op. cit.*, 29–40.

27. Crutchfield, 'The Marine Fisheries', *op. cit.*, 206.

28. An outstanding example of an international agreement involving an explicit distributive mechanism is the Fur Seal Convention between the United States, the Soviet Union, Japan, and Canada.

29. A collective good is a good that exhibits the following characteristics:

120

a) if it is supplied to any member of a given group, it will be supplied to the other members of the group as well, and b) consumption of the good by one member of the group does not reduce its value to others. For theoretical background consult Mancur Olson, Jr., *The Logic of Collective Action*, (Cambridge 1965), and Norman Frohlich, Joe A. Oppenheimer, and Oran R. Young, *Political Leadership and Collective Goods*, (Princeton 1971).

30. On 'free-rider' tendencies see Olson, *op. cit.*

31. *Ibid.*

32. On the relevance of intervening factors (e.g. the possibility of introducing marginal-cost-sharing arrangements) in this context see Frohlich, Oppenheimer, and Young, *op. cit.*

33. Anatol Rapoport, *N-Person Game Theory*, (Ann Arbor 1971).

34. Thomas C. Schelling, *The Strategy of Conflict*, (Cambridge 1960).

35. Crutchfield, 'The Marine Fisheries', *op. cit.*, 213.

36. For various conceptualizations of bargaining see Oran R. Young editor and contributor, *Bargaining: Formal Theories of Negotiation*, (Urbana 1975).

37. For an extensive survey see *ibid.*

38. Knauss, *op. cit.* and J. A. Gulland, *The Management of Marine Fisheries*, (Seattle 1974).

39. Crutchfield, 'Economic and Political Objectives in Fishery Management', *op. cit.*, 81.

40. Crutchfield, 'The Marine Fisheries', *op. cit.*, 210.

41. Gulland, *The Fish Resources of the Ocean, op. cit.*, 73. See also Buck, *op. cit.*, 1 for the conclusion that 'The variability found in fishery statistics, as reported by the various agencies and nations, also negates a pure emphasis on numerical tables which might seem to imply greater accuracy than is recognized.'

42. Gulland, Tussing *et. al., op. cit.*, 77.

43. For example, actors have incentives to underreport their catches in the context of distributive bargaining.

44. Harry L. Rietze, 'Alaska Fisheries', Sidney Shapiro ed., *Our Changing Fisheries*, (Washington 1971), 258–279.

45. These summary arguments are drawn from a variety of sources. Among the best of these are Buck, *op. cit.*, Gulland, Tussing *et. al., op. cit.*, Rietze, *op. cit.*, Gulland, *The Fish Resources of the Ocean, op. cit.*, Hiroshi Kasahara and William Burke, 'North Pacific Fisheries Management', Paper No. 2, *RfF Program of International Studies of Fishery Arrangements*, (Washington 1973), and the 'Monthly Report' of the Northwest Fisheries Center, National Marine Fisheries Service, National Oceanic and Atmospheric Administration, United States Department of Commerce.

46. Gulland, Tussing, *et. al., op. cit.*, 78–83.

47. Crutchfield, 'The Marine Fisheries', *op. cit.*, 216.

48. More marginal to Beringia, there is also the Canadian-American International Pacific Salmon Fisheries Convention, which deals with the salmon stocks originating in the Fraser River.

49. Gulland, Tussing, *et. al., op. cit.*, 80–81.

50. Jeffrey A. Gorelik, 'The Eleventh Hour for Alaska's Salmon Fishery: A Proposed Regulatory Solution', *Ecology Law Quarterly*, 3 (1974), 393.

51. 'Monthly Report', Northwest Fisheries Centre, July 1974, 27.

52. Salvatore Comitini,'Prospects for Alaska-Japan Trade Relations in Marine Products', Tussing *et. al., op. cit.*, 147.

53. Gulland, *The Fish Resources of the Ocean, op. cit.*, 65–76.

54. For some helpful empirical estimates, however, consult Rietze, *op. cit.*, 263–264. Also, it is widely agreed that the Japanese practice of taking

salmon on the high seas is inefficient. As Tussing puts it, 'Both sides would benefit if the United States would grant Japan a quota of salmon approximately equal to their present high seas take, to be caught inshore in exchange for an end to the high seas fishery' (Tussing, *op. cit.*, 42).

55. Buck, *op. cit.*, 17–18.
56. Note also that Soviet high seas fishing for herring is not regulated by any existing agreements.
57. Compare Rietze, *op. cit.*, 265 with Gulland, Tussing, *et. al.*, *op. cit.*, 83–84.
58. Evidence for this and the preceding statements comes from 'Monthly Report', Northwest Fisheries Center, December 1974, 10–15.
59. Allan Gotlieb and Charles Dalfen, 'National Jurisdiction and International Responsibility: New Canadian Approaches to International Law', *AJIL*, 67 (1973), 229–258.
60. Gulland, *The Fish Resources of the Ocean, op. cit.*, 71.
61. *Loc. cit.* Note that the phrase 'Northeast Pacific' here is roughly equivalent to the area of Beringia as delineated in this study.
62. Kasahara and Burke, *op. cit.*, 1.
63. That is, it is more nearly feasible in physical terms for coastal states to exercise jurisdiction over these species, whatever the political repercussions might be.
64. Buck, *op. cit.*, 57–58.
65. 'Monthly Report', Northwest Fisheries Center, December 1974, 12–15.
66. Buck, *op. cit.*, 57 and 'Monthly Report', Northwest Fisheries Center, December 1974, 11.
67. 'Monthly Report', Northwest Fisheries Center, December 1974, 10.
68. Rietze, *op. cit.*, 264 Gulland, Tussing, *et. al.*, *op. cit.*, 84–95.
69. Kasahara and Burke, *op. cit.* Several informal bilateral agreements pertaining to these stocks have recently been negotiated between the United States and Japan and the United States and the Soviet Union, but they hardly amount to a comprehensive system of management for demersal stocks in Beringia.
70. Walter B. Parker, 'International Fisheries Regimes of the North Pacific', *Alaska and the Law of the Sea*, Arctic Environmental Information and Data Center, (Anchorage 1974), 1.
71. For an optimistic assessment of potential yields see Rietze, *op. cit.*
72. Gulland, Tussing *et. al.*, *op. cit.*, 95–105.
73. Rietze, *op. cit.*, 267.
74. Gulland, *The Management of Marine Fisheries, op. cit.*
75. Parker, *op. cit.*, 28–38.
76. *Ibid.*, 29.
77. George W. Rogers and Don C. Foote, 'The North Pacific Fur Seal Industry, the Record of International Management', *Inter-Nord*, 10 (1968), 151–154.
78. Marine Mammals Protection Act, 21 October 1972, (PL 92–522; 86 Stat. 1027).
79. For relevant data see Parker, *op. cit.*, 15–21.
80. George Small, *The Blue Whale*, (New York 1971), esp. Ch. VII.
81. Parker, *op. cit.*, 17.
82. William E. Schevill ed., *The Whale Problem: A Status Report*, (Cambridge 1974).
83. Rogers and Foote, *op. cit.* and Parker, *op. cit.*, 4–8.
84. Parker, *op. cit.*, 8. The idea is that the growing high seas fishing operations in the area have depleted the food supply of the fur seals.
85. Discussion with Dr. Francis Fay, University of Alaska, Fairbanks July 1974.
86. Christian Vibe, 'Can the Polar Bear Survive?', *Polar Times*, 77 (1973), 7.

87. Existing Polar Bear stocks are thought to number less than 20,000 in toto.
88. Jack Lentfer, 'Agreement on Conservation of Polar Bears', *Polar Record*, 17 (1974), No. 108, 327–330.
89. J. W. Devanney III, *The OCS Petroleum Pie*, MIT Sea Grant Program, Report No. MITSG 75–10, 28 February 1975.
90. This point applies specifically to production; the situation with respect to marketing is quite different.
91. For some relevant background information see Barbara Ward, 'Introduction', Robert Hallaman, *Towards an Environmentally Sound Law of the Sea*, (Washington 1974). In fact, it is probable that the annual value of these hydrocarbons will substantially exceed the value of the region's fish harvests during peak years. But it is important to note that under proper management the fisheries can continue to be highly productive indefinitely.
92. For a general discussion of common-pool problems see Richard James Sweeney, Robert D. Tollison, and Thomas D. Willett, 'Market Failure, the Common-Pool Problem, and Ocean Resource Exploitation', *Journal of Law and Economics*, XVII (1974), 179–192.
93. *U.S. Energy Resources: An Agenda for Research*, A Resources for the Future Staff Report, (Baltimore 1968), 29.
94. *Ibid.*
95. Devanney, *op. cit.*, 61. Unitization occurs whenever the relevant actors agree (or are required to agree) to manage a common reservoir of oil on a coordinated basis and to share the proceeds according to an explicitly negotiated formula.
96. Irvin L. White, Don E. Kash, Michael A. Chartock, Michael D. Devine, and R. Leon Leonard, *North Sea Oil and Gas*, (Norman, Oklahoma 1973).
97. With respect to ownership, therefore, hydrocarbons and land-based agriculture have much in common, though fishing and land-based agriculture share the problems of managing living resources.
98. Note that the delineation of jurisdictional boundaries will have the *de facto* effect of determining the distribution of oil and natural gas reserves among the states involved.
99. These factors include the level of uncertainty about the size of the reservoirs and various risks associated with offshore production. See Devanney, *op. cit.* for a discussion of the implications of these factors.
100. Developments along these lines with respect to the exploitation of North Sea oil are suggestive in this context (see White *et. al., op. cit.*).
101. A number of alternatives are assessed in detail in Devanney, *op. cit.*
102. Such decisions require the introduction of discount rates in order to compare the prospects of future benefits with estimates of current benefits from the exploitation of a given resource.
103. See, for example, Anthony Scott, *Natural Resources: The Economics of Conservation*, (Toronto 1973) and Robert M. Solow, 'The Economics of Resources or the Resources of Economics', *American Economic Review*, LXIV (1974), 1–14.
104. The establishment of jurisdictional boundaries implies the settlement of distributive controversies at the international level.
105. See, for example, *U.S. Energy Resources, op. cit.*
106. For a survey of theoretical work on externalities see Robert Staaf and Francis Tannian eds., *Externalities: Theoretical Dimensions of Political Economy*, (New York n.d.).
107. Discussions with Robert Meyer, Outer Continental Shelf Office, Bureau of Land Management, (Anchorage, August 1974 and July 1975).
108. Frank Gardner, 'Offshore Oil – Only the Beginning', *Oil and Gas Journal*,

72 (6 May 1974), 123–125.

109. Malcolm T. Baldwin, 'Public Policy on Oil – An Ecological Perspective', *Ecology Law Quarterly*, 1 (1971), 245–303. See especially pg. 280.
110. In the United States, those with prior experience in the Gulf of Mexico typically worry less about these problems than those with prior experience off the coast of California.
111. Devanney, *op. cit.* 116 and Richard B. Norgaard, 'Petroleum Development in Alaska: Prospects and Conflicts', *Natural Resources Journal*, 12 (1972), 83–107.
112. For an excellent discussion of these problems consult Devanney, *op. cit.*
113. Gas pressure provides the motivating force in the extraction of oil. Gas pressure typically gives out before all the oil in a given reservoir is removed, though the exact point at which this occurs is a function of a number of factors.
114. I am indebted to Lester Brockett of the Atlantic-Richfield Company (ARCO) office in Anchorage, Alaska for a discussion of these techniques and their limitations.
115. Note also that there is a high degree of corporate secrecy concerning estimates of oil reserves in various provinces and basins; available estimates do not always reflect the latest thinking on these matters.
116. George Rogers, 'International Petroleum and the Economic Future of Alaska', *Polar Record*, 15 (1971), 463–478.
117. In fact, it is large compared to onshore reservoirs in North America, though it is small compared to the reserves in the Prudhoe Bay area. See Devanney, *op. cit.* for relevant figures.
118. Nancy Munro, 'OCS Development – What it Means', *Alaska Seas and Coasts*, 3 (15 April 1975), 1–4.
119. Bob Potterfield, 'Pet-4: Alaska's Next Oil Bonanza', *Alaska Construction and Oil*, 15 (December 1974), 10–13. 16, 18–20.
120. *Ibid.*, 12.
121. Rogers, *op. cit.*
122. Richard S. Finnie, 'North American Arctic Petroleum Development', *Polar Notes*, XI (1971), 21–41. These leases involve land transferred to the State of Alaska under the terms of the Alaska Statehood Act of 1959.
123. For this and related figures see Devanney, *op. cit.*
124. Howard M. Wilson, 'Prudhoe Oil will Bring Profound Change to West Coast Crude-Flow Patterns', *Oil and Gas Journal*, 72 (18 March 1974), 96–100.
125. 'The Gas Line – El Paso or Arctic', *Alaska Construction and Oil*, 16 (April 1975), 32–33, 35–38, 40, 42, 44–45.
126. In American practice, lease sales ordinarily occur after geophysical exploration but before the drilling of exploration wells (Devanney, *op. cit.*, 99).
127. Potterfield, *op. cit.* and Howard M. Wilson, 'Alaska Report', *Oil and Gas Journal*, 73 (2 June 1975), 109–112.
128. 'Preserving Pet-4', *Alaska Construction and Oil*, 14 (September 1973), 64–68.
129. Potterfield, *op. cit.*, 11–12.
130. Howard M. Wilson, 'Pending Burst of Leasing Spells Big Alaskan Search', *Oil and Gas Journal*, 72 (2 December 1974), 27.
131. 'Preserving Pet-4', *op. cit.* and untitled report in *World Oil*, 178 (January 1974), 7.
132. Howard M. Wilson, 'Vast New Areas on North Slope Beckon Wildcatters', *Oil and Gas Journal*, 72 (18 March 1974), 21–24.
133. *Ibid.*, 21.

134. Richard Pollock, 'Introduction', Tom Brown, *Oil on Ice*, (San Francisco 1971), 14.
135. Stewart French, 'Alaska Native Claims Settlement Act', Arctic Development and the Environment Program, Arctic Institute of North America, (Montreal and Washington 1972).
136. Wilson, 'Pending Burst . . . ', *op. cit.* 28.
137. R. A. Rudkin, 'Petroleum of Arctic Canada', *Oil and Gas Journal*, 72 (4 March 1974), 136–137 and 'Petroleum Potential of Arctic Canada', *Oil and Gas Journal*, 72 (11 March 1974), 147–151.
138. Finnie, *op. cit.*, 28.
139. Rudkin, *op. cit.*
140. One proposal calls for a single pipeline to transport Prudhoe Bay gas and Mackenzie Delta gas to central Canada and the American Middlewest ('The Gas Line', *op. cit.*).
141. Richard Rohmer, *The Arctic Imperative*, (Toronto 1973), 81–83.
142. Rudkin, *op. cit.*
143. Terence Armstrong, 'Soviet Northern Development, With Some Alaskan Parallels and Contrasts', *ISEGR Occasional Paper No. 2*, (Fairbanks 1970), 15–19.
144. *Ibid.*, 18.
145. Bill Schultz, 'After Prudhoe Bay? The Outer Continental Shelf', *Alaska Construction and Oil*, 15 (1974), 48–50.
146. Wilson, 'Pending Burst . . . ', *op. cit.*, 26.
147. Schultz, *op. cit.*, 48.
148. Wilson, 'Alaska Report', *op. cit.*, 104–109.
149. Schultz, *op. cit.*, 50.
150. The lower Inlet lies to the south of the point at which the distance across the entire Inlet is 24 miles. This point is in the vicinity of Kalgin Island.
151. Robert M. Klein, William M. Lyle, Patrick L. Dobey, and Kristina M. O'Connor, 'Estimated Speculative Recoverable Resources of Oil and Natural Gas in Alaska', *Open File Report No. 44*, State of Alaska, Department of Natural Resources, Division of Geological and Geophysical Surveys, January 1974.
152. Wilson, 'Pending Burst . . . ', *op. cit.*, 26–27.
153. United States vs. Alaska, United States Supreme Court No. 73–1888, decided 23 June 1975.
154. Wilson, 'Vast New Areas . . . ', *op. cit.*, 22.
155. Ed McGhee, 'Drillers Weigh Their Options for the Ice-Covered Arctic Seas', *Oil and Gas Journal*, 72 (6 May 1974), 134.
156. Wilson, 'Pending Burst . . . ', *op. cit.*, 27.
157. Klein *et. al.*, *op. cit.*
158. Donat Pharand, *The Law of the Sea of the Arctic with Special Reference to Canada*, (Ottawa 1973), 312–318.
159. See, for example, Robert B. Weeden and David R. Klein, 'Wildlife and Oil: A Survey of Critical Issues in Alaska', *Polar Record*, 15 (1971), 489–490.
160. Schultz, *op. cit.*, 50–51.
161. Rudkin, *op. cit.*, 136.
162. Martin Loken, 'Special Report – Dividing the Continental Shelf', *Alaska Construction and Oil*, 10 (December 1969), 23.
163. Klein *et. al.*, *op. cit.*
164. Wilson, 'Pending Burst . . . ', *op. cit.*, 28.
165. Loken, *op. cit.*
166. Weeden and Klein, *op. cit.*; Loken, *op. cit.*, and Rudkin, *op. cit.*
167. Klein *et. al.*, *op. cit.*

168. Wilson, 'Pending Burst . . . ', *op. cit.*, 28.
169. *Oil and Gas Journal*, 72 (1 April 1974), 46.
170. *Loc. cit.*
171. Worldwide, commercial shipping now generates approximately $40 billion of revenue annually. Accordingly, maritime commerce constitutes one of the major uses of the natural resources of marine regions. See Charles C. Bates and Paul Yost, 'Where Trends the Flow of Merchant Ships?', John K. Gamble and Giulio Pontecorvo eds., *Law of the Sea: The Emerging Regime of the Oceans*, (Cambridge 1974), 249.
172. *Arctic Marine Commerce*, Summary of Final Report, Arctic Institute of North America, (Contract No. 2–36288, Maritime Administration, United States Department of Commerce), August 1973).
173. *Arctic Marine Commerce*, Final Report, Arctic Institute of North America, (Contract No. 2–36288, Maritime Administration, United States Department of Commerce), August 1973, 229.
174. The major channels are Unimak Pass, Amukta Pass, and Amchitka Pass.
175. Terence Armstrong, 'International Transport Routes in the Arctic', *Polar Record*, 16 (1972), 375–382.
176. *Arctic Marine Commerce*, Final Report, *op. cit.*, 196–199.
177. Armstrong, 'International Transport Routes . . . ', *op. cit.*
178. The only major metropolitan area in Beringia is Anchorage (current population approximately 165,000), and it is not a large center of maritime operations. On the other hand, Kodiak is now the second largest fishing port in the United States.
179. *Arctic Marine Commerce*, Final Report, *op. cit.*, esp. 79–80.
180. That is, flow resources are generally not subject to crowding or rivalry until the pattern of usage becomes very heavy, On these concepts see Olson, *op. cit.* and Frohlich, Oppenheimer, and Young, *op. cit.*
181. See Ross D. Eckert, 'Exploitation of Deep Ocean Minerals: Regulatory Mechanisms and United States Policy', *Journal of Law and Economics*, 17 (1974), 151–163.
182. For background information consult Bates and Yost, *op. cit.*
183. Moreover, this is a case in which 'The spread of pollution transcends national ownership' [Abel Wolman, 'Pollution as an International Issue', *Foreign Affairs*, 47 (1968), 175].
184. That is, there have been numerous efforts to introduce exclusion mechanisms relating to navigation and commerce in marine areas. For a theoretical discussion of exclusion mechanisms consult Norman Frohlich and Joe A. Oppenheimer, *An Entrepreneurial Theory of Politics*, unpublished Ph.D. dissertation, (Princeton University 1971), Ch. V.
185. Olson, *op. cit.*
186. For a highly relevant case study, which deals in depth with these matters, see Richard B. Bilder, 'The Canadian Arctic Waters Pollution Prevention Act: New Stresses on the Law of the Sea', *Michigan Law Review*, 69 (1970), 1–54.
187. The resultant institutions would be collective goods of the type that Olson calls 'organizations' (Olson, *op. cit.*).
188. Once again, the North Sea offers clearcut illustrations of the kinds of problems that are likely to arise in the Beringian region during the next 20–30 years.
189. Bates and Yost, *op. cit.*
190. *Arctic Marine Commerce*, Summary of Final Report, *op. cit.*
191. *Ibid.*, 13.
192. *Arctic Marine Commerce* Final Report, *op. cit.*, 79–80.
193. *Ibid.*, 278 *et. seq.*

126

194. Parker, *op. cit.*, 15.
195. The 1970 census recorded a population of 2,375 for Nome; during gold-rush days at the turn of the century, there were 12—15 thousand people in Nome.
196. Armstrong, 'International Transport Routes . . . ', *op. cit.*
197. Armstrong, 'Soviet Northern Development', *op. cit.*, 6.
198. *Ibid.*, 8.
199. Pharand, *op. cit.*, 24—26.
200. Armstrong, 'International Transport Routes . . . ', *op. cit.*, Data on the use of the Northern Sea Route are also published annually in the *Polar Record*.
201. See Robert Trumbull, 'Japan Seeks Use of Arctic Route', *New York Times*, 12 June 1967 [reprinted in *Polar Times*, 64 (June 1967), 30].
202. William E. Butler, 'The Legal Regime of Russian Territorial Waters', *AJIL*, 62 (1968), 51—77 and S. M. Olenicoff, 'Territorial Waters in the Arctic: the Soviet Position', Rand, R-907-ARPA, July 1972.
203. Raymond Anderson, 'Soviet to Open its Arctic Route', *Polar Times*, 64 (1967), 30 (originally published in the *New York Times*).
204. Consult generally William E. Butler, *The Soviet Union and the Law of the Sea*, (Baltimore 1971).
205. Pharand, *op. cit.* The usual route, passing from east to west, involves passage through the Davis Strait, Baffin Bay, Lancaster Sound, the Barrow Strait, and Melville Sound, and thence either through McClure Strait directly into the Beaufort Sea or through the Prince of Wales Strait into the Amundsen Gulf.
206. See V. Stefansson, *Northwest to Fortune*, (New York 1958).
207. Bern Keating, *The Northwest Passage*, (Chicago 1970), 139—152 and Brown, *op. cit.*, 86—96.
208. This experiment apparently cost approximately $50 million, most of which was put up by Exxon (Brown, *op. cit.*, 86—87).
209. But see the comments in *Arctic Marine Commerce*, Final Report, *op. cit.*, 222.
210. *Ibid.*, 223.
211. Gordon W. Smith, 'Sovereignty in the North: The Canadian Aspect of an International Problem', R. St. J. Macdonald ed., *The Arctic Frontier*, (Toronto 1966), 228—236.
212. Gotlieb and Dalfen, *op. cit.* and 'Arctic Pact Sought by U.S. and Canada', *Polar Times*, 70 (1970), 24 (originally published in the *New York Times*).
213. These issues are discussed at length in Pharand, *op. cit.*
214. Armstrong, 'International Transport Routes . . . ', *op. cit.*
215. The first submarine to make the passage was the *USS Nautilus* under the command of Captain William R. Anderson. See William R. Anderson, 'The Arctic as a Sea Route of the Future', *National Geographic Magazine*, CXV (1959), 21—24.
216. *Ibid.*, 22.
217. *Arctic Marine Commerce*, Final Report, *op. cit.*, esp. 195—199 and 222.
218. *Ibid.*, 195—199.
219. Smith, *op. cit.*, 194—255 and Pharand, *op. cit.*, esp. Part IV.
220. *Arctic Marine Commerce*, Summary of the Final Report, *op. cit.*, 13.
221. Armstrong, 'International Transport Routes . . . ', *op. cit.*
222. *Ibid.*, 380.
223. Alaska Airlines experimented with tour flights during the summer from Anchorage to Khabarovsk in the early 1970s [Stu Rothman, 'Alaska's Highway in the Sky', *Arctic Oil Journal*, 14 (June/July/August 1971), 18].
224. Moreover, these developments undoubtedly constitute one of the major

factors accounting for the speed with which Anchorage has outstripped Fairbanks as the dominant urban center in Alaska during recent years.

225. Smith, *op. cit.*, 248 *et. seq.*
226. The most important issue here concerns the prospect of a 200-mile economic zone. However, it is highly unlikely that jurisdiction over superjacent airspace will be extended to the boundaries of the economic zones.
227. See George S. Robinson, 'Military Requirements for International Airspace: Evolving Claims to Extensive Use of a *Res Communis* Natural Resource', *Natural Resources Journal*, 11 (1971), 162–176.
228. See, for example, Pharand, *op. cit.*, 240–241 and Olenicoff, *op. cit.*, 23.
229. Smith, *op. cit.*, 253. Little has happened to alter this conclusion since it was published in 1966.
230. A study that illustrates the advantages of this perspective is J. H. Dales, *Pollution, Property and Prices*, (Toronto 1968).
231. John C. Hendee, 'A Scientist's Views on Some Current Wilderness Management Issues', *Western Wildlands*, 1 (1974), 27–32.
232. Consult, *inter alia*, M. J. Dunbar, 'Stability and Fragility in Arctic Ecosystems', *Arctic*, 26 (1973), 179–185 and the collection of articles published in the *Marine Pollution Bulletin*, 1 (May 1970).
233. Dunbar, *op. cit.*, 182.
234. *Ibid.*, 180.
235. *Ibid.*, 181.
236. Though Dunbar is quite cautious on this issue, he generally supports the argument developed in the text (*ibid.*, 183–185).
237. 'Ice fogs' occur when pockets of extremely cold air containing dust particles are pinned near ground level by overlying layers of warmer air. Some authorities regard this form of pollution as so serious that it could substantially restrict the growth potential of communities like Fairbanks.
238. Carl S. Benson, 'The Role of Air Pollution in Arctic Planning and Development', *Polar Record*, 14 (1969), 783.
239. For concrete examples see Frank T. Bachmura, 'The Economics of Vanishing Species', *Natural Resources Journal*, 11 (1971), 674–692.
240. On the case of birds, see Cyrille de Klemm, 'The Conservation of Migratory Animals Through International Law', *Natural Resources Journal*, 12 (1972), 271–277.
241. That is, they are problems involving negative externalities. For relevant theoretical background consult the essays in Staaf and Tannian eds., *op. cit.*
242. Alan Randall, 'Coase Externality Theory in a Policy Context', *Natural Resources Journal*, 14 (1974), 35–54.
243. There is considerable disagreement, however, concerning the circumstances in which government intervention is desirable in dealing with externalities. In recent years, this debate has often focused on arguments about the Coase theorem [R.H. Coase, 'The Problem of Social Costs', *Journal of Law and Economics*, 3 (1960), 1–44].
244. Olson, *op. cit.*
245. See Frohlich, Oppenheimer, and Young, *op. cit.* for an analysis of the programs of political leaders in situations involving the supply of collective goods.
246. For example, this perspective makes it easier to understand the story of efforts to conserve blue whale stocks reported in Small, *op. cit.*
247. For an interesting case study see William M. Ross, *Oil Pollution as an International Problem*, (Seattle 1973).
248. Oscar Schachter and Daniel Serwer, 'Marine Pollution Problems and Remedies', *AJIL*, 65 (1971), 111.

249. See also Albert E. Utton, 'Environmental Policy and International Institutional Arrangements: A Proposal for Regional and Global Environmental Protection Agencies', *Natural Resources Journal*, 11 (1971), 513–517.

250. Bachmura, *op. cit.*

251. International Convention for the Regulation of Whaling, 1946 (TIAS 1849; 62 Stat. 1716); Agreement on the Conservation of Polar Bears, *signed* 15 November 1973 [*International Legal Materials*, XIII (January 1974), 13].

252. Bachmura, *op. cit.*, 692.

253. Compare, for example, salmon with such slow-turnover species as most of the great whales. An unusually good year can quickly reinstate a depleted salmon stock, but it may take decades to restore a depleted whale stock even under favorable conditions.

254. Japanese experts, for example, often stress arguments of this type in discussing the viability of whale stocks.

255. In the case of the blue whale, for example, it is easy to harvest remaining members of this species as an incidental catch in efforts to harvest fin or sei whales (Small, *op. cit.*).

256. For example, there is considerable evidence to suggest that the loss of certain strains of rice could produce a situation in which there is no form of rice resistant to some diseases. There may well be analogs to this phenomenon with respect to stocks of fish and marine mammals.

257. Note also that it is possible to imagine circumstances under which it would be rational to exterminate deliberately a given species (Bachmura, *op. cit.*, 689–690).

258. This point is raised explicitly with respect to whales in J.Z. Young, 'Save the Whales!', *New York Review of Books*, XXII (17 July 1975), 3–6.

259. See, for example, Scott, *Natural Resources* . . . , *op. cit.*

260. Rogers and Foote, *op. cit.* and Parker, *op. cit.*, 4–7.

261. Compare Ross' analysis of the problems of pollution control in the Puget Sound and the Straits of Georgia (Ross, *op. cit.*).

262. Baldwin, *op. cit.* Note that the Santa Barbara Channel case did not involve a transportation disaster.

263. 'New Perspectives on International Environmental Law', *Yale Law Journal*, 82 (1973), 1659–1680.

264. Thus, 'Oil pollution from vessels results from collisions, mechanical failures, pumping accidents, and, most importantly, from deballasting and cleaning operations' (Baldwin, *op. cit.*, 265).

265. Weeden and Klein, *op. cit.* 486.

266. This is the case, for example, with respect to ballast cleansing operations – discussion with D. W. Hood, Fairbanks, Alaska (July 1974).

267. Weeden and Klein, *op. cit.*, 491.

268. Schachter and Serwer, *op. cit.* and Michael Hardy, 'International Control of Marine Pollution', *Natural Resources Journal*, 11 (1971), 296–348.

269. William S. Osburn, Jr., 'Large-Scale Examples', Jack D. Ives and Roger G. Barry eds., *Arctic and Alpine Environments*, (London 1974), 925–951.

270. *Ibid.*

271. Ross, *op. cit.*, esp. Chapters 4 and 5.

272. For a comprehensive discussion of these issues see Baldwin, *op. cit.*

273. These include: International Convention for the Prevention of Pollution of the Sea by Oil, 1954 (TIAS 4900; 12 UST 2989); International Convention on Civil Liability for Oil Pollution Damage, 1969 [*International Legal Materials*, IX (January 1970), 45–64]; International Convention Relating to Intervention on the High Seas in Cases of Oil Pollution Casualties, 1969

[*International Legal Materials*, IX (January 1970), 25–44], and Convention on the Prevention of Marine Pollution by Dumping Wastes and Other Matters, 1972 (U.N. Doc. A/Ac. 138/Sc. III/L. 29).

274. Hallaman, *op. cit.* Note that most of the existing international agreements deal only with vessel-based pollution.

275. Bilder, *op. cit.*

276. These are precisely the issues raised by the Canadian Arctic Waters Pollution Prevention Act of 1970 (See 'New Perspectives on International Environmental Law', *op. cit.*).

277. Randall, *op. cit.*

278. 'New Perspectives on International Environmental Law', *op. cit.*

279. John V. Krutilla, 'Conservation Reconsidered', *American Economic Review*, LVII (1967), 777–786.

280. Nathaniel Wollman, 'The New Economics of Resources', *Daedalus*, 96 (1967), 1099–1114.

281. See, for example, Bryan Cooper, *Alaska – The Last Frontier*, (London 1972), esp. 206–227.

282. On the distributive implications of liability rules see Randall, *op. cit.*

283. See Krutilla, *op. cit.* and the parallel remarks on living resources in Bachmura, *op. cit.*

284. Krutilla, *op. cit.*, 783.

285. *Ibid.*, 778.

286. This theme is now emerging more and more frequently in discussions about the future of Beringia (see, for example, Brown, *op. cit.* and Cooper, *op. cit.*).

287. See, for example, the essays in George W. Rogers ed., *Change in Alaska*, (College and Seattle 1970).

288. Krutilla, *op. cit.*

289. Munro, *op. cit.*

290. Of course, many others will be affected by such things on an indirect basis, especially in an era of television reporting and frequent travel. Nevertheless, the impact of these indirect effects is small in the utility functions of most individuals.

291. This statement should *not* be read as implying that concern with the preservation of the habitat is more pronounced at the level of the government of the State of Alaska than at the level of the federal government.

292. For background information see Donald Hood and C. Peter McRoy, 'Uses of the Ocean', Donald W. Hood ed., *Impingement of Man on the Oceans*, (New York 1971), 689–695.

293. For a more general discussion of interdependencies among marine species see Christy, *op. cit.*, 10–14.

294. On the Kachemak Bay controversy see Munro, *op. cit.*

295. Such choices are particularly difficult in areas, like those covered in this discussion, characterized by the absence of a common denominator in terms of which to compare the expected consequences of various options.

296. On the case of fisheries see Crutchfield, 'The Marine Fisheries', *op. cit.*, 213–214. More generally, consult Richard B. Norgaard, 'Petroleum Development in Alaska', *op. cit.*

297. For a clear illustration see Brown, *op. cit.*

298. Crutchfield, 'Economic and Political Objectives . . . ', *op. cit.*, 76. Though this remark was made with reference to marine fisheries, it is equally relevant to the broader questions of resource management under discussion here.

299. There may be cases in which the intrinsic problems of resource management prove insurmountable at the international level. Note, however, that failure

to achieve international coordination as a consequence of these problems should be distinguished sharply from failure due to the intrusion of politico-military sensitivities.

300. Pharand, *op. cit.*, esp. Part IV.
301. Robert E. Chasen, 'Distant Early Warning Systems in the North American Arctic', *Polar Record*, 13 (1967), 595–596.
302. See, for example, Butler, 'The Legal Regime . . . ', *op. cit.*
303. Oran R. Young, *The Politics of Force*, (Princeton 1968), 110.
304. The United States has conducted several underground tests in the Aleutians, the most recent being the Cannikin test on Amchitka Island in November 1971 (Osburn, *op. cit.*).
305. *Arctic Marine Commerce*, Final Report, *op. cit.*, 18.
306. Terence E. Armstrong, *The Northern Sea Route*, (Cambridge 1952).
307. For a fuller discussion consult Smith, *op. cit.*
308. In this light, consider such recent developments as the Agreement on Cooperation in the Field of Environmental Protection Between the U.S.A. and the U.S.S.R., 1972 (TIAS 7345; 23 UST 845). For a discussion of the terms of this agreement see Weldon L. Merritt, 'The Soviet – U.S. Environmental Protection Agreement', *Natural Resources Journal*, 14 (1974), 275–281.
309. For details see Butler, *The Soviet Union . . .* , *op. cit.*
310. Rogers, 'International Petroleum . . . ', *op. cit.*
311. Olenicoff, *op. cit.* and Terence Armstrong, 'Soviet Sea Fisheries Since the Second World War', *Polar Record*, 13 (1966), 155–186.
312. Colin S. Gray, *Canadian Defense Priorities: A Question of Relevance*, (Toronto 1972), 184–193.
313. Alexander Rich and Aleksandr P. Vinogradov, 'Arctic Disarmament', *Bulletin of the Atomic Scientists*, 20 (1964), 22.
314. The Antarctic Treaty, 1959 (TIAS 4780; 12 UST 794); Seabed Treaty, 1970 [*Disarmament Negotiations and Treaties: 1946–1971*, (New York 1972), 283–287].
315. For further comments on these questions see Terence Armstrong, 'Arms Control in the Arctic', *Nature*, 206 (29 May 1965), 865–866.
316. See, for example, Gordon, *op. cit.*; Crutchfield, 'The Marine Fisheries', *op. cit.*; Christy and Scott, *op. cit.*, and Christy, *op. cit.*
317. Note that the reference here is to the maximization of aggregate profit or rent for the relevant fishery as a whole.
318. This figure is from Christy, *op. cit.*, 10.
319. Tussing, *op. cit.*, esp. 40–41.
320. There may be compelling reasons to move factors of production away from relatively more profitable industries in some cases. One such reason is the argument in favor of certain government subsidies to agricultural enterprises on the grounds that food products are normatively preferable to other products under a wide range of conditions.
321. Note that this 'economic' issue is apt to become highly politicized wherever the fishing industry has political influence.
322. The fishermen of the Bristol Bay who are dependent upon the sockeye salmon runs for their livelihood illustrate this point clearly.
323. As Crutchfield has argued, 'Where national economies are organized on radically different principles, as in the case of the socialist nations, comparisons of alternative arrangements for fishery management in monetary terms are virtually meaningless' (Crutchfield, 'Economic and Political Objectives . . . ', *op. cit.*, 79).
324. Christy, *op. cit.*, 12–14 and Knauss, *op. cit.*

325. In this connection, consider Crutchfield's conclusion that 'The extreme uncertainty about long- and short-run input-output relations colors every aspect of the high seas fisheries' (Crutchfield, 'The Marine Fisheries', *op. cit.*, 210).
326. Ole A. Mathiesen and Donald E. Bevan, 'Some International Aspects of Soviet Fisheries', *Mershon Center Pamphlet Series No. 7*, (1968), 51–52.
327. Crutchfield, 'Economic and Political Objectives . . . ', *op. cit.*, 75.
328. See, for example, 'Alaska Fishery May Close', *Polar Times*, 77 (1973), 4 and Gorelik, *op. cit.*
329. This will remain true even if large 'economic zones' emerge from the ongoing negotiations on the law of the sea. Though such zones would increase the relative influence of coastal states in the management of high seas fisheries, they would not offer any neat solutions to the issue of optimal harvests. See also Kasahara and Burke, *op. cit.*, 60 *et. seq.*

CHAPTER IV

THE EXISTING REGIME IN BERINGIA

The purpose of this chapter is to characterize the regime that is presently operative in Beringia. In the course of this examination, it will become evident both that the existing regime is not comprehensive in the sense that it contains few provisions relating to several important functional areas and that it is inchoate in the sense that it is currently changing quite rapidly. It is not, however, the aim of this chapter to analyze methods of alleviating these problems; this question is examined in considerable detail in the next chapter. This chapter assesses the existing regime in order to provide background material required for any effort to evaluate alternative regimes for Beringia.

Several general characteristics of the existing regime deserve mention at the outset. This regime incorporates a fundamental clash between expansive jurisdictional claims advanced by the relevant coastal states and the more inclusive claims of a common property regime coupled with some elements of coordinated management at the supranational level. Therefore, the regime exhibits a dual character that inevitably produces somewhat confusing results. The jurisdictional claims of coastal states are presently growing in influence relative to common property claims, at least in worldwide terms. Stevenson and Oxman, for example, describe a movement toward ' . . . broad coastal state resource management jurisdiction beyond the 12-mile territorial sea that does not result in interference with navigation and other non-resource uses.'[1] Nevertheless, there are reasons to question the impact of this worldwide trend in the Beringian region. Several of the major actors in this region are among the world's most influential distant-water states, and the region's other leading actors have traditionally been prominent among supporters of policies involving freedom of the seas.

Since Beringia is a marine region, the existing regime rests squarely on the foundation provided by the law of the sea. But this foundation is currently characterized both by ambiguity and by flux. It lacks generality in the sense that a number of influential states have failed to ratify one or more of the conventions that comprise the prevailing law of the sea. Moreover, it contains important substantive gaps. To illustrate, the prevailing law of the sea does not specify the width of the territorial sea; it is unclear with respect to the operational definition of baselines for use in demarcating the territorial sea, and it leaves major questions unresolved concerning the management of the resources of the continental shelf. Under the circumstances, it is not surprising that many states have begun to attack the prevailing law of the sea with increasing vigor during recent years. It is no doubt true that coastal states pursuing expansive jurisdictional claims have spearheaded these attacks, but it would be erroneous to conclude that they constitute the only source of objections to the prevailing law of the sea. All this has precipitated the organization of a new Law of the Sea Conference under the auspices of the United Nations.[2] Though it is not yet possible to predict the results of this Conference with precision, it is certain to have a substantial impact on the prevailing law of the sea.[3]

The existing regime in Beringia is also deeply affected by the fact that the core interests of the region's major actors have been shifting continuously during the postwar years. The Soviet Union, which previously exhibited the interests of a coastal state, has become a leading maritime power and increasingly displays the policy orientation of a distant-water state. The United States, by contrast, has come to occupy a more crosspressured position in this realm with the passage of time. While it has traditionally advocated policies involving freedom of the seas, it has recently found itself with rapidly expanding coastal state interests in the realm of jurisdiction over resources. Canada, another traditional supporter of internationalist policies with respect to maritime affairs, has been moving dramatically toward more nationalistic or protectionistic postures in this realm since the 1960s.[4] Furthermore, though Japan has always exhibited the interests of a distant-water state, a number of developments in recent years have combined to make Japan a more insistent advocate of common property arrangements in Beringia.[5] These changing interests suggest that there is considerable potential for conflict concerning fundamental features of the Beringian regime. But they also help to explain the prevailing ambiguity concerning these issues, since shifting interests are difficult to pin down precisely at any given moment in time and often induce actors to depart from earlier policy orientations in confusing ways.

A. The Geneva System

The prevailing law of the sea is encapsulated in a series of four interlocking conventions that emerged from the 1958 Geneva Conference on the Law of the Sea (as supplemented by an additional Conference in 1960).[6] These conventions are broad in scope, but they do not constitute a total regime for the oceans. For example, they have little to say about such matters as naval hostilities, pollution control, or dispute settlement at the international level, though they contain extensive provisions relating to matters like jurisdiction over the territorial sea and the continental shelf.

There are also real questions concerning the legal status of the four conventions that make up the Geneva system.[7] None of them has been ratified by two-thirds of the members of the international community, and the Fisheries Convention has received less than thirty ratifications to date. Therefore, it is possible to question the legislative force of these conventions (though the whole issue of international legislation is a controversial one among students of international law).[8] Some observers suggest that the central provisions of these conventions reflect prevailing practice in the international community so that they possess the status of customary international law. Given the fact that a new Law of the Sea Conference is now underway, this argument hardly seems compelling. Nevertheless, the fact that an abrupt rejection of the legal force of the Geneva system would produce a situation of extreme chaos in the law of the sea is enough to make even the severest critics of the existing system hesitate.

With respect to the Beringian region, the legal status of the Geneva system is particularly ambiguous. Though the United States has ratified all of the Geneva Conventions of 1958, the Republic of Korea has failed to adhere to any of them, and the other major actors in the region occupy various intermediate positions in these terms. Table III summarizes the current pattern of membership in the four Geneva Conventions on the part of the five states with the most extensive interests in the management of Beringia's natural resources. The

TABLE III

Convention	Country				
	Canada	Japan	South Korea	USSR	United States
1. Territorial Sea		X		X	X
2. Continental Shelf	X			X	X
3. Fisheries					X
4. High Seas	X	X		X	X

resultant mosaic does not license the conclusion that the Geneva system is irrelevant to Beringia, but it does constitute a clear warning against simple assumptions to the effect that the provisions of these conventions are automatically applicable in the region.[9]

1. *Convention on the Territorial Sea and the Contiguous Zone.*[10] This Convention establishes a system of three jurisdictionally separable domains between the land mass of a state, which is subject to full national sovereignty, and the high seas, which are conceptualized as *res communis. Internal waters* encompass waters lying inside the baselines used to demarcate territorial seas, seas wholly surrounded by a state's territorial domains, and historic bays or seas. For all practical purposes, internal waters are simply treated as an extension of the state's territorial domains in jurisdictional terms. Starting at the outer boundary of a state's internal waters, the Convention calls for a band or belt of *territorial sea.* While the exact demarcation of the territorial sea is a complicated matter in specific cases, the jurisdictional status of this belt is conceived as being intermediate between that of internal waters and that of the high seas. The coastal state's jurisdiction over its territorial sea is extensive, but it is qualified by certain rights of other states to freedom of navigation in such waters.[11] Between the outer boundary of the territorial sea and the high seas, the Convention provides for a *contiguous zone.* Coastal state jurisdiction within this contiguous zone is conceived as being highly restricted and limited to specific functional areas involving such matters as customs, immigration, and sanitation.[12] In the context of this study, it is worth emphasizing that this Convention does *not* conceptualize the contiguous zone in terms of the regulation of fishing and other activities associated with the utilization of resources.

While the Territorial Sea Convention draws clear distinctions among these jurisdictional domains, it leaves unresolved a number of issues that are of considerable importance in Beringia. First, it does not set forth precise criteria to determine the extent of internal waters, especially with respect to historic bays or seas.[13] Second, it is somewhat unclear concerning the nature of the baselines to be used in demarcating the inner boundary of the territorial sea. The Convention undoubtedly moves toward the concept of 'straight' baselines, which was articulated in the Anglo-Norwegian Fisheries Case of 1951 and which has the effect of expanding the domain of internal waters by projecting the inner boundary of the territorial sea outward.[14] But this hardly amounts to an operational specification of baselines, and the Convention gives little guidance concerning the role of islands in the demarcation of the territorial sea. Third, the Convention fails to specify the width of the territorial sea.[15] This failure was the result of irreconcilable disagreements among the participants at the conference, and these disagreements have continued to plague the international community during the intervening years. However, it is widely believed that the 1974 Fisheries Case has finally given formal status to the 12-mile rule for the width of the territorial sea,[16] and this development may well be confirmed by the new Law of the Sea Conference. Fourth, the Convention has little to say about the jurisdictional status of the waters surrounding major archipelagos. This is a matter of real importance in Beringia since the region encompasses all or part of two of the world's principal archipelagos (i.e. the Aleutian chain and the Canadian Arctic Islands).[17] Fifth, the Territorial Sea Convention is not precise concerning the jurisdictional content of the contiguous zone. Thus, it is difficult to determine whether or not the extension of coastal state jurisdiction to cover problems of resource management in the contiguous zone is in keeping with the spirit of this Convention.

A brief summary of prevailing practice in the Beringian region may be helpful in this context. The United States presently claims a 3-mile territorial sea together with an additional 9-mile contiguous zone which is conceived as extending to jurisdiction over fishing activities.[18] The Soviet Union continues to adhere to its traditional policy of claiming a 12-mile territorial sea.[19] This makes any claims to a contiguous zone under the terms of the Territorial Sea Convention irrelevant, since the Convention conceptualizes contiguous zones as extending no more than 12 miles beyond the baselines used to demarcate the inner boundary of the territorial sea. For its part, Canada adopted a 12-mile exclusive fishing zone in 1964 but replaced this claim in 1970 with a more general claim to a 12-mile territorial sea.[20] Thus, Canada and the Soviet Union presently maintain identical policies on these issues. Japan exhibits a very different policy

137

orientation on these matters. The Japanese continue to claim a 3-mile territorial sea and to deny the legitimacy of extending claims to contiguous zones into the realm of resource management. Finally, the Republic of Korea now combines claims to a 3-mile territorial sea with claims to jurisdiction over adjacent fisheries ranging from 20 to 200 miles.[21] Korea has also failed to adhere to the Territorial Sea Convention.

2. *Convention on the Continental Shelf*.[22] This Convention deals with control over resources located on or beneath the seabed of the continental shelf. In general, it codifies postwar trends toward the expansion of coastal state jurisdiction over these resources.[23] With reference to Beringia, however, it is important to note that Japan and Korea have refused to adhere to this Convention and that Japan, at least, has publicly rejected some of its major provisions.

The Convention defines the term 'continental shelf' to include:[24]

(a) the seabed and subsoil of the submarine areas adjacent to the coast but outside the area of the territorial sea, to a depth of 200 metres or, beyond that limit, to where the depth of the superjacent waters admits of the exploitation of the natural resources of the said areas; (b) the seabed and subsoil of similar marine areas adjacent to the coasts of islands.

This formulation is obviously rather ambiguous. While the 200-metre criterion is clear enough, the limits of exploitability beyond a depth of 200 metres are a function of prevailing technology.[25] Consequently, the limits of coastal state jurisdiction are apt to expand outward as new technology is developed. Asymmetries among states with respect to the technology at their disposal are bound to pose severe problems for any efforts to develop a general rule to demarcate the outer boundary of coastal state jurisdiction over the resources of the continental shelf.

The Continental Shelf Convention is also imprecise concerning the demarcation of jurisdictional boundaries over the continental shelf between *adjacent* states and, especially, *opposite* states.[26] That is, when two or more states share the same continental shelf, what procedures are to be used in determing the limits of the jurisdiction of each state? Article 6 of the Convention outlines the so-called 'triad' concept as a response to this problem.[27] It refers first to the desirability of negotiated agreements between the relevant states. It then suggests boundaries 'justified by special circumstances'. And failing all else, it suggests that the ' . . . boundary is the median line, every point of which is equidistant from the nearest points of the base lines from which the breadth of the territorial sea is measured.' But even this final criterion fails to resolve the problem unambiguously since the specification of the relevant baselines remains a matter of substantial disagreement in the international community.[28]

Beyond this, the Continental Shelf Convention has provoked considerable debate concerning the operational definition of a 'shelf resource'. It seems clear that resources located under the seabed, such as oil and natural gas, are shelf resources and therefore subject to the jurisdiction of the coastal state. However, the case of renewable resources (i.e. various types of crabs and shellfish) living in close proximity to the seabed of the continental shelf is more ambiguous.[29] In this realm, a substantial controversy has arisen. So, for example, the Soviet Union has taken an expansive view of the concept 'shelf resource' and included a wide range of shellfish under this rubric. Japan, by contrast, refuses to accept the contention that crabs and other species of sedentary fish belong to the category of shelf resources, and this is a major source of the unwillingness of Japan to adhere to the Continental Shelf Convention. On this issue, the United States has adopted an intermediate position, but the policy implications of this position are much more similar to those of the Soviet position than of the Japanese position.

3. *Convention on Fishing and Conservation of the Living Resources of the High Seas.*[30] This Convention was one of the major innovations of the 1958 Conference on the Law of the Sea since it introduces certain restrictions on the traditionally unlimited conception of the doctrine of the freedom of the high seas. The authority of coastal states to regulate fishing in the territorial sea has been accepted for some time, but the Fisheries Convention contemplates a limited extension of the regulatory authority of coastal states with respect to high seas fisheries.[31] As such, it impinges, at least potentially, on the freedom of action of distant-water states in the fisheries of the high seas, and this helps to explain the refusal of leading distant-water states like Japan and the Soviet Union to adhere to this Convention.

In general, the Fisheries Convention establishes the obligation of *all* states to take seriously the objective of conserving fish stocks in the high seas. In this connection, the Convention calls for efforts to achieve the ' . . . optimum sustainable yield . . . so as to secure a maximum supply of food and other marine products.'[32] And as Jessup has pointed out, ' . . . it deals with various methods for the conservation of fish stocks, indicates priorities, and proposes methods for negotiation and for the solution of conflicting claims.'[33] But the Convention goes further in Article 7 to contemplate certain situations in which relevant coastal states may take unilateral measures to deal with urgent conservation problems.[34] These provisions are highly restricted, and it is explicitly stated that such unilateral measures must ' . . . not discriminate in form or in fact against foreign fishermen.' Nevertheless, Article 7 of the Fisheries Convention constitutes a genuine departure from traditional arrangements concerning the freedom of the high seas.[35] However, the significance of this development is circumscribed by the fact that the Convention has substantially fewer adherents than the other Geneva Conventions. This is a clear indication of the unwillingness of many states to accept this shift in the traditional arrangements relating to the freedom of the high seas.

4. *Convention on the High Seas.*[36] This Convention is, in a sense, a residual agreement; it establishes a common property regime governing human activities in those maritime areas not explicitly covered by the other three conventions. In this connection, there are certain initial problems associated with efforts to demarcate the domain of the high seas with precision. The establishment of the relevant boundaries depends, for example, on the nature of the baselines used in demarcating the territorial sea as well as on prevailing views concerning the width of the territorial sea and the contiguous zone. Moreover, there are situations in which it is difficult to draw a clear distinction between 'land' and 'sea', a phenomenon that leads inevitably to serious jurisdictional ambiguities. In the Beringian region, this problem arises with respect to the Arctic Ocean, and I shall revert to this subject in greater detail in a later section of this chapter.

In general terms, the Convention on the High Seas reaffirms the principal freedoms that have traditionally been associated with human activities on the high seas.[37] These include: a) freedom of navigation, b) freedom of fishing, c) freedom to lay submarine cables and pipelines, d) freedom to fly over the high seas, and e) freedom of scientific research. For the first time, however, the Convention suggests the possibility of explicit restrictions relating to human activities on the high seas. That is, it is formulated in such a way as to make it compatible with the Fisheries Convention. Moreover, it is important to emphasize that this general area has become a focus of debate during the years since this Convention was negotiated. While the principal freedoms of the high seas are among the most entrenched doctrines of the prevailing law of the sea, many jurisdictional proposals that are now being vigorously pursued by various influential states logically imply a substantial restriction of some of these freedoms.[38]

5. *Ongoing negotiations.*[39] The first substantive session of the Third Law of the Sea Conference took place in Caracas during the summer of 1974. A second session was held in Geneva in the spring of 1975, and another substantive session is now scheduled for New York. At this time, it is impossible to predict whether this Conference will eventually produce a comprehensive convention setting forth a new regime for the oceans. There are compelling reasons to doubt that a clear and unambiguous regime will emerge from these negotiations.[40] Nevertheless, the Conference seems certain to have a far-reaching impact on the evolution of attitudes and expectations in the international community concerning the law of the sea. Some of these developments will have important implications for the governance of Beringia.

The most critical issue in this connection undoubtedly involves the movement toward the creation of 'exclusive economic zones'.[41] Numerous states have now endorsed the general idea of establishing economic zones which would have the effect of extending the jurisdiction of coastal states in the realm of resource management well beyond the boundaries of the territorial sea. The most common idea suggests the delineation of economic zones extending outward 200 miles from the baselines used to demarcate the inner boundary of the territorial sea. There is considerable debate concerning the appropriate jurisdictional content of such zones. Virtually all the major proposals are couched in terms of extensive coastal state jurisdiction over the management of the renewable resources located within the economic zones. Some proposals would extend the rights of coastal states to formal ownership of these resources as well. Many suggestions would also accord coastal states far-reaching authority to deal with such matters as the control of marine pollution within the economic zones. And some influential states are vigorously advocating the establishment of special regimes to ensure coastal state control of anadromous fish (e.g. salmon) over and above the 200-mile economic zones.[42]

Leaving aside the issue of economic zones, several additional developments in these negotiations have significant implications for the governance of Beringia. First, there is an emerging consensus on a 12-mile rule with respect to the width of the territorial sea, and support for the doctrine of 'straight' baselines is growing. Concomitantly, some proposals suggest a retention of the concept of contiguous zones together with an extension of such zones to 24 miles from the inner boundary of the territorial sea. Second, considerable discussion has arisen about jurisdictional boundaries with respect to the continental shelf. Thus, some influential actors are now proposing that the limits of coastal state jurisdiction over the resources of the seabed should be made congruent with the boundaries of the economic zone (i.e. fixed at the 200-mile point) regardless of depth or exploitability.[42a] Third, there is a movement toward the formulation of strong statements relating to pollution control and general obligations to preserve the marine environment. But it is much less clear what provisions will prove acceptable concerning the articulation and enforcement of specific standards relating to the preservation of the environment.[43] Fourth, it is quite unlikely that coastal states will acquire jurisdiction over the airspace above their economic zones. Nevertheless, the extension of the territorial sea will lead to broader coastal state jurisdiction over airspace, and the underlying political atmosphere produced by the Conference may lend support to claims pertaining to such things as contiguous air defense zones. Fifth, there has been a good deal of discussion about the desirability of international coordination in efforts to manage the resources of enclosed or semi-enclosed seas. Such ideas are highly relevant to Beringia since large segments of the region can plausibly be thought of as belonging to the category of semi-enclosed seas.[44]

Broadly speaking, what impact are these negotiations likely to have on Beringia? There can be little doubt that the trends referred to in the preceding paragraphs will strengthen the coastal state claims advanced by actors like Canada and the United States in Beringia. Still, it would be a mistake to overemphasize the significance of this development. Much will depend on such things as whether a formal convention ultimately emerges from the Law of the Sea Conference, whether a convention of this type is widely ratified within the international community as a whole, and whether it proves acceptable to the major actors in Beringia. Moreover, the detailed application of new jurisdictional arrangements to specific regions like Beringia will require extensive negotiations, and distant-water states such as Japan and the Soviet Union will certainly not be altogether devoid of bargaining strength in negotiations of this type.[45] The general implications of this situation are captured nicely in the following statements about the marine fisheries:

No matter what is agreed at the third LOS Conference on substantive principles of fisheries management or on fishing zones, there is almost certain to be a continuing need for improved institutional mechanisms in the North Pacific.[46]

... it is realistic to expect that future changes in the international fishery regime, which will probably continue to exhibit the currently predominant trend toward extension of national jurisdiction, will result in more international negotiation rather than less.[47]

B. Functional Agreements

Though the Geneva system constitutes the foundation of the existing regime in Beringia, a superstructure of more specific agreements between and among the states of the region has been erected on this foundation. These agreements involve binding commitments on the part of those actors who are parties to them. Unlike the Geneva Conventions, however, they have no legislative implications of a general sort. Currently, all these functional agreements relate to problems associated with the management of the renewable resources of Beringia.[48] This situation is attributable to the facts that these resources have so far been subjected to heavier usage than the region's other natural resources and that the management problems relating to renewable resources are intrinsically more complex than those of other functional areas.

Some of the Beringian functional agreements have a relatively long history (e.g. the Fur Seal Convention was originally negotiated in 1911 and the International Pacific Halibut Convention dates back to 1923). Nevertheless, the set of these agreements has evolved in an *ad hoc* fashion and can hardly be said to form a comprehensive and coherent managerial system. As of 1973, for example, Kasahara and Burke were able to assert that ' . . . despite the numerous international treaties and agreements, more than 90 percent of the total catch in the North Pacific comes from fisheries that are outside international regulation.'[49] Certain marginal developments in this area have occurred since that time (e.g. the new bilateral agreements between the United States and Japan and the United States and the Soviet Union).[50] But the overall picture remains unchanged. So, for example, the harvests of demersal fish (other than halibut) in the Bering Sea and the Gulf of Alaska are subject to little effective international regulation. Additionally, the herring harvests of Beringia now fall largely outside the terms of any of the functional agreements. None of this is intended to suggest that these agreements, taken individually, are undesirable or altogether ineffective. But it is important to bear in mind that they amount to a thicket of criss-crossing responses to particularistic problems rather than a coherent system of international coordination based on any general principles of biological conservation or economic efficiency.[51]

This section presents a classification of the functional agreements pertaining to resource management currently in force in Beringia.[52] While many of these agreements are complex, I have grouped them into four categories on the basis of their strongest provisions relating to international coordination.[53] The weakest agreements are straightforward technical arrangements designed to alleviate problems of congestion caused by overlapping fishing operations. Next, there are conservation agreements whose purpose is to protect various stocks in biological terms without introducing provisions for the allocation of these resources. A third category encompasses agreements having pronounced distributive consequences that emanate from superordinate-subordinate relationships rather than from processes involving bargaining among relative equals. Finally, there are several agreements that go beyond *de facto* allocation to establish clearcut and mutually agreed-upon distributive formulas as well as conservation arrangements.

1. *Congestion problems*. When a number of actors harvest fish in the same geographical area, various forms of mutual interference are apt to occur. This is particularly true when there is competition for the same stocks of fish or when different species are harvested with incompatible types of gear.[54] Though procedures designed to alleviate the resultant congestion are incorporated in a number of functional agreements pertaining to Beringia, there are two agreements whose primary emphasis lies in this area. These are the Soviet-American 'Kodiak' Gear Agreement of 1964[55] and the American-Japanese Agreements of 1970.[56]

The 'Kodiak' Gear Agreement emerged as a response to conflicts in the general vicinity of Kodiak Island between American fishermen using pot gear to harvest crabs and Soviet fishermen engaged in mobile trawling operations for demersal fish. Briefly, the agreement involves the demarcation of several areas of the high seas in which the Soviets have agreed to refrain from the use of mobile gear during the American king crab season. The use of such gear is permitted at other times as well as in other areas.[57] The American-Japanese Agreements of 1970 '... provide that Japan will refrain from dragnet and longline fishing in designated areas and periods.'[58] Though the details are somewhat complex, the effect of these agreements is to protect American fishing operations during certain periods of the year off Kodiak Island, off Unimak Island in the Aleutians, and in the eastern Bering Sea halibut grounds.

144

2. *Conservation agreements.* It is possible to negotiate agreements concerning the conservation of marine species or stocks without proceeding to deal with the problem of apportioning the total harvest among the relevant participants.[59] Agreements of this type often have unfortunate economic consequences. They typically produce an annual rush to harvest the allowable quota of the stocks in question, a situation likely to generate both overinvestment in equipment and underemployment of men and equipment during large parts of the year.[60] On the other hand, conservation is an objective that has widespread normative appeal in its own right, and it is usually easier to arrive at overall quotas and restrictions among competitors than to deal explicitly with the problems of allocation or distribution. Thus, it is worth stressing that conservation agreements in the absence of distributive formulas may produce results that are desirable in biological and environmental terms quite apart from their economic consequences.

Several functional agreements operative in Beringia focus primarily on conservation. Perhaps the most important of these is the International Pacific Halibut Convention negotiated originally in 1923 by the United States and Canada to protect the viability of the halibut stocks of the North Pacific and superseded in 1953 by a successor convention that emphasizes management of the halibut stocks on a maximum sustained yield basis.[61] Some successes in protecting the halibut stocks have been achieved under this agreement through a combination of catch limits, seasons, gear restrictions, size limits, and geographical zones. However, it has not prevented the occurrence of a long-term decline in the annual harvest of halibut in convention waters. Of crucial importance in this context is the fact that the agreement is confined to the United States and Canada so that it is incapable of regulating the incidental catch of halibut associated with high seas trawling for other demersal species on the part of Japan and the Soviet Union.[62]

A more general conservation agreement, which is nevertheless fully applicable in Beringia, is embodied in the International Whaling Convention of 1946.[63] This is a 14-nation agreement providing for ' . . . control of the whale harvest on a worldwide basis' and establishing a International Whaling Commission (IWC) to supervise the particular regulations.[64] In earlier years, attention was devoted primarily to problems associated with the Antarctic harvests, but there has been growing interest in the regulation of the North Pacific harvests during recent years. From the perspective of conservation, the results achieved under this Convention have generally left a great deal to be desired.[65] Overall quotas for the annual harvests of whales have been laboriously negotiated. But these quotas have only recently been established on a species-by-species basis (rather than in blue whale units),[66] and the overall quotas have seldom been set low enough to prevent the depletion of important whale stocks.[67] Moreover, the tendency to set overall quotas without specifying national quotas has aggravated the situation by giving several major whaling countries (e.g. Japan and the Soviet Union) powerful incentives to avoid the retirement of any of their whaling fleets. More recently, informal efforts have been made to arrive at national quotas outside the official meetings called for by the Whaling Convention. Agreement on such quotas emerged some years ago in the case of the Antarctic and some steps have now been taken along these lines with respect to the North Pacific.[68] Nevertheless, the *overall* quotas for the North Pacific remain high enough to produce serious dangers of stock depletions regardless of the allocation of the harvests among the leading participants. The contrast between this situation and the case of Polar Bears (outlined below), constitutes a dramatic illustration of the problems posed by entrenched commercial interests for the development of effective conservation arrangements.[69]

A rather different conservation arrangement with implications for Beringia is the new Polar Bear agreement negotiated during the fall of 1973.[70] This 5-nation agreement (Canada, Denmark, Norway, the Soviet Union, and the United States) aims to protect the limited remaining stocks of Polar Bears by establishing what amounts to a sanctuary for this species.[71] There is no commercial harvest of Polar Bears, and the agreement requires a virtual cessation of hunting for these animals except on the part of certain native peoples.[72] Therefore, it is not necessary to pursue the goal of conservation against pressure for commercial exploitation in this case, and there are no powerful economic groups whose fundamental interests are severely damaged by this agreement. Conservation under these circumstances is clearly a simpler proposition than in situations involving large-scale commercial operations.[73]

3. *De facto distribution.* The most influential (though not the most popular) functional agreements currently operative in Beringia are those that produce distributive consequences on a *de facto* basis. Most of these agreements also aim at conservation, but their distinguishing feature is that they lead to *de facto* distributions of harvests. It is possible to identify three different distributive mechanisms within this set of agreements. First, there is the Soviet principle of exclusion under

which a coastal state unilaterally prohibits other states from fishing, or exceeding clearcut catch quotas, in areas of the high seas adjacent to its own coasts.[74] Second, there is the Canadian-American 'abstention principle'.[75] Though this mechanism often has a somewhat more sophisticated gloss than the principle of exclusion, it yields much the same results in distributive terms. Briefly, the central idea is to negotiate international agreements in which certain stocks of fish are singled out and in which there is agreement on ' . . . abstention from these stocks by some member nations where it can be shown that, historically, they have not fished the stock . . . and that the other member nations are fully utilizing the resource and have it under study and scientific management.'[76] That is, the abstention principle seeks to legitimize efforts to preserve traditional fisheries from the inroads of new entrants. Third, negotiated quotas emanating from highly asymmetrical bargaining processes lead to results that are quite similar to those associated with outright exclusion. This is particularly true, in cases where the quotas are renegotiated from time to time in such a way as to increase the superordinate actor's share of the harvest while reducing the share of the subordinate actor.

Two agreements involving *de facto* distributive mechanisms are especially prominent in Beringia. The most well known is the International North Pacific Fisheries Convention of 1952.[77] It originated as an element in the postwar peace settlement with Japan; included are the United States, Canada, and Japan as members. It is supervised by an international commission whose headquarters are in Vancouver. In essence, the Convention calls for a set of applications of the abstention principle. Presently, the major provisions are as follows: 1) Japan agrees to abstain from fishing for salmon east of 175°W longitude (the so-called abstention line), 2) Canada agrees not to fish for salmon in the Bering Sea east of the abstention line, and 3) Japan agrees to refrain ' . . . from fishing for halibut of North American origin in convention waters off the coast of Canada and the U.S., exclusive of the Bering Sea'.[78] Originally, the Convention placed additional restrictions on Japanese fishing for halibut in the eastern Bering Sea and for herring throughout convention waters, but these provisions were dropped in 1959, 1961, and 1963.[79] The crucial provisions of this agreement concern the salmon stocks of the Bering Sea, and these arrangements have become highly controversial in recent years.[80] There is growing pressure from the American side to take steps aimed at restricting the Japanese harvest of North American salmon on the high seas west of the abstention line, while Japanese objections to the basic idea of the abstention principle have become increasingly vigorous.[81] Controversy concerning these issues is likely to become more prominent in the next decade though it is noteworthy that neither side has so far seriously threatened to exercise its right to abrogate the Convention.[82]

The other prominent *de facto* distributive agreement operative in Beringia is the Soviet-Japanese Northwest Pacific Fisheries Convention of 1956.[83] This Convention ' . . . covers the northwest Pacific generally west of 175° West and north of 45° North latitutde, including the Sea of Okhotsk, parts of the Sea of Japan, and the Bering Sea.'[84] Convention waters thus encompass an important segment of Beringia, though they also extend beyond the boundaries of the region as demarcated in this study. This Convention was occasioned by the postwar resurgence of Japanese fishing operations in the north-west Pacific. It establishes a bilateral commission and makes provisions for annual bargaining sessions to deal with catch quotas, fishing areas, and inspection procedures. In this case, the Soviet Union has played the role of coastal state with vigor, taking active steps to protect Soviet interests in stocks of such species as Asian salmon and king crab. To this end, the Soviets have generally sought to negotiate from a superordinate position and often invoked the exclusion principle in their efforts to restrict the inroads of Japanese high seas fishing in Convention waters. There is an obvious parallel between this situation and the American efforts to make use of the abstention principle in the northeast Pacific, though many observers regard Soviet restrictions on Japanese fishing under the 1956 Convention as even more severe than the restrictions associated with the International North Pacific Fisheries Convention.[85]

Beyond this, bilateral agreements relating to the harvest of North American crabs have been negotiated (and subsequently renegotiated) between the United States and Japan since 1964 and between the United States and the Soviet Union since 1965.[86] Each biennial renegotiation of these agreements has yielded new quotas for the relevant Japanese and Soviet operations. The basic effect of this process has been continuously to reduce Soviet and Japanese harvests of crabs in North American waters. The scope of the restrictions has also been expanded to encompass tanner crabs as well as king crabs. By 1973,

> Five rounds of bilateral negotiations with Japan and the Soviet Union in regard to king crab and tanner crab resources of the continental shelf of the eastern Bering Sea and the Gulf of Alaska [had] resulted in *de facto* recognition that America has the

exclusive exploitation rights to these resources. It is apparent that a continued U.S. effort in the fisheries will eventually eliminate all but token foreign quotas.[87]

Though every effort has been made in these negotiations not to prejudice the legal status of the Japanese position concerning the concept of shelf resources, it is apparent that these developments have operated to buttress the positions of the United States and the Soviet Union in this area.[88]

Since the mid-1960s, the United States has also entered into a series of bilateral agreements relating to foreign fishing operations in the so-called contiguous fishery zone. These agreements were called forth by the passage of the Contiguous Fishery Zone Act of 1966 (the 'twelve mile' bill)[89] which asserts exclusive American jurisdiction over all fishing activities in a band of water extending 9 miles from the outer edge of the territorial sea. Roughly parallel agreements were negotiated with Japan and the Soviet Union in 1967 and they have since been renegotiated on several occasions.[90] Briefly, these agreements permit continued Japanese and Soviet fishing in the contiguous zone but they impose well-defined restrictions on these activities. They grant the use of several 'loading areas' to Japan and the Soviet Union in the contiguous zone, specify gear restrictions on Japanese and Soviet fishing in the zone, and further reduce Japanese and Soviet harvests of crabs in North American waters.[91] Along somewhat similar lines, the United States and Canada negotiated a Reciprocal Fishing Agreement in 1970.[92] The purpose of this agreement is to resolve problems stemming from the unilateral establishment of contiguous fishing zones by Canada in 1964 and the United States in 1966. The result is a collection of detailed provisions setting forth various rights and obligations pertaining to the fishing operations of each country in the other's fishery zone.

Finally, the United States and the Republic of Korea entered into a 5-year agreement in 1972 dealing with the fisheries of the northeastern Pacific.[93] While this agreement contains a number of technical provisions, its essential feature is the extension of the abstention principle of the International North Pacific Fisheries Convention to the operations of Korea.[93a] Specifically, Korea has agreed to refrain from fishing for salmon and halibut east of the abstention line at 175° W longitude. Given the fact that there has been a marked upsurge during the 1970s of American criticisms concerning the location of this abstention line with respect to Japanese fishing operations, it is interesting that the locus of the line remains unchanged in the American-

Korean agreement.

4. *Allocation principles.* The distinctive feature of the agreements in this category is the inclusion of explicit and mutually agreed-upon distributive formulas to go along with conservation arrangements.[94] Agreements of this type are capable of controlling the unfortunate economic consequences that often accompany conservation arrangements not coupled with formulas for the allocation of overall quotas. Nevertheless, they are difficult to negotiate in most situations. They require explicit resolutions of the conflictual aspects of competitive-cooperative relationships, and the outcomes must be mutually acceptable since agreements of this type are essentially voluntary undertakings rather than the results of sharply asymmetrical bargaining processes.

Two significant agreements of this type are currently operative in Beringia. The most well known is the North Pacific Fur Seal Convention, whose members are the United States, the Soviet Union, Canada, and Japan. This agreement dates back to 1911 and has been in force ever since, with the exception of a short period starting just prior to World War II when Japan withdrew from the arrangement. The current managerial arrangements for the fur seal herds were negotiated in 1957.[95] Briefly, the major provisions of the Fur Seal Convention are as follows: 1) all pelagic sealing is prohibited, 2) all harvesting of fur seals is to be carried out by the designated managers (the United States for the Pribilof herds and the Soviet Union for the Komandorski and Robben Island herds),[96] and 3) each manager is to share its harvest with Japan and Canada according to an explicit formula stated in percentage terms.[97] By and large, this Convention has been remarkably successful. The Pribilof herds, for example, have increased over the years from a low of approximately 150,000 to something in the neighborhood of 1.5 million, and the commercial value of the annual harvest is not insignificant. In recent years, however, the crucial Pribilof herds have declined somewhat, probably as a consequence of the expanding high seas fishing operations in the area by Japanese and Soviet fleets.[98]

The other agreement of this type is considerably more marginal to Beringia in geographical terms. This is the Canadian-American International Pacific Salmon Fisheries Convention negotiated in 1930 but ratified only in 1937.[99] The agreement deals with the sockeye salmon fishery (it was extended in 1956 to cover pink salmon as well) of the Fraser River-Puget Sound area. In addition to a variety of measures aimed at conservation and the achievement of maximum sustained yields, the Convention introduces the so-called equalization principle. Specifically, it establishes a commission which is '... empowered to make rules about gear and open days so as to equalize the catch of both members.'[100] Though certain controversies have arisen in conjunction with this agreement in recent years, it is widely regarded as an outstanding example of serious international coordination concerning the management of renewable resources.

It is impossible to escape the conclusion that these functional agreements, taken as a set, constitute a highly inadequate response to the growing need for coordinated resource management in Beringia, though some of them are defensible in their own right. They offer little assistance in coping with the region's emerging problems of resource management outside the realm of renewable resources. Many of them. fail to tackle the central problem of managing renewable resources (i.e. the restriction of entry) on any effective, economically rational, or equitable basis. There are enormous gaps in the coverage of these agreements even in the realm of renewable resources (e.g. the absence of effective regulations pertaining to most demersal fish in the Bering Sea and the Gulf of Alaska). And they offer no basis for responding, from a managerial point of view, to the growing interdependencies both among the various species of fish in the region and between the renewable resources and the other resources of the region. In short, these agreements amount to a piecemeal approach to a set of problems that have become insoluble on any such basis. Many of them originated in an era of much lighter usage of the renewable resources of Beringia, and they are simply inadequate to cope with the contemporary problems of management occasioned by the increasingly heavy usage of the region's resources.

C. Unilateral Claims and Unresolved Conflicts

All regimes are dynamic rather than static in the sense that they change continuously. A regime ultimately reflects the fundamental political, economic, and social realities of the social system in which it functions, and these realities are never perfectly stationary in any social system. Shifts in major features of a social system ordinarily precipitate a process in which the principal actors in the system assert streams of claims and counterclaims intended to shape the content of the regime of the system to conform to their own interests. At any given moment in time, there are apt to be numerous unresolved conflicts among these competing claims pertaining to the content of the system's regime.[101] This is especially true in decentralized social systems, such as the international system as a whole or international regions, which lack authoritative and effectively institutionalized procedures for the resolution of conflicts among such claims and counterclaims. In systems of this type, changes in existing regimes typically flow from *ad hoc* bargaining processes in contrast to clearcut legislative procedures. Though such bargaining processes are sometimes effective in *de facto* terms, they seldom yield results that are as unambiguous or authoritative as those that emanate from well-developed legislative processes.[102]

The Beringian resource region reflects this general pattern clearly. It is highly decentralized politically so that major developments in the region's regime can only stem from *ad hoc* bargaining processes among its principal actors. Moreover, it is a social system experiencing rapid and, probably, accelerating change with respect to a number of its fundamental features. The preceding chapter documents the most important of these changes pertaining to the utilization of natural resources in detail. Under the circumstances, it is hardly surprising that unilateral claims concerning management, use, and ownership of the region's resources are proliferating rapidly at the present time, and new claims of this type are certain to emerge with growing force in future years. The purpose of this section, then, is to round out the picture of the existing regime in Beringia presented in the preceding sections by identifying and evaluating the major unresolved conflicts about the region's regime which exist at this time.

1. *Internal waters, territorial seas, contiguous zones.* Beringia is the scene of a variety of conflicting claims relating to the jurisdiction of coastal states over the belt of water between the land masses and the high seas of the region. In the first instance, there are disagreements concerning the demarcation of internal waters. The Soviet Union has, from time to time, advanced especially far-reaching claims concerning the extent of its internal waters in Beringia and in the Arctic in general.[103] As Figure IX indicates, the Soviets have periodically advanced claims to full sovereignty over the Kara, Laptev, and East Siberian Seas as well as the Sea of Okhotsk. Though such claims have not been extended to encompass the Bering Sea in recent times, the Soviet attitude toward the Chukchi Sea is less clear. All such claims have been disputed vigorously by the United States (in some cases with the backing of Japan), which has a strong interest in maintaining freedom of navigation and scientific research in these areas. Moreover, the Soviet position regarding these claims may now be shifting sifnificantly as a consequence of the emergence of the Soviet Union as a major maritime power with worldwide maritime interests.[104]

Figure IX

Soviet Maritime Claims

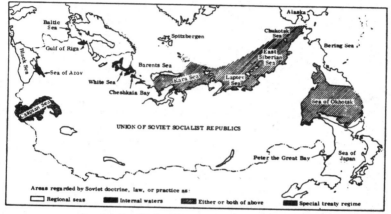

Some Areas Treated in Soviet Doctrine, Law, or Practice as Closed Seas, Historic Bays or Seas, or Internal Waters

Source: William E. Butler, *The Soviet Union and the Law of the Sea*, (Baltimore 1971), 105.

The Soviet Union is not, however, the only actor in Beringia which has exhibited an interest in expansive claims relating to internal waters. There has been some discussion in Canadian circles of claiming the waters of the Canadian Arctic as internal waters on the basis of certain archipelago doctrines, though Canadian efforts to construe these waters as part of the Canadian territorial sea may surface even more vigorously during the near future.[105] In either case, the United States will undoubtedly take steps to oppose such claims.[106] Nevertheless, there are also certain American claims which involve efforts to expand the scope of the internal waters of the United States. In Beringia, these claims have been articulated largely through the activities of the State of Alaska. The Supreme Court has finally ruled against the view that the Cook Inlet should be regarded as internal water on the basis of the historic bay doctrine.[107] But there remain influential groups in Alaska with an interest in advancing similar claims to all or part of the Bristol Bay.[108] In short, positions concerning the boundaries of internal waters fluctuate dramatically as a function of the particularistic interests at stake.

The basic problems pertaining to the territorial seas of Beringia, as of other regions of the world, stem from indeterminacies in the prevailing law of the sea. Expansive views about baselines have the double effect of pushing the outer boundary of internal waters seaward and of extending the outer boundary of the territorial sea in the same direction, thereby enlarging the jurisdiction of coastal states over offshore resources lying close to land. Current examples in Beringia involve efforts on the part of the United States Navy to redefine the baselines used in demarcating the territorial sea off Naval Petroleum Reserve No. 4,[109] and on the part of the State of Alaska to employ expansive baselines in the Beaufort fringe area off Prudhoe Bay.[110] Similarly, the role accorded to islands has significant implications for the demarcation of territorial seas in a region like Beringia. This is especially true when islands are utilized in the process of drawing straight baselines. Furthermore, various doctrines concerning the status of archipelagos have substantially different implications for the demarcation of the American territorial sea around the Aleutian chain and the Canadian territorial sea throughout the Canadian Arctic. Claims and counterclaims concering these matters are not now being advanced with sufficient precision and force to generate serious international conflicts in the Beringian region, but the development of such conflicts is quite probable during the next 10–20 years. In this context, it is not difficult to foresee significant Soviet-American, Canadian-American, and Japanese-American disputes emerging in this realm.[111]

Unresolved problems are also beginning to surface in Beringia with respect to the somewhat imprecise notion of contiguous zones. The Geneva system suggests a rather restrictive conception of contiguous zones in functional terms and conceives of such zones as extending no more than 12 miles beyond the inner boundary of the territorial sea. In fact, however, states like Canada and the United States have taken steps explicitly to extend the scope of contiguous zones to encompass fishing operations and other matters pertaining to the exploitation of resources.[112] There now appears to be widespread consensus on the idea of expanding the width of the territorial sea to 12 miles, a development that undermines the initial Geneva conception of contiguous zones.[113] Nevertheless, various states have advanced *ad hoc* claims on a unilateral basis which appear to rest upon expanded conceptions of contiguous zones if they have any clear juridical basis at all. Recent examples in Beringia include Canadian initiatives concerning vessel-based pollution[114] and Soviet claims to restrict foreign activities in a 30-mile zone surrounding the Komandorski Islands for the stated purpose of safeguarding the Komandorski fur seal herds.[115] Though such claims have not yet led to severe clashes in the Beringian region, they are associated with the more general movement toward expansive jurisdictional claims on the part of coastal states and they will undoubtedly meet with resistance from time to time on the part of states with important distant-water interests.

2. *The continental shelf.* In much of Beringia, the continental shelf is a large, continuous underwater plain stretching from the west coast of North America to the east coast of Siberia. There are few areas in the Chukchi Sea in which water depths exceed 200 metres, and the same is true of the Bering Sea approximately as far south as the Pribilof Islands. Moreover, the continental shelves in other parts of Beringia (e.g. the Beaufort Sea, the Gulf of Alaska, and the coast of the Kamchatka Peninsula) are relatively large. Accordingly, the region includes a large segment of the earth's total continental shelf, and this shelf is unusually rich in renewable and, probably, non-renewable resources. Presently, three unresolved issues of some significance relate explicitly to these shelf areas.[116]

Undoubtedly the most important of these issues stems from the fact that the United States and the Soviet Union are 'opposite' states with respect to the continental shelves of the Chukchi Sea and the Bering Sea. That is, the provisions of the Continental Shelf Convention permit overlapping jurisdictional claims in this area on the part of these states so that a problem of demarcation or boundary specification arises.[117] This issue, which was somewhat academic in earlier terms, has recently begun to loom larger with the emergence of indications of major offshore oil reserves in the area and the possibility of other valuable resources as well.[118] In this connection, it is important to note that the 'convention line' of the 1867 treaty between Russia and the United States applies only to jurisdiction over islands and has no significance with regard to the demarcation of shelf boundaries.[119] Therefore, the issue comes under the terms of the somewhat ambiguous 'triad' concept incorporated in Article 6 of the Continental Shelf Convention. In this case, it is unclear whether there are any significant 'special circumstances',[120] and the exact location of the median line would be highly sensitive to decisions on such matters as the relevance of islands and the appropriate baselines for the demarcation of the territorial sea. Figure X indicates graphically the scope of the ambiguities associated with efforts to resolve this boundary problem on the basis of such criteria. Both the United States and the Soviet Union have so far exhibited a reluctance to enter into serious negotiations concerning this issue, though it is clear that both countries are acutely aware of its potential importance.[121] This evidently stems from the reluctance of '. . . both countries to make the Bering Sea 'grab' before each has collected more data on the Shelf's undersea mineral potential'[122] as well as from a mutual desire to avoid contentious issues that might strain the somewhat delicate *detente* that has grown up between the two countries in recent years. Consequently, while the issue raised in this paragraph is virtually certain to crystalize as a significant conflict sometime during the next decade or so, there exists at present a tacit agreement to avoid (at least temporarily) an overt confrontation in this area.

A lesser issue in this realm arises from the fact that the United States and Canada are 'adjacent' states in Beringia. That is, their land masses adjoin each other so that it is necessary to agree on some basis on which to project their territorial boundaries onto the adjacent shelf areas. In fact, the two countries are adjacent states in two different parts of Beringia: 1) the Mackenzie basin and 2) the juncture of British Columbia and Southeast Alaska. This boundary problem has not yet produced any overt conflict between Canada and the United States;[123] it is intrinsically less contentious than the Soviet-American case discussed above since the affected areas are smaller in this case of adjacent states than in the preceding case of opposite states.[124]

156

Figure X
Continental Shelf Boundaries

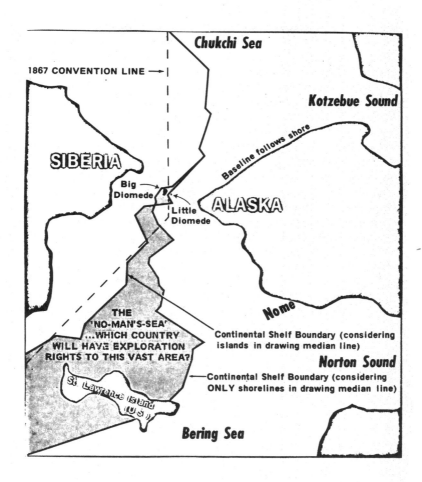

Source: Martin Loken, 'Special Report — Dividing the Continental Shelf', *Alaska Construction and Oil*, 10(12), December 1969, 25.

Nevertheless, the importance of crabs and other crustaceans in the British Columbia-Southeast Alaska area and the probable presence of hydrocarbons in the Mackenzie basin will almost certainly make it necessary for the two countries to confront this boundary problem in a serious fashion during the near future. In this context, it is worth noting that at least in the Mackenzie basin area there are 'special circumstances' to be considered. Thus, ' . . . the 141st meridian . . . might be deemed to constitute a special circumstance. Its historical significance goes back to the 1825 boundary treaty between Russia and Great Britain.'[125] Moreover, ' . . . the Canadian government has been issuing oil and gas permits in the Beaufort Sea for some time, using the 141st meridian as the westerly limit.'[126]

A further source of contention relating to the Beringian shelf stems from the conflict between the United States and the Soviet Union on the one hand and Japan on the other with respect to the operational definition of shelf resources. Specifically, the Japanese maintain that king crabs and tanner crabs are high seas resources while the two coastal states view these crabs (as well as other crustaceans) as shelf resources under their control or jurisdiction. In addition, Japan has refused to adhere to the Continental Shelf Convention so that it is not possible to seek a settlement of this conflict in terms of the provisions of that Convention. To date, the Japanese have consistently refused to make concessions of principle concerning this issue. Nevertheless, a pattern is emerging from a series of *ad hoc* agreements (e.g. the United States — Japan King Crab Agreements) which indicates that the effective jurisdiction of coastal states over living shelf resources in Beringia will soon be more broadly defined.[127] The Japanese are obviously not enthusiastic about this outcome, and they may well attempt to trade concessions on this issue for reciprocal concessions in some other area. But there can be no doubt that the jurisdictional claims of the coastal states are gaining the upper hand with regard to the issue of control over the living resources of the continental shelf.

3. *High Seas fishing*. The problems of managing and, implicitly, allocating the living resources of the high seas may well generate the sharpest and most dramatic conflicts among claims and counterclaims pertaining to the regime of the Beringian region during the next 10—20 years. The central issue is clear: how to alter or replace the existing modified common property system in this realm to cope with the consequences of heavy usage and to produce an allocation of resources which is defensible on grounds of distributive justice. The

major battlelines have also emerged in a clearcut fashion. In short, the conflict pits distant-water fishing interests against coastal fishing interests.[128] In Beringia, the principal actors vary in the extent to which they are crosspressured along these lines,[129] but it is clear that it will be difficult for any of these actors to avoid taking a definite stand on this issue in the coming struggle over high seas fishing. It now seems probable that this conflict will be couched largely in terms of debates about the increasingly fashionable notion of exclusive economic zones.[130] Canada and the United States may well advocate the establishment of such zones in Beringia. For its part, the Soviet Union would benefit from their introduction in the western portion of the region, though the Soviets stand to lose more than they would gain from a general movement in this direction in Beringia. The concept of 200-mile economic zones has become highly popular in the context of the new Law of the Sea Conference, despite the fact that the jurisdictional content of these zones is still a matter lacking consensus.[131] Moreover, political pressures in the United States are now building in support of the idea of taking unilateral steps to establish 200-mile fishing zones along the country's coasts if there is no agreement on economic zones at the Law of the Sea Conference in the near future.[132]

Therefore, it would be a serious mistake to underrate the growing movement toward the creation of economic zones in the context of this discussion of high seas fishing. But it would be equally erroneous to assume that the mere promulgation of such zones either unilaterally or as part of a revised law of the sea will automatically and un-ambiguously resolve the existing conflicts concerning the management and allocation of the resources in question. Efforts to assess the probable impact of exclusive economic zones on high seas fishing in Beringia raise several complicated questions. In the first instance, the exact demarcation of these zones would be highly sensitive to such matters as the specification of acceptable baselines and the role accorded to islands (e.g. St. Lawrence Island) in this process.[133] In Beringia, variations along these lines might be substantial in terms of the extent to which specific stocks of fish would fall within various economic zones. Under the circumstances, the demarcation of economic zones in this region would require extensive international negotiations.

The introduction of 200-mile economic zones would also produce confusing and, in some cases, unintended results in Beringia. For example, such arrangements would probably reduce coastal state control over the region's salmon stocks (in comparison with current applications of the exclusion and abstention principles). Thus, it is not surprising that American policymakers are now advocating a supplementary formula designed to ensure coastal state control over anadromous fish stocks over and above the 200-mile economic zone.[134] Similarly, such zones would not guarantee coastal state control over all stocks of pelagic fish (e.g. saury and some herring stocks) or over stocks of most species of great whales. Next, it is important to remember that control over the exploitation of crabs and other sedentary fish in Beringia is already going decisively to the coastal states under various *de facto* interpretations of the jurisdictional status of the living resources of the continental shelf. Moreover, 200-mile economic zones would not decisively alter the current situation with regard to marine mammals since these animals are either already managed on a co-ordinated basis (e.g. the fur seals) or sufficiently migratory to be unmanageable within individual economic zones. Consequently, the most striking impact of 200-mile economic zones in Beringia would be to increase coastal state control over the harvesting of stocks of demersal fish.[135] This would be a rather curious outcome in view of the fact that the major stocks of demersals (other than halibut) in the region are highly important to distant-water states like Japan and the Soviet Union but of only marginal economic significance to the relevant coastal states (i.e. the United States and Canada).

Beyond this, it is far from clear whether the introduction of a system of economic zones would noticeably improve the management of Beringia's high seas fisheries. It is perhaps true that the consequences of common property arrangements have now become so unfortunate that '. . . even an agreement dictated by any one of the participants would be preferable to unrestructured exploitation.'[136] Nevertheless, the division of Beringia into sharply separated jurisdictional zones would not necessarily lead to great improvements over the existing situation in terms of either biological conservation or economic efficiency. A greatly reduced, though still significant, portion of the high seas would remain unregulated. Inadequate coordination among states operating different economic zones could lead to severe depletions with respect to certain species (e.g. salmon, herring, some species of whales). Moreover, the results with regard to stocks lying predominantly within individual economic zones would depend on the policies of the relevant states both toward the fishing activities of their own nationals and toward the fishing activities of others under systems of permits or licenses.[137] In this context, it is likely that

160

many of the defects of a common property system would reemerge on a smaller scale within individual economic zones.

Nor is there any reason to suppose that a system of economic zones in Beringia would yield particularly desirable results from the point of view of distributive justice. Even if outsiders were permitted to harvest some stocks in the zones through the use of permits or licenses, the general effect of the introduction of economic zones would be a shift in the distribution of wealth toward the relevant coastal states. It is hard to identify any intrinsic reason why the normative claims of coastal states are superior to those of distant-water states with respect to marine fisheries. This is especially true in cases like Beringia where the coastal states are highly industrialized countries and where the resources in question are typically more important to the distant-water states as sources of animal protein.[138] Moreover, a system based on exclusive economic zones harbors a conservative bias insofar as it increases barriers against the emergence of new entrants in specific fisheries.[139] And such a system might well lead to the under-utilization of important stocks (e.g. eastern Bering Sea demersals) for a considerable period of time,[140] an unfortunate outcome during a period of worldwide food shortages.

Finally, it would be a mistake to assume that the implementation of a system of exclusive economic zones in Beringia would be a simple matter in political terms. Even if the new Law of the Sea Conference produces a convention sanctioning economic zones of some sort, the promulgation of such zones in a specific geographical region will remain a highly complex matter. So, for example, Japan and the Soviet Union have refused to adhere to the Fisheries Convention of the Geneva system, and they might well enter explicit reservations to the provisions of any new convention concerning extensive economic zones. The exact language of the provisions dealing with the jurisdiction of coastal states within their economic zones is also likely to be imprecise. At present, there are numerous formulations which have been advanced by various interested parties.[141] The United States is now advocating provisions giving ' . . . the coastal state exclusive rights for the purpose of regulating fishing in the 200-mile economic zone, subject to a duty to conserve and to ensure full utilization of fishery stocks taking into account environmental and economic factors,'[142] but there are many other proposals that differ from this one in crucial ways. Moreover, the language of each of these proposals is hardly self-explanatory when it comes to concrete applications in specific regions, and in any case, the language finally agreed to is apt to

161

be particularly ambiguous since it will inevitably be the result of numerous compromises among divergent interests.[143]

It is also important to remember that powerful distant-water states such as Japan and the Soviet Union will not be altogether devoid of bargaining strength in their dealings with states like Canada and the United States concerning the high seas fisheries of Beringia, regardless of the formal arrangements relating to economic zones which emerge in the near future. In this connection, it is important to bear in mind the fact that the major harvests in question are far more important to the Soviets and, especially, the Japanese in economic terms than they are to either the Canadians or the Americans.[144] Consequently, it is highly probable that the future allocation of the harvests of the high seas fisheries of Beringia will be strongly influenced by the push and pull of political interactions among the United States, the Soviet Union, Japan and Canada.[145] This is not to say that the final result will be any more desirable in terms of biological conservation, economic efficiency, or distributive justice than the result that would flow from a more mechanical application of the concept of exclusive economic zones. But it would be a mistake to make predictions in this area on the basis of the assumption that economic zones will be implemented in a more or less routine fashion in Beringia.

4. *Pollution control.* The identification and the initial stages of development of hydrocarbon resources in Beringia during recent years have precipitated a rapid growth of concern about the dangers of marine pollution in the region. There is little doubt that the regulation of land-based pollution will remain primarily under the jurisdiction of the state of origin, though pollution of this type may have far-reaching effects throughout marine regions. With respect to seabed-based and vessel-based pollution, however, the situation is considerably less clear. The central issues here are not questions of ownership but rather problems relating to the locus of jurisdiction concerning such matters as the formulation of standards, the assessment of liability, the enforcement of rules, and the administration of penalties.[146]

A number of general international conventions relating to marine pollution are now in existence.[147] But the resultant regulatory system deals primarily with vessel-based pollution, focuses on remedial rather than preventive actions, is weak in the realm of compliance mechanisms, and fails to deal with the special problems of individual resource regions.[148] As we move toward an era of large-scale offshore production of hydrocarbons and extensive tanker operations in Beringia, the weaknesses of this overarching system are becoming dramatically apparent.[149] But the most appropriate alternative is far from self evident, and there are certain to be major jurisdictional conflicts in this realm during the near future in Beringia.

To date, the most striking unilateral claim in this area is symbolized by the Canadian Arctic Waters Pollution Prevention Act of 1970.[150] This act

> . . . draws a loosely defined 100-mile zone outside the Canadian islands in the Arctic and stipulates that within this zone Canada will exercise certain antipollution measures. Specifically, the Act prohibits and prescribes penalties for the deposit of 'waste' in Arctic waters or on the islands or mainland under conditions which may cause such waste to enter the Arctic waters.[151]

Though it is easy to sympathize with the concerns underlying this Canadian initiative, it is difficult to construct a compelling justification for it in terms of prevailing international law.[152] Accordingly, the fate of this claim is far from clear at this time.[153] It was called forth by the voyages of the *Manhattan* in 1969 and 1970, and its operative provisions concerning liability, enforcement, and penalties have not yet been tested directly.[154] The Act is certainly compatible with the general move toward the expansion of the jurisdictional claims of coastal states, and this factor may work in its favor. Also, it is possible to justify it to some extent on the basis of the doctrine of self-protection.[155] Nevertheless, states (like the United States) with powerful interests in the maintenance of freedom of navigation and commerce have lodged vigorous protests against the Act and might well attempt to ignore its provisions in concrete cases. A Canadian-American clash concerning this issue is by no means improbable during the next 10–15 years. There has been some discussion of a Canadian-American (or perhaps more inclusive) treaty aimed at the establishment of mutually agreed-upon mechanisms for pollution control in the Arctic.[156] But the positions of the principal actors in this conflict remain relatively far apart at this time.[157]

It is not easy to specify the optimal method of pollution control for a marine region like Beringia. The expansion of coastal state jurisdiction in this realm holds certain attractions because it seems probable that this would produce more effective control than some system involving regulation on the part of poorly equipped international institutions. But coastal state regulation in the area of pollution control is not without drawbacks.[158] The regulations devised by individual states will often reflect parochial interests that are not congruent with the goal of maintaining environmental quality in the region as a whole. Inconsistencies among disparate national systems can generate serious complications.[159] And above all, many pollution problems in a region like Beringia are inherently regional in scope so that they can only be dealt with effectively through some form of international coordination.[160] Consequently, it is hardly self evident that the problem of pollution ccntrol should simply be turned over to coastal states (or flag states or port states) to be handled as they see fit. A more desirable system for Beringia, as well as for other resource regions, might involve hybrid arrangements in which coordinated efforts to formulate common standards and liability rules for the region as a whole are combined with decentralized enforcement procedures.[161]

5. *Claims to the Arctic.* The Arctic is now one of the last real frontiers on the earth. Until recently, the level of human activity in this area was so low that problems of government were virtually nonexistent. Desultory jurisdictional claims were advanced from time to time, but they appeared rather academic and were generally ignored by those who did venture into the Arctic. Now, however, the Arctic has become a focal point of expanding human interest.[162] It may well contain large reserves of hydrocarbons, and it encompasses flow resources of considerable potential importance. But it is also increasingly clear that the Arctic is a fragile area from an ecological point of view. All this has produced a situation in which various states are beginning to advance serious claims and counterclaims relating to human activities in the Arctic. In general, these claims fall neatly into two categories: claims relating to sovereignty and claims asserting jurisdiction over specific activities in the Arctic.[163]

Is the Arctic subject to meaningful claims of sovereignty on the part of individual states?[164] No doubt the Arctic islands are capable of being brought within the purview of national sovereignty, and serious claims along these lines have been advanced by Canada, the Soviet Union, and Norway. But the case of the Arctic Ocean is far more complex since it ' . . . has the characteristics of both land and sea, and yet, is totally unlike both.'[165] It is an ocean in technical terms. But the Arctic has so far failed to sustain significant maritime commerce, the traditional basis of legal doctrines concerning the freedom of the high seas.[166] By the same token, the permanent ice of the Arctic is usable as a base for human activities similar to those pursued on land (e.g. the operation of airfields and fixed-base research programs). But ice islands move continuously within the Arctic basin and the contours of the pack ice change greatly over time so that the analogy between land-based activities and Arctic operations is highly imperfect at best. Beyond this, it is difficult to predict how the pattern of human activities in this area will evolve in the future. Therefore, the status of the Arctic is not only currently inchoate in legal terms, it is also quite unclear what basic concepts to employ in efforts to come to grips with this problem. In short, ' . . . international law has not as yet taken particular note of the circumstances peculiar to polar waters, and there do not appear to be any special international conventions or agreements to cover them.'[167]

Under the circumstances, the Arctic presently constitutes a rather fertile field for competing claims concerning sovereignty. Undoubtedly the most far-reaching and important claims along these lines have been advanced under the rubric of the so-called 'sector principle.'[168] In its more modest forms, this principle ' . . . asserts that each state with a continental Arctic coastline automatically falls heir to all the islands lying between the coastline and the North Pole, which are enclosed by longitudinal lines drawn from the eastern and western extremities of the same coastline to the Pole.'[169] However, various publicists and statesmen have periodically attempted to expand the scope of this doctrine to encompass Arctic waters and ice formations as well as islands lying within these sectors. The sector principle dates back to the early twentieth century, and both Canada and the Soviet Union (the major potential beneficiaries) have advanced sector claims in the Arctic from time to time. Figure XI outlines the boundaries of sovereign jurisdiction that would emerge from an application of this principle in the Arctic. Not surprisingly, the sector principle has been vigorously opposed by other states, such as the United States, with substantial interests in the Arctic. At present, it is widely agreed that none of the versions of the principle possesses the status of law in the international community.[170] Nevertheless, arguments concerning the issues raised by this principle are virtually certain to increase during the foreseeable future as interest in the exploitation of Arctic resources continues to grow.[171]

Setting aside the underlying question of sovereignty, several states have exhibited an interest in extending their *de facto* jurisdiction in the Arctic for various functional purposes. While the issues at stake are complex, they are generally likely to pit Canada and the Soviet Union as advocates of expansive jurisdiction against the United States and perhaps Japan as supporters of common property arrange-

165

Figure XI
The Sector Principle

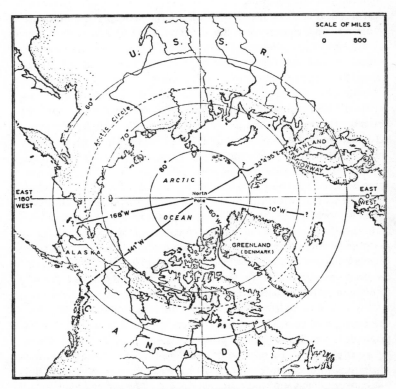

Arctic sectors. The line along 10° W shows Danish and Norwegian-Finnish sectors as proposed in 1927 by L. Breitfuss, who also assigned an Alaskan sector to the United States. Scale of miles is approximately accurate only near the Pole.

Source: Gordon W. Smith, 'Sovereignty in the North: The Canadian Aspect of an International Problem', in R. St. J. Macdonald ed., *The Arctic Frontier*, (Toronto 1966), 219.

ments. For its part, the Soviet Union has exhibited great sensitivity about jurisdiction in Arctic areas lying along its Siberian coastline from the point of view of security, and it has periodically asserted the 'national character' of the Northern Sea Route.[172] Juridically, the Soviet position concerning the Sea Route rests primarily on claims relating to internal waters. But the basic objectives of this stance are to achieve control over the use of the Sea Route by non-Soviet vessels and to create a basis for levying user's fees in the event that foreign vessels do begin to use the Route.[173] Canada, by contrast, appears to be concerned with potential foreign (especially American) encroachments on the exploitation of the resources of the Canadian Arctic archipelago as well as with the possibility of commercial use of the Northwest Passage.[174] In this connection, Canada's legal position rests on emerging doctrines concerning the jurisdictional status of archipelagos and on the fact that 'Under a strict interpretation of even the three-mile rule, much of the archipelago waters lie within Canada's territorial sea, because of the multiplicity of islands, each one having, according to recognized international law, its own marginal belt.'[175] There is little doubt that Canada's legal claims with regard to the Arctic archipelago are substantial, though the Canadian position in this area exhibits important political and economic weaknesses.

The United States and Japan, on the other hand, have every reason to resist such jurisdictional claims on the part of the Soviet Union and Canada. Both stand to profit from freedom of navigation and commerce in the area. The United States has both security interests and resource interests in the Arctic that could be damaged by the extension of these claims. Not surprisingly, then, the United States has been particularly active in combatting claims along these lines. It rejects all claims that appeal in any way to the sector principle. It denies Soviet claims concerning the national character of the Northern Sea Route (the Vilkitski Strait incident of 1967 is relevant in this context).[176] Also, it vigorously opposes Canadian efforts to solidify national jurisdiction over the Northwest Passage and the Canadian Arctic archipelago in general. At present, it is difficult to predict how the resultant conflicts will evolve, though they are apt to become increasingly salient as the level of human activity in the Arctic rises. As Olenicoff has recently suggested, however,

In recent years . . . , the importance of the Arctic Basin as an arena for scientific, economic, and military activities has been rapidly increasing. This has accentuated the need for an international agreement on Arctic waters or, at least, a clear mutual understanding of the individual positions taken by the various Arctic-exploiting nations.[177]

D. Conclusion

The existing regime in Beringia does not have a good performance record in terms of the criteria of evaluation employed in this study. Harvesting in the marine fisheries of the region is typically carried out in an economically inefficient fashion and frequently exhibits little regard for the requirements of biological conservation. It is highly probable that initial production operations in the realm of Beringia's offshore hydrocarbons will be conducted hastily and without taking full account of non-economic values involving such things as pollution control and the preservation of the habitat.[178] Serious problems of overinvestment and unregulated use are likely to emerge with respect to the flow resources of the region as the growing exploitation of nonrenewable resources creates a heightened demand for the use of these flow resources. The existing regime can hardly be said to facilitate efforts to cope effectively with the extensive interdependencies among various functional areas which are surfacing with the advent of heavier usage of Beringia's natural resources.

Moreover, the existing regime is open to serious criticisms concerning its distributive consequences. Not only is distribution currently a source of contention and confusion in Beringia since many unresolved conflicts in the region focus on distributive questions; it is also difficult to construct a normatively persuasive defense of the distributive results of the existing regime. Is the Canadian-American abstention principle ultimately fair as applied to the fishing operations of Japan and Korea? Why should the coastal states have exclusive rights to all the offshore hydrocarbons of Beringia? Even more important, the existing regime is open to the charge that it permits the management of Beringia as a preserve of a small number of highly industrialized states which presently exhibit little interest in utilizing the region's resources in such a way as to contribute significantly to the welfare of the less developed countries of the world.

It also seems accurate to conclude that the political acceptability of the existing regime in Beringia is increasingly open to question. Both external and internal challenges to the regime are now on the rise. Externally, there are the developments symbolized by the new Law of the Sea Conference. Even if this Conference fails to produce a comprehensive convention on the law of the sea, there is no doubt that it will substantially alter the expectations associated with the Geneva system, which forms the foundation of the existing regime in Beringia. Internally, the challenges to the existing regime seem even more pressing. Rapid increases in the usage of the region's resources are now highlighting the defects of this regime in a dramatic fashion. This has encouraged the articulation of a wide range of unilateral claims and counterclaims which will inevitably lead to major changes in the Beringian regime during the foreseeable future.

It is evident that this situation harbors considerable potential for international conflict. A somewhat less obvious, though equally important, feature of the situation, however, is the fact that the emerging conflicts exhibit a definite pattern of cross-cutting cleavages rather than a dominant axis of conflict pitting the same actors against each other on issue after issue.[179] Thus, the Soviet Union and the United States have divergent interests concerning jurisdictional boundaries on the continental shelf, but they have strong common interests vis-à-vis Japan with respect to the operational definition of shelf resources. Similarly, the United States and Canada have serious disagreements in the realm of pollution control in Beringia, but they are increasingly in the same camp regarding the regulation of high seas fisheries. By the same token, Japan and the Soviet Union are often at odds over the fish stocks of the Western Bering Sea, but they have powerful common interests vis-à-vis Canada and the United States in connection with the regulation of the region's high seas fisheries. It would be possible to identify numerous additional cross-cutting cleavages along these lines.

All this suggests that the international conflicts associated with the management of natural resources in Beringia in the future will exhibit a fundamental element of moderation, though they are apt to be highly complex and hard to unravel. As students of politics have often observed, cross-cutting cleavages produce pressure for moderation in conflict situations since every principal actor is apt to view each of the others not only as an opponent but also as a potential coalition partner with respect to one or more important issues.[180] Under the circumstances, it does not pay to alienate any other actor completely. At the same time, the resultant interactions are likely to become highly complex as non-congruent coalition structures form with respect to different issues and efforts are made to arrange package deals and side payments across separable issues in the interests of striking mutually acceptable bargains.[181]

Notes

1. John R. Stevenson and Bernard H. Oxman, 'The Preparations for the Law of the Sea Conference', *AJIL*, 68 (1974), 9.
2. See John R. Stevenson and Bernard H. Oxman, 'The Third United Nations Conference on the Law of the Sea: The 1974 Caracas Session', *AJIL*, 69 (1975), 1–30.
3. For a variety of perspectives on this issue consult Francis T. Christy, Jr., Thomas Clingan, Jr., John King Gamble, Jr., H. Gary Knight, and Edward Miles eds., *Law of the Sea: Caracas and Beyond*, (Cambridge 1975).
4. Allan Gotlieb and Charles Dalfen, 'National Jurisdiction and International Responsibility: New Canadian Approaches to International Law', *AJIL*, 67 (1973), 229–258.
5. The most important of these are the growing demand for animal protein on the part of the Japanese population and the deterioration of harvests in the fisheries closer to the Japanese islands.
6. For a general survey consult Philip C. Jessup, 'The United Nations Conference on the Law of the Sea', *Essays on International Law from the Columbia Law Review*, (New York 1965), 197–231.
7. Esther C. Wunnicke, 'The Legal Framework Governing Alaska's Fisheries', Arlon R. Tussing, Thomas A. Morehouse, and James D. Babb, Jr. eds., *Alaska Fisheries Policy*, (Fairbanks 1972), 224.
8. For a review of the relevant arguments see Nicholas G. Onuf, 'Law-Making in the Global Community: A Working Paper', Princeton Center of International Studies (1974).
9. For a case in point see *Emergency Marine Fisheries Protection Act of 1974*, Hearing before the Committee on Foreign Relations of the United States Senate (U.S. Government Printing Office 1974), 13–16.
10. Convention on the Territorial Sea and the Contiguous Zone, done at Geneva on 29 April 1958 (entered into force on 10 September 1964), [TIAS 5639; 15 UST 1606].
11. There is general agreement that the coastal state has full jurisdiction over the management and exploitation of resources in its territorial sea.
12. Article 24.
13. See the discussion in William E. Butler, 'The Legal Regime of Russian Territorial Waters', *AJIL*, 62 (1968), 51–77.
14. Reports of Judgments, Advisory Opinions and Orders, 1951, Fisheries Case (United Kingdom v. Norway), Judgment of 18 December 1951, The Hague, Cour Internationale de Justice, 1951.
15. For discussion see Jessup, *op. cit.*
16. Fisheries Jurisdiction Case (United Kingdom v. Iceland), Judgment of 25 July 1974, I.C.J. Rep. 1974 and Fisheries Jurisdiction Case (Federal Republic of Germany v. Iceland), Judgment of 25 July 1974, I.C.J. Rep. 1974.
17. Note that these cases fall under the heading of 'oceanic archipelagos belonging to continental states' rather than under the rubric of 'archipelagic states'.
18. The key provisions are in Contiguous Fishery Zone Act, 14 October 1966, (PL 89–658; 80 Stat. 908).
19. Butler, *op. cit.*
20. Gotlieb and Dalfen, *op. cit.*
21. Walter B. Parker, 'International Fisheries Regimes of the North Pacific', *Alaska and the Law of the Sea*, (Anchorage 1974), 59.
22. Convention on the Continental Shelf, done at Geneva on 29 April 1958 (entered into force on 10 June 1964), [TIAS 5578; 15 UST 471].

23. This trend is commonly dated from the American 'Proclamation with Respect to the Natural Resources of the Subsoil and Sea Bed of the Continental Shelf', 28 September 1945 (10 Fed. Reg. 12303).
24. Article 1.
25. For further discussion see Jessup, *op. cit.*
26. See also Juraj Andrassy, *International Law and the Resources of the Sea*, (New York 1970), esp. 94–99.
27. Article 6. The quotations in the following sentences are from this article.
28. The North Sea Continental Shelf Cases (Federal Republic of Germany v. Denmark and Federal Republic of Germany v. Netherlands), decided by the International Court of Justice in 1969, also deal with these problems of boundary specification. Germany is not a member of the Continental Shelf Convention, whereas the relevant states in Beringia have adhered to the Convention. Nevertheless, these cases lend weight to the proposition that opposite and adjacent states should attempt to negotiate mutually agreeable boundaries relating to jurisdiction on the continental shelf.
29. Article 2. See also Wunnicke, *op. cit.*, 231.
30. Convention on Fishing and Conservation of the Living Resources of the High Seas, done at Geneva on 29 April 1958 (entered into force on 20 March 1966), [TIAS 5969; 17 UST 138].
31. Wunnicke, *op. cit.*, 232–233 and Jessup, *op. cit.*
32. Article 2.
33. Jessup, *op. cit.*, 222.
34. Article 7. The quotation in the following sentence is from the article. Note, however, that Article 7 does not lend support to the so-called 'abstention principle' developed by the United States and Canada.
35. On the other hand, the procedures outlined in Article 7 of this Convention have never been actively used. This fact coupled with the relatively small number of adherents to this Convention raises serious questions about the legal status of the provisions of Article 7.
36. Convention on the High Seas, done at Geneva on 29 April 1958 (entered into force on 30 September 1962), [TIAS 5200; 13 UST 2312].
37. Article 2.
38. For example, the introduction of economic zones, discussed in later sections of this chapter, would necessitate significant restrictions on the freedom to fish on the high seas.
39. For background material see Stevenson and Oxman, 'The Preparations . . . ', *op. cit.*; Stevenson and Oxman, 'The Third United Nations Conference . . . ', *op. cit.*, and Christy *et. al., op. cit.* For texts of many of the draft articles now under consideration consult U.N. document A/Conf. 62/WP. 8/Part II, 7 May 1975.
40. Ann L. Hollick, 'What to Expect from a Sea Treaty', *Foreign Policy*, No. 18 (1975), 68–78.
41. See the discussion in Christy *et. al.*
42. Stevenson and Oxman, 'The Third United Nations Conference . . . ', *op. cit.* The United States is undoubtedly the most vigorous supporter of arrangements of this type.
42a. In comparison with the 200-metre rule, this criterion would expand coastal state jurisdiction in some areas but reduce it in others. In the case of Beringia, the most important of the continental shelf resources would be enclosed by either a 200-metre rule or a 200-mile rule.
43. Stevenson and Oxman, 'The Third United Nations Conference . . . ', *op. cit.*
44. See also Lewis M. Alexander, 'Special Circumstances: Semienclosed Seas', John K. Gamble, Jr. and Giulio Pontecorvo eds., *Law of the Sea: The*

Emerging Regime of the Oceans, (Cambridge 1974), 201–215.

45. Hiroshi Kasahara and William Burke, 'North Pacific Fisheries Management', *RfF Program of International Studies of Fishery Arrangements*, Paper No. 2, (Washington 1973), 60–69.

46. *Ibid.*, 60.

47. *Ibid.*, 61.

48. For a general study of international agreements relating to marine fisheries see Douglas M. Johnston, *The International Law of Fisheries*, (New Haven 1965).

49. Kasahara and Burke, *op. cit.*, 43.

50. These are conservation agreements dealing with stocks of crabs and demersal fish in the northeastern Pacific. See 'Monthly Report', Northwest Fisheries Center, National Marine Fisheries Service, National Oceanic and Atmospheric Administration, United States Department of Commerce, December 1974, 13–16.

51. Specific changes relating to this collection of functional agreements occur regularly. However, I do not think the general conclusions reached in this section are likely to be altered by specific changes of this type.

52. The information presented in this section comes from many sources, but the most comprehensive accounts are Parker, *op. cit.*; Wunnicke, *op. cit.*; Ronald C. Naab, 'The Role of International Agreements in Alaskan Fisheries', *Commercial Fisheries Review*, 30 (October 1968), 46–56, and Ronald C. Naab, 'Revisions of International Agreements Affecting Alaskan Fisheries', *Commercial Fisheries Review*, 31 (June 1969), 30–34.

53. Thus, agreements involving the allocation of harvests among participants are stronger than straightforward conservation agreements. Moreover, agreements calling for explicit joint management procedures as well as distributive formulas are even stronger than those that stop at the issue of allocation.

54. Francis T. Christy, Jr., 'Alternative Arrangements for Marine Fisheries: An Overview', *RfF Program of International Studies of Fishery Arrangements*, Paper No. 1, (Washington 1974), 12–14.

55. Agreement between the U.S.A. and the U.S.S.R. Relating to Fishing Operations in the Northeastern Pacific Ocean, 14 December 1964 (TIAS 5703; 15 UST 2179).

56. Agreement between the Government of Japan and the Government of the U.S.A. concerning Certain Fisheries off the U.S. Coast and Salmon Fisheries, 11 December 1970 (TIAS 7020; 21 UST 2746). This agreement was replaced by a subsequent agreement on 20 December 1972 (TIAS 7528; 23 UST 3781).

57. Naab, 'The Role of International Agreements . . . ', *op. cit.*, 50.

58. Wunnicke, *op. cit.*, 242.

59. It is possible to formulate a variety of goals under the general rubric of conservation. In recent years, the goal of maximum sustained yield (MSY) from specific stocks has undoubtedly been the most influential guideline in the realm of conservation, but it is certainly not the only feasible goal.

60. James A. Crutchfield, 'Economic Aspects of Fishery Management', Tussing, Morehouse, and Babb eds., *op. cit.*, 15–39.

61. Convention Between the U.S.A. and Canada for the Preservation of the Halibut Fishery of the Northern Pacific Ocean and Bering Sea, 2 March 1953, (TIAS 2900; 5 UST 5).

62. Parker, *op. cit.*, 23–27.

63. International Convention for the Regulation of Whaling, 1946 (TIAS 1849; 62 Stat. 1716).

64. Parker, *op. cit.*, 15.
65. For recent developments concerning the international regulation of whaling see William E. Schevill ed., *The Whale Problem: A Status Report*, (Cambridge 1974).
66. Until recently, the total annual catch was determined in terms of blue whale units. This made it perfectly acceptable to continue harvesting endangered species (e.g. the blue whale itself) as an incidental catch in operations aimed primarily at other species. For a detailed discussion of the problems associated with this system see George L. Small, *The Blue Whale*, (New York 1971).
67. Parker, *op. cit.*, 15−21 and Small, *op. cit.*
68. See, for example, Agreement on the Regulation of North Pacific Whaling, 30 July 1971 (TIAS 7188; 22 UST 1616). This is a tripartite agreement among Japan, the Soviet Union, and the United States.
69. Ole A. Mathisen and Donald E. Bevan, 'Some International Aspects of Soviet Fisheries', *Mershon Center Pamphlet Series No. 7*, (September 1968), 40−43.
70. Jack Lentfer, 'Agreement on Conservation of Polar Bears', *Polar Record*, 17 (1974), 327−330.
71. Agreement on the Conservation of Polar Bears, 15 November 1973 [*International Legal Materials*, XIII (January 1974), 13].
72. 'Polar Bear Protected in Arctic Region', *Polar Times*, 77 (1973), 7.
73. The new bilateral agreements referred to in note No. 50 should also be mentioned in connection with this discussion of conservation agreements.
74. George W. Rogers, 'The North Pacific as an International Marine Region: Patterns of Conflict and Cooperation', *Inter-Nord*, 8 (1966), 161.
75. Parker, *op. cit.*, 23−27.
76. Naab, 'The Role of International Agreements . . . ', *op. cit.*, 49.
77. International Convention for the High Seas Fisheries of the North Pacific Ocean, 9 May 1952 (TIAS 2786; 4 UST 380).
78. Naab, 'The Role of International Agreements . . . ', *op. cit.*, 49.
79. Parker, *op. cit.*, 26.
80. For background information consult Kasahara and Burke, *op. cit.*
81. Parker, *op. cit.*, 27 and Rogers, *op. cit.*, 161−162.
82. After ten years of operations, according to the terms of the Convention, each member shall have the right to withdraw after giving one year's notice to the other members.
83. Convention Concerning the High Seas Fisheries of the Northwest Pacific Ocean, 14 May 1956 [*AJIL*, 53 (1959), 763−773].
84. Francis T. Christy, Jr. and Anthony Scott, *The Common Wealth in Ocean Fisheries*, (Baltimore 1965), 203.
85. See, for example, Georg Borgstrom, *Japan's World Success in Fishing*, (London 1964), 155.
86. Agreement between Japan and the U.S.A. in Regard to the King Crab Fishery of the Eastern Bering Sea, 25 November 1964 (TIAS 5688; 15 UST 2076) and Agreement between the U.S.A. and the U.S.S.R. Relating to Fishing for King Crab, 5 February 1965 (TIAS 5752; 16 UST 24).
87. Parker, *op. cit.*, 36.
88. *Ibid.*, 31−33.
89. Contiguous Fishery Zone Act, 14 October 1966 (PL 89−658; 80 Stat. 908).
90. Wunnicke, *op. cit.*, 240−245. See also Agreement between the U.S.A. and the U.S.S.R. on Certain Fishery Problems in the Northeastern Part of the Pacific Ocean off the Coast of the United States, 13 February 1967 (TIAS 6218; 18 UST 190).
91. Parker, *op. cit.*, 39−40.

92. U.S.-Canada Agreement Regarding Reciprocal Fishing Privileges, 24 April 1970 (TIAS 6879; 21 UST 1283).
93. Agreement between the U.S.A. and the Republic of Korea Concerning Cooperation in Fisheries, 24 November 1972 (TIAS 7517: 23 UST 3702).
93a. Parker, *op. cit.*, 47.
94. That is, agreements of this type are not imposed on one or the other of the participants as a consequence of highly asymmetrical bargaining positions.
95. The original agreement was the Convention between the United States and Other Powers Providing for the Preservation and Protection of Fur Seals, 1911 (UST 564; 37 Stat, 1542). The 1957 Agreement is the Interim Convention on Conservation of North Pacific Fur Seals, 1957 (TIAS 3948; 8 UST 2283).
96. The fact that actual harvesting is done under a joint management system makes it possible, at least in principle, to achieve economic efficiency in the utilization of this resource.
97. Specifically, Japan and Canada each receive 15% of the harvests of the United States and of the Soviet Union. For more detailed information on the provisions of this agreement see George W. Rogers and Don C. Foote, "The North Pacific Fur Seal Industry, the Record of International Management", *Inter-Nord*, 10 (1968), 151–154.
98. Parker, *op. cit.*, 8. See also 'The Northern Fur Seal Industry: Populations and Perspectives', *Monthly Report*, Northwest Fisheries Center, (November 1974), 1–7.
99. Convention between the U.S.A. and Canada for the Protection, Preservation, and Extension of the Sockeye Salmon Fisheries in the Fraser River System, 26 May 1930 (TS 918; 50 Stat. 1355). The addition of pink salmon is contained in a protocol of 28 December 1956 (TIAS 3867; 8 UST 1057).
100. Christy and Scott, *op. cit.*, 198.
101. This conception parallels, in considerable measure, that of McDougal. See Myres S. McDougal and Associates, *Studies in World Public Order*, (New Haven 1960), 3–42.
102. Such processes are also apt to be slow so that the adaptation of regimes to changing circumstances is typically quite inefficient in highly decentralized social systems.
103. Consult also Butler, *op. cit.*
104. William E. Butler, *The Soviet Union and the Law of the Sea*, (Baltimore 1971), esp. 132 and 167.
105. Donat Pharand, *The Law of the Sea of the Arctic with Special Reference to Canada*, (Ottawa 1973), Pts. II and III and Richard B. Bilder, 'The Canadian Arctic Waters Pollution Prevention Act: New Stresses on the Law of the Sea', *Michigan Law Review*, 69 (1970), 1–54.
106. See, for example, H. L. Dickstein, 'International Law and the Envirionment', George Keeton and Georg Schwarzenberger eds., *Yearbook of World Affairs 1972*, (New York 1973), 245–266.
107. United States v. Alaska, U.S. Supreme Court No. 73–1888, decided on 23 June 1975.
108. Wunnicke, *op. cit.*, 227. For background consult the Arctic Maid case [Alaska v. Arctic Maid, 366 U.S. 199 (1961)].
109. George W. Skladel, 'The Coastal Boundaries of Naval Petroleum Reserve No. 4', Alaska Sea Grant Report No. 73–12, (May 1974).
110. Howard M. Wilson, 'Pending Burst of Leasing Spells Big Alaskan Search', *Oil and Gas Journal*, 72 (2 December 1974), 27.
111. Note that there are also certain to be important intra-national disputes in this realm. Relations between the State of Alaska and the federal

government of the United States illustrate this point clearly.
112. See also Bilder, *op. cit.*
113. See, for example, the discussions in *Emergency Marine Fisheries Protection Act of 1974, op. cit.*
114. Bilder, *op. cit.* and 'New Perspectives on International Environmental Law', *Yale Law Journal*, 82 (1973), 1659–1680.
115. 'Soviet Bans Ships from Seal Region', *Polar Times*, 70 (1970), 13 (a UPI report).
116. If the new Law of the Sea Conference should settle on a 200-mile rule with respect to coastal state jurisdiction over the continental shelf, this will raise additional problems of boundary specification in Beringia.
117. That is, the two states could simultaneously claim jurisdiction over certain portions of the Beringian shelf without violating the basic concepts of the Continental Shelf Convention.
118. Martin Loken, 'Special Report – Dividing the Continental Shelf', *Alaska Construction and Oil*, 10 (December 1969), 22–25.
119. Wunnicke, *op. cit.*, 229.
120. It might perhaps be argued that the 'convention line' of the 1867 treaty constitutes a special circumstance in this context. See the Convention for the Cession of the Russian Possessions in North America to the United States, 30 March 1867, [U.S. Department of State, *Treaties and Conventions 1795–1887*, (Washington 1889)].
121. Loken, *op. cit.*
122. *Ibid.*, 24.
123. Pharand, *op. cit.*, 312–318.
124. That is, even under the most extreme interpretations, the portions of the continental shelf that can figure in such claims are severely restricted.
125. Pharand, *op. cit.*, 318.
126. *Loc. cit.* Note also the following observations advanced by Pharand:
The geography there gives the United States a fairly convex coast whereas, in the same area, the Canadian coastline is markedly concave, thus being to the disadvantage of Canada. (pg. 312)
Canada might then wish to argue that this exceptional configuration of the coast constitutes a special circumstance and that the 141st meridian would be a more equitable boundary line to divide the continental shelf between itself and the United States. (pg. 318)
127. See, for example, Parker, *op. cit.*, 28–36.
128. Superimposed on this conflict is the problem of how to treat new entrants. See James Crutchfield, 'The Marine Fisheries: A Problem in International Cooperation', *American Economic Review*, LIV (1964), esp. 213–214.
129. So, for example, whereas Japan is essentially an uncrosspressured distant-water state, the Soviet Union has significant coastal interests despite the fact that it is primarily a distant-water state in Beringia.
130. For background see Christy *et. al.*
131. Lawrence G. Mallon, 'A Multi-Disciplinary Analysis of the Various Proposals Presented for the 1974 Law of the Sea Conference on Exclusive Fisheries Zones', Sea Grant Technical Bulletin No. 28, University of Miami Sea Grant Program, (1974).
132. See the discussions in *Emergency Marine Fisheries Protection Act of 1974, op. cit.*
133. So, for example, Parker's formulation (Parker, *op. cit.*, 60) rests on assumptions about the role of the Aleutian Islands and the American islands in the Bering Sea, which might be rejected by Japan and the Soviet Union.
134. See John R. Stevenson's statement in *Emergency Marine Fisheries Protection*

175

Act of 1974, op. cit., 39–40.
135. There is, in fact, some disagreement concerning the probable consequences of economic zones with respect to demersal fish. To illustrate, compare the argument developed by the National Oceanic and Atmospheric Administration in *ibid.*, 44–47 with Crutchfield's statement (Crutchfield, 'The Marine Fisheries . . . ', *op. cit.*, 216) to the effect that

> In few of the critical areas would extension of . . . special fishery control zones actually exclude participation by other nations. It might well make fishing more expensive, but the ability of highly efficient large-scale fishing units to harvest fish outside the limits of territorial waters is sufficiently great to undermine seriously even the conservation argument for extension of control by a single nation.

136. Crutchfield, 'The Marine Fisheries . . . ', *op. cit.*, 215.
137. See, for example, Salvatore Comitini, 'The Influence of Management Regimes on the Availability of Capital for Fishery Development', Tussing, Morehouse, and Babb eds., *op. cit.*, 41–72.
138. So, for example, the Japanese are far more dependent upon fish for animal protein than the Americans. It could be argued that this dependency gives the Japanese some normative claim to a substantial share of the harvest of fish in Beringia as well as generating powerful incentives for them to engage in hard bargaining rather than relinquishing their catch from this area.
139. Crutchfield, 'The Marine Fisheries . . . ', *op. cit.*, 213–214.
140. For example, American fishermen currently engage in relatively little high seas fishing in the Bering Sea. To avoid underutilization following the introduction of a 200-mile economic zone in this area it would be necessary to expand the American harvest of the relevant demersal stocks and/or negotiate some licensing system to permit harvesting by the Japanese, Soviets, or Koreans. It seems probable that the implementation of either of these alternatives would involve the passage of considerable time. See also Kasahara and Burke, *op. cit.*, 70.
141. Mallon, *op. cit.*
142. Stevenson, *Emergency Marine Fisheries Protection Act of 1974, op. cit.*, 39.
143. Most states appear to agree that the nature of coastal state jurisdiction in the 200-mile economic zone would be more limited than in the territorial sea, though even this distinction is not universally accepted.
144. There are local exceptions to this generalization, which are relevant to Beringia. So, for example, the residents of some American communities in the Bristol Bay area are heavily dependent on fishing for their livelihood. See George W. Rogers, 'Fisheries Management: The Cook Inlet and Bristol Bay Cases', Tussing, Morehouse, and Babb eds., *op. cit.*, 333–384.
145. Kasahara and Burke, *op. cit.*, 60–61.
146. Samuel A. Bleicher, 'An Overview of International Environmental Regulation', *Ecology Law Quarterly*, 2 (1972), 1–90.
147. Michael Hardy, 'International Control of Marine Pollution', *Natural Resources Journal*, 11 (1971), 296–348.
148. See Barbara Ward, 'Introduction', Robert Hallman, *Toward an Envirionmentally Sound Law of the Sea*, (Washington 1974), 10–11.
149. For background material see Hallman, *op. cit.*
150. Arctic Waters Pollution Prevention Act of 1970, Revised Statues of Canada, RSC Ch. 2, 1st. Supplement, c. 47, 1969–1970. This Act did not come into force until 8 February 1972.
151. Dickstein, *op. cit.*, 263.
152. For a general discussion see Pharand, *op. cit.*, 224–244.
153. Bilder, *op. cit.*

154. See also 'New Perspectives on International Environmental Law', *op. cit.*
155. Pharand, *op. cit.*, 238–240.
156. 'Arctic Pact Sought by U.S. and Canada', *Polar Times*, 70 (1970), 24 (reprinted from the *New York Times*) and Malcolm F. Baldwin, 'Public Policy on Oil – An Ecological Perspective', *Ecology Law Quarterly*, 1 (1971), 245–303.
157. For a discussion of Soviet claims concerning pollution control in the Arctic see Pharand, *op. cit.*, 250–251.
158. Bilder, *op. cit.*
159. See the essays in Thomas A. Clingan, Jr. and Lewis M. Alexander eds., *Hazards of Marine Transit*, (Cambridge 1973).
160. For a case study that demonstrates this conclusion with respect to the Puget Sound – Straits of Georgia area see William M. Ross, *Oil Pollution as an International Problem*, (Seattle 1973).
161. See also Dickstein, *op. cit.* and 'New Perspectives on International Environmental Law', *op. cit.*
162. See, for example, S. M. Olenicoff, 'Territorial Waters in the Arctic: the Soviet Position', Rand R-907-ARPA, 1972, 1 *et. seq.*
163. The legal dimensions of these issues are discussed at length in Pharand, *op. cit.*
164. Gordon Smith, 'Sovereignty in the North: The Canadian Aspect of an International Problem', R. St. J. Macdonald ed., *The Arctic Frontier*, (Toronto 1966), 194–255.
165. Olenicoff, *op. cit.*, 2.
166. On the future prospects of maritime commerce in the Arctic see *Arctic Marine Commerce*, Final Report, Arctic Institute of North America, Contract No. 2–36288 (Maritime Administration, United States Department of Commerce), August 1973.
167. Smith, *op. cit.*, 228.
168. For extensive discussions of the sector principle consult *ibid.* and Pharand, *op. cit.*
169. Smith, *op. cit.*, 214.
170. Smith, for example, concludes that 'So far as the status of the sector principle in international law is concerned, the most favorable thing that can be said is that it remains unsettled' (*ibid.*, 225).
171. It is also worth noting here that Canada has become increasingly concerned in recent years with refforts to assert its sovereignty unambiguously in the area of the Canadian Arctic, without reference to the status of the sector principle. For background consult Gotlieb and Dalfen, *op. cit.*
172. Olenicoff, *op. cit.*, 28.
173. Since the substantial costs of maintaining the Sea Route are borne by the Soviet Union, it is not entirely unreasonable for the Soviet government to think in terms of user's fees for foreign vessels passing through the Sea Route. For relevant factual information consult Terence Armstrong, 'International Transport Routes in the Arctic', *Polar Record*, 16 (1972), 375–382.
174. On the prospects for commercial use of the Northwest Passage see *Arctic Marine Commerce*, *op. cit.*
175. Smith, *op. cit.*, 236.
176. See, for example, Donat Pharand, 'Soviet Union Warns United States Against Use of Northeast Passage', *AJIL*, 62 (1968), 927–935.
177. Olenicoff, *op. cit.*, 1.
178. On the current pace of development in this realm see Nancy Munro, 'OCS Development – What it Means', *Alaska Seas and Coasts*, 3 (15 April 1975),

1—4.

179. It is, of course, also relevant to make enquiries about the intensity of these cleavages. Roughly speaking, it seems reasonable in the case at hand to conclude that it is impossible to single out one or two of the relevant issues as being far more intense than the remaining members of the set.

180. See, for example, Douglas Rae and Michael Taylor, *The Analysis of Political Cleavages*, (New Haven 1970).

181. For a wealth of interesting ideas concerning interactions of this type consult Thomas C. Schelling, *The Strategy of Conflict*, (Cambridge 1960).

CHAPTER V

ALTERNATIVE REGIMES FOR BERINGIA

The preceding chapters leave no doubt that the existing regime in
Beringia exhibits serious defects, and the whole argument of this essay
licenses the conclusion that these defects will become more severe as
the resources of the region are subjected to heavier usage. Therefore, it
seems appropriate at this juncture to turn to an examination of alternative regimes that could be introduced in Beringia. The present chapter
initiates this process through an exercise in comparative statics. Specifically,
it identifies the distinctive features of what appear to be the principal
alternative regimes for the region and assesses the probable consequences
of each of these alternatives in terms of the criteria of evaluation set
forth in Chapter II.

Before embarking on this enterprise, however, a few general comments
are relevant. The next two decades will undoubtedly witness rapid and
extensive changes in Beringia's regime. There currently exist numerous
claims and counter-claims relating to the regime of the region which will
produce significant changes as time passes. Even more important, the
region exhibits a deepseated volatility with respect to its governing
arrangements attributable to the impact of rapid increases in the usage
of its natural resources. It seems inevitable, then, that change itself will
be a prominent feature of the Beringian regime during the near future.
Accordingly, the critical question for this analysis is not whether substantial changes in the Beringian regime are feasible but whether it is
possible to guide forthcoming changes to achieve certain desired results
and to avoid some of the unfortunate developments now occurring in

other international regions (e.g. the Mediterranean Sea). Guided change, in contrast to change *per se*, at the level of the regime for a whole international region is undoubtedly difficult to achieve, but it constitutes a challenge that is both practically important and intellectually interesting.

The substantive sections of this chapter differentiate rather sharply among the principal alternative regimes that could be introduced in Beringia. In this connection, it is important to bear in mind that the resultant constructs are at least 'extreme types' and that some of them may well be 'ideal types'.[1] Constructs of this type are useful in many fields of study, and are of utility for thinking systematically about future regimes for international resource regions like Beringia. But it would be a mistake to expect the occurrence of a neat transition from the present situation to any one of these alternatives at some point in the future. Beyond this, it is worth emphasizing that regimes are highly complex phenomena involving a multiplicity of interdependent components. Consequently, it will be necessary to make use of certain simplifications in efforts to spell out clearly the basic structure of individual regimes, and there will inevitably be an element of speculation associated with assessments of the probable consequences of specific regimes. Nevertheless, the issues involved are of great importance, and there is a compelling case to be made for the proposition that future development of the Beringian regime should not simply be left to chance.

The next three sections of this chapter deal with the most important of the alternative regimes that could be introduced in Beringia: 1) national zones, 2) functional authorities, and 3) a Beringian regional authority. The final substantive section of this chapter contains briefer comments on three minor options.

A. National Zones

It has become commonplace to assert that there is a global trend toward the replacement of modified common property regimes in marine areas with regimes in which the role of coastal states is far more prominent.[2] Publicly, the key argument in favor of this shift rests on the proposition that common property arrangements are incapable of coping effectively with the problems of heavy resource usage and that only coastal states have sufficient power and authority to deal with these problems adequately. Privately, there is little doubt that many coastal states are motivated, in considerable measure, by the distributive gains they expect to reap from developments along these lines. Regardless of one's evaluation of these motivating forces, however, it is clear that the idea

180

of a system of national zones must be taken seriously as an alternative regime for the Beringian region.

The essential feature of a regime of this type is the decentralization of both power and authority in the social structure or region in question to some or all of the constituent members of the system. In the case of Beringia, this would mean decentralization of power and authority to the relevant coastal states (i.e. the United States, the Soviet Union, and Canada). Note, however, that such decentralization does *not* imply an absence of rules or behavioral prescriptions accepted by all the active participants in the region.[3] In fact, the specific alternative examined in this section explicitly assumes the development of common rules concerning such matters as coastal state jurisdiction and the rights of non-coastal states. Nor does this type of regime require a total ban on the exploitation of the region's resources by non-coastal states; they would simply have to operate under the regulations laid down by the relevant coastal states.

A major issue in the introduction of a regime of this type in a resource region like Beringia would be the delineation of specific national zones. Here there is a distinction between the demarcation of all-purpose zones and the demarcation of zones whose boundaries would differ from one functional area to another (e.g. one set of zones for marine fisheries and another set for hydrocarbons).[4] There is also the question of whether the whole region would be divided into national zones (the so-called 'national lakes' scheme)[5] or whether there would remain some area outside the zones regulated on some other basis. The logic of the argument underlying this type of regime suggests that there is little reason to leave part of a region outside the system of zones, though this might occur as a consequence of various political processes.[6] In any case, it is evident that the distributive implications of such a regime would be significantly affected by the precise boundaries of the national zones that ultimately emerged.

Regimes of this type may also vary greatly with respect to the jurisdictional content of the national zones. There are different levels of jurisdictional control that could be allocated to zonal authorities within the general framework of a system characterized by the decentralization of power and authority.[7] It would be feasible to construct a system in which the jurisdictional control of the coastal states varied significantly from one functional area to another. Moreover, there is the question of whether such a regime would involve the delegation of ultimate authority to individual coastal states for their own zones or whether it would include some system of dispute settlement through which appeals against the decisions of zonal authorities could be heard.[8]

The concept of national zones, then, actually encompasses a family of regime types all of which share certain fundamental attributes. In this section, I propose to examine in some detail the probable consequences for the Beringian region of introducing a zonal regime with the following specific characteristics. The entire region would be divided into national zones under the jurisdiction of the relevant coastal states. Each national zone would be an all-purpose zone regarding issues pertaining to resource management and environmental quality. Coastal state jurisdiction would include ownership of zonal resources as well as the authority to promulgate managerial regulations.[9] Nevertheless, there would be political pressures on the coastal states to refrain from total exclusion with respect to the utilization of zonal resources on the part of outsiders.

1. *Social (or group) consequences.* What would be the impact of introducing a system of national zones in Beringia in terms of various measures of production? In the marine fisheries, such a regime would be incompatible with the achievement of economic efficiency with regard to highly migratory species such as salmon, saury, and whales. The movement of these fish across zonal boundaries would produce powerful incentives to overharvest since fishermen in each zone would have to assume that the relevant stocks would be subject to harvest by others as soon as they crossed zonal boundaries.[10] On the other hand, national zones would be compatible, at least in principle, with the achievement of economic efficiency in the harvesting of less migratory species (e.g. many demersals and sedentary fish). The stocks in question would be fully under the jurisdiction of zonal authorities and could be subjected to unified management. Nevertheless, the achievement of this result in practice would certainly not flow automatically from the introduction of national zones. It would require extensive developments in the realm of unified management practices, including overall entry restrictions and methods of distributing entry permits to outsiders as well as nationals.[11]

It is unlikely that a system of national zones would actually lead to economic efficiency in the marine fisheries of Beringia. There is no compelling reason to expect such a regime to lead to significant reductions in the current harvests of highly migratory species like salmon.[12] Even with respect to zonal species, the achievement of economic efficiency would require improbable changes in the impact of political factors (e.g. the provision of employment opportunities),

182

prevailing conceptions of the goals of fisheries management, and attitudes toward the activities of outsiders.[13] In the short tun, national zones would almost certainly lead to substantial reductions in the harvests of zonal species in Beringia.[14] Coastal states like the United States and Canada have little capacity to harvest many of these stocks,[15] and political sensitivities would impede the development of an effective licensing system to permit the operation of Japanese and Soviet high seas fleets in these zones. The impact of each of these factors might decline over time, but it is probable that Beringian harvests of many zonal species would remain below current levels under a system of national zones.

There is no intrinsic incompatibility between a regime based on national zones and the achievement of economic efficiency with respect to the production of oil and natural gas in Beringia. There is no serious 'common pool' problem at this level.[16] Each national zone would be large enough to permit the use of procedures like spacing and unitization, and it would be possible to negotiate unitization agreements to govern production from oil or gas fields straddling zonal boundaries. Efficient production would require a willingness on the part of zonal authorities to permit foreign firms to hold leases within their zones.[17] But there is nothing in the concept of national zones to prevent such arrangements, though they might be politically unacceptable to some countries.

At the same time, it is improbable that the actual level of production of Beringian hydrocarbons would conform to the requirements of economic efficiency under a regime based on national zones. There is little doubt that the Soviets intend to concentrate their attention on the development of the massive reserves of oil and natural gas in western Siberia in the near future.[18] Consequently, the hydrocarbon reserves of the Soviet zone in Beringia would remain largely untapped, except in the rather unlikely event of effective joint ventures with Japanese and/or American corporations.[19] The hydrocarbons of the American zone, on the other hand, would almost certainly be exploited more rapidly than the criterion of efficiency would suggest under a system of national zones. This is partly due to the impact of various political factors (e.g. the drive for energy independence) which are likely to generate powerful pressures for the rapid exploitation of hydrocarbon reserves under American jurisdiction.[20] It also stems from the proposition that ' . . . among the domestic alternatives, oil and gas from the [outer continental shelf] and Alaska have become among the most attractive from an environmental standpoint.'[21]

A regime based on national zones would be inappropriate for the achievement of economic efficiency with respect to maritime commerce in Beringia. It is true that national zones would serve to eliminate the prospect of overuse associated with traditional common property arrangements, but this is unlikely to be a serious concern in Beringia.[22] More importantly, the division of the region into national zones would severely impede the achievement of unified management in this functional area so that there would be a strong tendency toward under-investment in such regional collective goods as coordinated navigational systems, improvements to marine highways, and maintenance facilities. Also, the uncertain legal environment produced by a system of sharply differentiated national zones would make shippers hesitant to invest in the expansion of maritime commerce in the region.[23] Under such a regime, then, there would be a marked tendency for maritime commerce in Beringia to fall considerably short of the level suggested by the criterion of economic efficiency.

Nevertheless, the absolute level of maritime commerce would probably rise considerably in the region even under a system of national zones.[24] This mode of shipment is inexpensive relative to other modes, especially for the movement of heavy cargoes. Rapid developments in the production of nonrenewable resources in Beringia are almost certain to generate extensive new demands for the shipment of heavy freight in the region during the near future. Technological advances will make it easier to operate large vessels under arctic and sub-arctic conditions regardless of the jurisdictional provisions of the prevailing regime in the Beringian region. Under the circumstances, it would take extreme measures on the part of zonal authorities in the realm of user's fees (i.e. taxes) or outright prohibitions to prevent a significant increase in maritime commerce in Beringia in the next few years.

How would the introduction of a system of national zones affect the utilization of various environmental resources? Where the problems in question cut across zonal boundaries such a regime would produce serious difficulties. With respect to the preservation of species and stocks, for example, a zonal system would impede efforts to prevent the depletion of salmon, Polar Bear, and some herring stocks, though it would not be incompatible with efforts to conserve stocks of many demersals and sedentary fish. In the realm of pollution control, a regime of this type would exhibit serious drawbacks since many forms of pollution would not remain localized within individual zones.[25] There would be numerous differences in regulatory arrangements from zone to zone, and there would be a strong tendency for regional outcomes to be determined by the weakest arrangements wherever the relevant problem cut across zonal boundaries. Problems relating to the preservation of the Beringian habitat, on the other hand, seem less likely to generate immediate regionwide repercussions. Accordingly, there is no compelling reason to conclude that national zones would have unfortunate consequences in this realm.

Beyond this, the environmental effects of a regime of this type would clearly vary significantly from zone to zone. The United States is the most advanced of the three relevant zonal states with respect to the political influence of environmental concerns.[26] But it is also under the greatest pressure at this time to exploit the oil and gas reserves of Beringia regardless of the consequences of such activities for commercial fishing and various environmental resources. The Soviet Union, by contrast, has little incentive to exploit Beringia's hydrocarbons at this time, but it might utilize some of the renewable resources of its zone without placing much emphasis on the requirements of biological conservation. For its part, Canada has exhibited great sensitivity concerning the dangers of marine pollution in arctic and sub-arctic areas, but Canadian policy is currently much less attuned to the probable consequences of offshore oil and gas production for various environmental resources.[27] In short, many of the environmental consequences of this regime in Beringia would vary substantially as a function of the policies of the local zonal authorities.

2. *Distributive implications.* Leaving aside questions of production, let us consider the distributive implications of a regime based on national zones in Beringia. In the realm of marine fisheries, such a regime would produce, at least potentially, a major shift of wealth to the relevant coastal states and/or their nationals.[28] Under such a regime, it would be feasible for these actors to appropriate all the economic profits or rents associated with the harvest of zonal species (e.g. many demersals and sedentary fish). The ultimate distributive results of a regime of this type would depend upon a number of additional factors such as: a) the success of zonal authorities in developing unified managerial arrangements to prevent the dissipation of profits, b) the allocation of profits between the state and various entrepreneurs, c) the nature of the provisions governing the fishing activities of outsiders within individual zones, d) the level of direct investment by outsiders in the fishing industries of the coastal states,[29] and e) the extent to which coastal states choose to distribute any of the profits from the marine fisheries to others

(e.g. the less developed countries) through various forms of revenue sharing. Nevertheless, there is no escaping the fact that the outcome of a zonal system would be at least an initial shift in wealth derived from the marine fisheries to the relevant coastal states.

A regime of this type would also permit the coastal states and/or their nationals to appropriate all profits or rents stemming from the production of hydrocarbons in Beringia. Instead of producing a major shift in the distribution of wealth, however, this consequence of a zonal system would merely confirm the essential results of the present system incorporated in the Continental Shelf Convention of 1958. Here too the types of factors outlined above in the discussion of marine fisheries would affect the ultimate distribution of wealth emanating from the production of hydrocarbons in Beringia. But in the case of hydrocarbons, it is worth noting both that the relevant corporations possess considerable influence with respect to distributive questions[30] and that the Beringian coastal states have so far shown little inclination to share any revenues derived from the production of oil or natural gas with others.

The distributive implications of a zonal system in the realm of maritime commerce are actually somewhat more complex than in the realms of marine fisheries and hydrocarbons. In the event that such a system retards the development of maritime commerce in Beringia, the amount of divisible wealth flowing from this source would be limited accordingly. The actual distributive effects of a regime of this type, however, would depend on the managerial arrangements employed in the various zones. If the zonal authorities refrained from levying user's fees in this realm, all profits or rents from the use of the region's flow resources would accrue to the relevant shippers. The coastal states, then, might well have to bear any costs associated with the maintenance of the most oft-commuted marine highways. Under the circumstances, a more probable arrangement would involve the introduction of user's fees on the part of the various zonal authorities.[31] Such fees might be established at a level at which they would just offset upkeep and improvement costs associated with the operation of the marine highways. Though the direct distributive impact of such fees would not be great, their *de facto* effect would be to leave most profits or rents arising in this functional area to the shipping interests. Therefore, coastal states might proceed to establish higher user's fees in order to capture all or part of the profits associated with the use of flow resources within their jurisdictional zones. This would produce a substantial shift of wealth from the

186

various shipping interests in the region (and perhaps those states in which they pay taxes) to the relevant coastal states.

Would the distributive consequences of a regime of this type be fair or just either for the major actors in the Beringian region or for various outsiders? In the marine fisheries, the probable results are not easy to justify in normative terms. It is true that national zones might serve to protect the interests of various sub-national groups (e.g. the fishermen in certain Bristol Bay communities). And it is possible to justify coastal state jurisdictional claims with respect to fish stocks where the relevant coastal state is making substantial investments in well-considered managerial arrangements.[32] However, it is difficult to identify any general normative principle on which to erect a satisfactory defense of the general shift of wealth from the marine fisheries which would flow from the introduction of a system of national zones. In the case of Beringia, many of the affected stocks (e.g. eastern Bering Sea demersals) have been exploited by Japanese and Soviet high seas fleets for some time so that it is even difficult for the relevant coastal states to justify exclusive jurisdictional claims on the basis of the somewhat ambiguous concept of 'historic rights'.[33]

Under a zonal system, the prospects for new entrants in the marine fisheries of Beringia would depend on: a) the willingness of zonal authorities to grant outsiders access to entry permits and b) the extent to which outsiders and nationals of the zonal state received equal treatment in the competition for such permits.[34] Though there is no intrinsic incompatibility between the idea of national zones and the periodic emergence of a new entrant in a given fishery, it is highly probable that a regime of this type would severely restrict the prospects for new entrants in practice. More generally, it seems accurate to conclude that a zonal system in the marine fisheries of the region would have a distinct 'conservative' bias in distributive terms. The principal beneficiaries would be the United States and Canada (as well as the Soviet Union to the extent that it has coastal state interests), states that are prominent among the ranks of industrialized, 'have' nations in global terms. Therefore, except in the unlikely event of these states introducing an effective system of revenue sharing in this realm, the net effect of national zones for the Beringian fisheries would be to reinforce the current unequal distribution of wealth at the international level.

Many of the same comments are applicable to the distributive implications of a zonal system in the realm of hydrocarbons. It is true that coastal state claims to the wealth derived from the production of

187

oil and natural gas in marine regions are already solidly established in *de facto* terms. The issue of new entrants does not arise here in the same way that it typically does in the area of marine fisheries.[35] Nevertheless, it is hard to construct a justification of this situation on the basis of anything other than the principle of might makes right. In effect, the extension of coastal state jurisdiction over the oil and gas reserves of the outer continental shelves of regions like Beringia is little more than a latter day application of the concept of 'manifest destiny'.

If anything, the underlying conservatism of a system of national zones would be more pronounced as applied to the hydrocarbons of Beringia than in the realm of marine fisheries. Zonal authorities would be unlikely to introduce managerial arrangements that would allow outsiders to obtain any entry rights in this area. The oil and gas reserves of the Soviet zone would probably remain largely untapped for the foreseeable future (as they have considerable reserves elsewhere), thereby making no contribution to the welfare of the less developed countries of the world. Moreover, the production of hydrocarbons in the American and Canadian zones would almost certainly serve primarily to sustain the positions of extreme advantage which these states already hold in global terms. Such results would be inevitable unless the three coastal states set up revenue sharing mechanisms with respect to the wealth derived from the exploitation of Beringian oil and natural gas, a development that, for the time being, seems highly improbable.

In the case of maritime commerce, the basic idea of user's fees seems perfectly justifiable in normative terms. There is no persuasive reason why coastal states should bear the upkeep and improvement costs associated with marine highways while shipping interests are acquiring profits or rents from the use of these resources. Whether or not coastal states would be justified in raising user's fees above the level at which they just offset the costs of upkeep and improvement, however, is a harder issue to resolve. There is of course no special reason why shipping interests should be allowed to capture the bulk of the profits arising from the use of the marine highways of a region like Beringia.[36] Nevertheless, the claims of the coastal states are not particularly compelling in this case. Presumably, the benefits accruing to the coastal states from high user's fees would eventually be reflected, to some extent at least, in higher prices paid by consumers of goods transported by sea in Beringia.[37]

At the same time, user's fees in the realm of maritime commerce in Beringia probably would not produce appreciable negative consequences for outsiders. The marine highways of Beringia are unlikely to be used extensively by vessels belonging to outsiders. Such fees are not apt to have a major impact on world market prices for goods purchased in large quantities by outsiders. And there is certainly no basis for concluding that outsiders would benefit more from the accrual of profits or rents from maritime commerce in the region to the major shipping interests than from a system involving relatively high user's fees. Therefore, outsiders might well exhibit little interest in the distributive implications of zonal arrangements for the flow resources of Beringia.

Overall, it seems exceedingly difficult to justify persuasively the probable effects of a regime based on national zones in Beringia from the point of view of distributive justice. It is of course always possible to rely upon standards that boil down to the assertion that might makes right, and it is not unreasonable to argue that some deserving sub-national groups would probably benefit from a regime of this type. Furthermore, some may wish to defend a zonal regime for Beringia on non-distributional grounds, dismissing the distributive implications of the regime as relatively unimportant side effects.[38] However, it seems difficult to justify the distributive implications of such a regime in terms of any such criteria as: equality, just desserts, divine will, the greatest good for the greatest number, or environmental protection.[39] Virtually any criterion of this type capable of operational interpretation appears to conflict with the probable distributive results of a zonal system in Beringia. This in no way implies that a regime of this type will not emerge in Beringia, but it should give pause to those who seek blindly to encourage developments along these lines.

3. *Feasibility.* Would a regime based on national zones be acceptable politically to the principal actors in the Beringian region? It is now widely believed that movement toward some such system is almost inevitable, at least in global terms.[40] The forceful articulation of coastal state claims in international forums such as the new Law of the Sea Conference seems to support this view. Several powerful states, including the United States, are now actively considering unilateral steps that would have the effect of establishing something akin to national zones off their coasts.[41]

Nevertheless, there are good reasons to question the force of this view as applied to the particular case of Beringia. Among the region's major actors, only Canada has interests that could produce unmitigated support for a system of national zones.[42] Korea and, especially, Japan can be counted on to oppose forcefully all developments leading toward a regime of this type. The evolving interests of the Soviet Union suggest waning, rather than increasing, support for any regime of this type in Beringia. The Soviets have growing interests in high seas fisheries and freedom of navigation in this region, while solidifying Soviet control over the hydrocarbons of their sector of Beringia is not a matter of critical importance to the Soviet Union.[43] The United States is severely cross-pressured in this realm. Its fishery interests and desire to control recoverable hydrocarbons suggest a growing receptivity to the idea of a system of national zones in Beringia. But the United States has powerful interests in freedom of navigation as well as a long tradition of support for the policy of freedom of the seas which cut in the other direction. Thus, many would agree with the proposition that 'In order to secure a narrow territorial sea or free transit through straits, the United States will very probably be willing to sacrifice its alleged fishery interests.'[44] Therefore, whatever the circumstances may be in other parts of the world, it seems unwise simply to assume that a regime based on national zones would be acceptable politically in Beringia during the foreseeable future.

Defenders of zonal systems tend to argue that such regimes would display great strengths in the realm of compliance. So, for example, many would agree with the view that ' . . . it is clear that the effective implementation of any regime is probably most effective when carried out by coastal states.'[45] Once again, however, there are good reasons to adopt a cautious view concerning this general proposition in the specific case of Beringia.

The advantage of zonal systems with respect to compliance presumably lies in the realm of direct enforcement, and it is likely that the enforcement capabilities of states will continue to look highly impressive relative to those of international institutions. However, the distinctive features of the Beringian region pose serious problems with respect to the rigorous enforcement of rules relating to the exploitation of natural resources even when individual states are taken as the relevant enforcement agents. The region is so large and so sparsely populated that questions often arise concerning the physical feasibility of enforcement and, in any case, effective enforcement is apt to become extremely costly.[46] American experiences with the abstention line of the International North Pacific Fisheries Convention illustrate these problems clearly,[47] and the difficulties would undoubtedly become far more severe in the face of determined opposition, in contrast to the rather sporadic violations of the abstention line on the part of Japanese high seas fishing fleets.

Therefore, though individual states would clearly possess distinct advantages in the realm of enforcement in a region like Beringia, there is reason to question the viability of any regime for the region compelled to rely primarily on enforcement as a source of compliance.

At the same time, there is no reason to conclude that a zonal system would exhibit great advantages with respect to the achievement of compliance in the absence of rigorous enforcement. It seems unlikely that nationals of states other than the zonal authority in a given zone would impute a generalized sense of legitimacy to the regulatory actions of coastal states under such a regime. On the contrary, to the extent that such zones were regarded as imposed, many actors might be unwilling to grant the authoritativeness of the regulatory actions of coastal states.[48] So, for example, Japanese and Korean nationals might well harbor deepseated reservations about the legitimacy of a system of national zones in Beringia. Moreover, it is probable that actors operating strictly in cost-benefit terms would often experience incentives to violate the regulations of zonal authorities under a regime of this type. Whenever the probability of apprehension and/or the probability of punishment was low, the expected value associated with the acquisition of resources through such violations might well exceed the cost of purchasing the relevant resources (or exploitation rights) from the zonal authority in question.[49]

Would a Beringian regime based on national zones be stable in the simple sense of exhibiting the capacity to endure over time? Such a regime might well have unfortunate consequences with respect to such things as marine pollution and the depletion of certain stocks of fish and marine mammals. But it would undoubtedly be a mistake to suppose that a zonal system would collapse in short order as a consequence of environmental crises associated with the growing usage of Beringia's resources.

On the other hand, a regime of this type might well contain the seeds of its own destruction in direct political terms. Thus, it would expand the regulatory burdens of several states in an era in which the legitimacy of the state as the dominant regulatory agency at the international level is no longer taken for granted.[50] It would also undoubtedly fan the flames of the distributive conflicts that are already emerging between 'haves' and 'have nots' in the international system. The division of Beringia into national zones on the part of three of the world's leading 'have' states could easily be taken as a particularly insulting gesture by many of the less developed countries of the world, quite apart from its implications for other industrialized states like Japan. The People's Republic of China has already begun to make extensive use of issues of this sort in efforts to exercise leadership in the third world, though it has not yet focused systematically on the case of Beringia in these terms.[51] Beyond this, the division of Beringia into clearcut national zones would almost certainly stimulate conflicts concerning jurisdictional control over the Arctic as a whole, and this is an area in which the two superpowers are highly sensitive on grounds of national security.[52] Any attempts to pursue the implications of the sector principle in the Arctic, for example, would undoubtedly elicit vigorous opposition from the United States and could precipitate serious international conflicts. In short, the implementation of a zonal system in Beringia might generate political consequences that could easily threaten the stability of the Beringian regime itself.

B. Functional Authorities

An alternative regime for a resource region like Beringia would involve the introduction of a set of functional authorities or agencies. Arrangements of this type have not been employed extensively in the context of marine regions; nor have they generally been applied to the problems of managing natural resources at the international level.[53] Nevertheless, experience with other forms of functional coordination in regional settings like Europe is suggestive;[54] functional authorities are widely used in the management of resources at the domestic level, and there is no intrinsic reason why similar arrangements should be ruled out in the case of Beringia. The purpose of this section, then, is to examine the probable consequences of a regime for Beringia based on a set of functional authorities.

The defining characteristic of this type of regime is a set of regional institutions organized on a function-by-function basis and endowed with independent regulatory authority in their respective functional areas.[55] The basic idea would be to separate the problems of resource management in a region into clearly differentiated domains and to deal with each of these domains through the operation of distinct institutional arrangements.[56] In the case of Beringia, there might be as many as four separate functional authorities established to manage renewable resources, hydrocarbons, flow resources, and environmental resources. Each agency would be accorded some regulatory capacity in its own functional area in the sense that the member states would transfer authority to make binding decisions about specified matters to the functional agency. In most cases, this partial centralization of authority would not be accompanied by an equivalent transfer of effective power. Consequently, there would typically be a gap between the authority of such functional agencies to make binding decisions and their ability to enforce these decisions, though they might be able to make good use of other sources of compliance.

In a regime of this type, each functional authority would include the actors relevant to its own concerns and encompass a geographical area demarcated in terms of the activities relating to the function in question. Moreover, such agencies could vary widely with respect to their jurisdictional scope and institutional characteristics. Such variations might involve: a) the scope of the authority accorded to the functional agency, b) the decision-making procedures employed by the authority, c) the extent of *formal* institutionalization of the authority, d) the capacity of the authority to raise and dispose of its own revenues, and e) the power of the authority to implement its decisions. Each functional authority would presumably evolve on an *ad hoc* basis in such a regime. It would not be surprising, therefore, if functional coordination along these lines were to reach substantial proportions in some areas in Beringia even while remaining rudimentary in other areas.

As in the case of national zones, the rubric of functional authorities encompasses a family of regime types all of which share certain fundamental attributes. This section will focus on the consequences for Beringia associated with the introduction of a system of functional authorities exhibiting the following specific characteristics. There would be four functional agencies to cope with the management problems of renewable resources, hydrocarbons, flow resources, and environmental resources. The United States, the Soviet Union, Canada, and Japan would be members of each of the authorities, though Japan might not be particularly influential in the authority for hydrocarbons. Other states, such as Korea and Taiwan, would be members of the authority for renewable resources, but such states would not become formal members of the other regional authorities. Geographically, the scope of the various authorities would vary significantly. Though this would be a subject for negotiation on a case-by-case basis, I shall assume in this discussion that the relevant geographical boundaries would conform roughly to those suggested in Chapter III. Each agency would have considerable authority to establish entry restrictions and licensing systems in its own domain, but they would not be operating authorities. That is, none of the agencies could undertake to harvest or produce resources directly. Finally, this regime would not include any coordinating mechanism above the individual functional authorities.

1. *Social (or group) consequences.* What would be the probable impact of a regime of this type in Beringia with respect to various measures of production? The geographical scope of the Beringian fisheries authority would permit the introduction of an effective system of unified management for the major fish stocks of the region. It would be extensive enough to cope with the region's migratory species, and all major harvesters in Beringia would be members of the authority. In principle, then, such an agency could take steps to achieve economic efficiency in the marine fisheries of the region. But it is not clear that this would in fact occur under such a regime. Not only would it require a highly effective functional authority; it is also quite possible that the authority would adopt some other standard in making decisions about harvest levels (e.g. maximum sustained yield).[57] In addition, non-economic factors, such as the provision of employment opportunities, might play a role in the authority's decision processes, though such factors would probably be less influential than under a system of national zones.

A regime of this type would almost certainly lead to the reduction of current harvests with respect to many Beringian stocks. In the short run, these reductions would be less drastic than in the case of a zonal system because there would not be problems with insufficient capacity and ineffective licensing systems. Long-run equilibrium under such a regime, however, might well occur at lower harvest levels than in the case of many national zones. This is so because the functional authority would be likely to display a firm commitment to the goal of high sustained yields if not the achievement of economic efficiency.[58] Nevertheless, there would be continuing pressures on such an agency for the expansion of harvests from the marine fisheries. These would include pressures to maximize the region's contribution to the world's supply of animal protein as well as various political pressures of a more localized nature.

It is highly probable that a functional authority for hydrocarbons in Beringia would run into stiff political opposition from the United States and perhaps others as well. Also, such an authority would not be required to achieve economic efficiency with respect to the actual production of oil and natural gas in the region. If an authority of this type were set up in Beringia, on the other hand, there is no intrinsic reason why it could not be utilized as a vehicle for the achievement of economic efficiency in this realm. This would require the development of a relatively complex regional leasing system, and it would of course be subject to the vagaries of the world oil market. However, it is worth noting that a Beringian hydrocarbon authority would probably not be drastically affected by certain political pressures (e.g. the drive for energy independence) that tend to divert national managers in this functional area from the goal of economic efficiency.

With respect to actual levels of production of oil and gas in Beringia a regional authority would be likely to have mixed results. It would tend to accelerate the movement toward production in the western (or Soviet) sectors of the region since American-based or Japanese-based firms would be able to obtain leases in this area under such a system. At the same time, it would probably operate to slow down the rate of exploitation in the eastern half of the region since the regional hydrocarbon authority would not be as strongly affected by the pressures of the 'energy crisis' as the governments of the United States and Canada.[59] It is also possible that major companies would regard the investment climate in the region as uncertain under a regime of this type, and this could have the effect of slowing down the rate of exploitation of Beringian oil and natural gas.

A Beringian regional authority in the realm of maritime commerce would have major advantages since it could institute a system of unified management for the region's flow resources. Accordingly, it could act to alleviate the tendency toward underinvestment in the areas of upkeep and improvements which would appear in the absence of unified management. Also, such an agency could make use of user's fees for regulatory purposes in the event that problems of overuse should emerge with respect to any of the region's marine highways. Would the Beringian region encompass a large enough area for optimal results in this functional domain? This is in fact a complex question. Briefly, however, it seems probable that the increased transactions costs associated with efforts to manage a larger area on a unified basis would more than offset costs arising from the fact that the Beringian region, as demarcated in Chapter III, would truncate certain marine highways in jurisdictional terms.[60]

As in the case of national zones, the actual use of Beringia's marine highways under a regime of this type would be heavily dependent upon the rate at which the region's other resources are utilized. In general, a regional authority for maritime commerce would probably encourage the growth of activity in this realm both by sponsoring improvements to the marine highways and by introducing a consistent regulatory system for the region which would minimize complications for shippers. Beyond this, much would depend on the nature of the user's fees established by the authority. Fees designed merely to offset the costs of upkeep and improvements would encourage the growth of maritime commerce in the region since they would keep the costs borne by shippers to a minimum. User's fees set to maximize rent for the regional authority, on the other hand, would tend to discourage the growth of maritime commerce in Beringia, though the extent of this effect would be a function of the level of the fees and the availability of alternative means of transportation or sources of resources.

What would be the consequences of a regime based on a set of differentiated functional authorities for various non-economic values and environmental resources in Beringia? Such a regime would tend to deemphasize planning for the whole region as an integrated unit from the point of view of resource management; it would place primary emphasis on problems of resource management arising in each functional area treated in its own terms. Under the circumstances, a regime of this type would not be well-equipped to deal with value trade-offs emerging as a consequence of interdependencies between separable functional areas (e.g. conflicts between fishing operations and the production of oil on the outer continental shelf). In view of the fact that issues of this type are certain to become more prominent as Beringia's resources are subjected to heavier usage, this feature must be regarded as a serious weakness of this type of regime for the region.

Beyond this, a separate functional authority for environmental resources would occupy a somewhat peculiar position under a regime of this type in Beringia. Though there is reason to believe that a regime based on functional authorities would have favorable implications for the conservation of species and stocks, actions in this area could probably be taken most effectively through the fisheries authority.[61] On the other hand, an environmental authority might play a role of some importance in efforts to control marine pollution and preserve the habitat in Beringia. Since these problems are largely the result of externalities of other activities (e.g. oil production) and since those responsible for these externalities have little incentive to regulate them on the basis of self-interest, there is a good case to be made for the introduction of an independent authority to cope with these problems. Such an authority could promulgate clearcut regulations regarding these matters and it might develop a set of liability rules to govern the exploitation of resources in Beringia. But it is probable that this authority would have trouble obtaining sufficient operating funds and enforcing its regulations.[62]

196

2. *Distributive implications.* What impact would the introduction of a system of functional authorities have on the distribution of wealth emanating from the exploitation of Beringia's resources? In the marine fisheries, the regional authority would presumably proceed either to distribute work permits on the basis of administrative decisions or to create an annual market in entry rights.[63] In the case of work permits, the initial gainers would be the actual harvesters of fish and marine mammals, rather than a specific group of states like the coastal states. The ultimate distributive impact of such a system, however, would depend upon such things as whether the regional authority levied fees on the holders of the work permits and if so, how the authority chose to expend the revenues arising from this source. The introduction of a market in entry rights, on the other hand, would result initially in a considerable shift of wealth to the regional fisheries authority. The ultimate distribution of this wealth would be a function of bargaining among the members of the authority (carried out by their designated representatives). This might lead to the allocation of resources for such things as research and biological conservation or aid to the less developed countries of the world. But there is no guarantee that such results would occur under a system of this type.

An essentially similar situation would obtain with respect to hydrocarbons in the event that a Beringian regional authority were established in this realm. But there are several special features of this functional area that would affect the distributive consequences of such an arrangement. The functional authority would not of course be an operating agency. Accordingly, it would have to deal with the powerful multinational corporations of this industry through some type of leasing system. In principle, the regional authority could capture the bulk of the profits or rents accruing in this area through the use of an appropriate leasing system. But the authority would face real problems in achieving this result. For various political reasons, it would probably occupy a weaker position than the regional fisheries authority. The oil companies might well engage in collusion or coordinated bidding in their dealings with the regional authority. And the authority might lack the resources to make sophisticated independent estimates of the recoverable reserves in various basins, thereby becoming dependent upon the judgments of the companies themselves. Under the circumstances, the division of profits or rents between the producers and the regional authority would probably be considerably more favorable to the producers than in the case of a market in entry rights for the region's fisheries.

In the realm of maritime commerce, there are again two important cases. If the regional authority set user's fees merely to offset the costs of upkeep and improvements, the distributive impact of the agency's operations would be minimal. The *de facto* beneficiaries of such a system would be the shipping interests. Presumably, this would ultimately be reflected in lower prices on the relevant world markets for goods transported on Beringia's marine highways, and most of these goods would probably be consumed in the developed countries of the northern hemisphere. On the other hand, the regional authority might set user's fees in such a way as to capture as much as possible of the profits or rents associated with the use of Beringia's marine highways. The distributive implications of this arrangement would parallel those of a market in entry rights for the region's marine fisheries. There would be an initial shift of wealth to the regional agency for maritime commerce. But once again, the ultimate distributive results would flow from bargaining processes among the constituent members of the authority.

To what extent would the distributive consequences of a regime based on functional authorities in Beringia be just or fair? In the case of the marine fisheries, several important issues arise in this context. Under a system of work permits, the allocation of harvests would involve extensive processes of bureaucratic bargaining.[65] Numerous criteria of fairness have been formulated for the assessment of bargaining processes, and there is no straightforward way of determining the extent to which the outcomes of such processes are just.[66] However, it is probable that the interests of outsiders would suffer under such a system in Beringia since the administrators associated with the regional authority would have few incentives to cater to the interests of these actors. The introduction of a market in entry rights, on the other hand, raises somewhat different questions. Such an arrangement would lead to the allocation of harvests to those actors willing to pay the highest prices for the relevant entry rights. This outcome is widely regarded as just, though it is by no means insensitive to the initial resource endowments of the actors involved.[67] Beyond this, considerable revenues would accrue to the regional authority from the operation of a market in entry rights. The ultimate distribution of these revenues would be a matter of bargaining among the members of the authority,[68] and the fairness of the outcome would once again be difficult to establish in any straightforward fashion.

An attractive feature of a market in entry rights of the type under consideration here is that it would allow for access to the Beringian fisheries on the part of new entrants and outsiders. Though imperfections might arise from time to time in this market, there is no intrinsic reason why it should work against the interests of any actor desiring to take part in the exploitation of these resources. With respect to the division of the proceeds from the sale of entry rights, however, outsiders would be at the mercy of the relevant bargaining processes among the members of the regional authority. In principle, these processes could yield benefits for outsiders in the form of such things as revenue sharing mechanisms designed to assist the less developed countries of the world. Nevertheless, it must be assumed that the interests of outsiders would typically fare rather poorly in these bargaining processes. Consequently, this arrangement for the Beringian fisheries would probably exhibit a 'conservative' bias in distributive terms since the authority would take the form of a club of 'have' nations.

In the case of hydrocarbons, much would depend on the outcome of the struggle over profits or rents between the actual producers and the regional authority. The producers would typically be large, multinational oil companies. Under the circumstances, it would be difficult to justify any outcome in which the bulk of the relevant profits went to the producers, though many observers argue that it is desirable for these companies to receive some of the profits since this will tend to encourage them to explore vigorously for new reserves.[69] To the extent that the regional authority succeeds in appropriating a large share of the profits, a situation might arise which is similar to that discussed above in conjunction with a market in entry rights in the Beringian fisheries. That is, distribution would result from bargaining processes whose fairness is not easy to judge.

It is unlikely that any real problem with respect to new entrants would arise under a regime of this type for Beringian hydrocarbons. It is not really meaningful to think of new entrants as countries in this realm since most efforts to produce oil and natural gas in Beringia would presumably be undertaken by large, multinational firms. Moreover, there is no intrinsic reason to expect that the regional authority would adopt a leasing system that would discriminate against the interests of any particular group of producers in this realm. However, a regional authority for hydrocarbons might produce even more unfortunate results from the point of view of outside states than a regional fisheries authority. Though it is possible that the authority would receive substantial revenues over a period of years,[70] this functional area is extremely sensitive politically and it is highly unlikely that the members of the authority would take a favorable view of revenue sharing mechanisms designed to assist the less developed countries of the world.

The key issue in the case of maritime commerce concerns the level at which user's fees should be set. The major beneficiaries of fees designed merely to offset upkeep and improvement costs would be the shipping interests. This might be justified as desirable in that it could ultimately lead to reductions in prices for consumers of certain important goods. On the other hand, the regional authority for maritime commerce could set user's fees in such a way as to capture profits or rents. There might well be some debate concerning the preferred basis for the levying of such fees. So, for example, the shipping interests might advocate a system in which each member state would pay a portion of the fees, though this seems even less justifiable than the idea of fees designed merely to offset upkeep and improvement costs. In any case, the ultimate distribution of the profits or rents accruing to the regional authority would be a function of bargaining among the members of the authority. Once again, therefore, judgments concerning the fairness of the relevant distributive outcomes would be difficult to make with confidence.

It is rather unlikely that any real issue concerning new entrants would arise in this realm. That is, shipping controlled by the principal member states of the regional authority will continue to account for the bulk of maritime commerce in Beringia during the foreseeable future.[72] In any case, outsiders could be accommodated with ease under an arrangement of this type. Fees could be levied on all vessels on a non-discriminatory basis, and it would even be possible to reduce fees for vessels from less developed countries if this should be deemed normatively desirable by the authority. However, it is not likely that outside countries would benefit from profits or rents arising from maritime commerce in Beringia under a system of this type. There is no reason to expect the major shipping interests to engage in revenue sharing with the idea of assisting the less developed countries. And though the regional authority itself could institute revenue sharing mechanisms of this type, it would be surprising if efforts along these lines produced significant redistributive effects.

3. *Feasibility.* Would a regime based on functional authorities be politically acceptable in Beringia? At the international level, functional coordination represents a departure not only from common property arrangements but also from the underlying tradition of indivisible state sovereignty.[72] Nevertheless, there is no obvious reason to conclude that any of the principal actors in Beringia would simply reject a regime

200

of this type out of hand. This conclusion applies specifically to the
United States and the Soviet Union which give every indication of being able
to coordinate effectively on matters of economics and resource management even while continuing to oppose each other in the realm of high
politics.[73] Moreover, it is important to bear in mind that a regime of this
type might yield mixed results. That is, some of the functional agencies
in the region might become highly effective while others remained
rudimentary.

The development of any given functional authority in Beringia
would undoubtedly involve hard bargaining among the region's
principal actors. Coastal states would express doubts about functional
authorities because they would be unlikely to produce distributive
results as favorable to these states as a system of national zones. There
would be extraordinary political barriers to overcome in conjunction
with any effort to introduce a regional authority for hydrocarbons.
There would also be numerous specific national sensitivites to
consider. The Japanese might be much happier about regional authorities
for renewable resources and hydrocarbons than for environmental
resources.[74] Though the United States would probably oppose such an
authority in the realm of hydrocarbons, it might favor such arrangements with respect to flow resources. The Soviet Union, on the other
hand, would almost certainly be happier about the idea of a regional
authority for renewable resources than such an arrangement for flow
resources. For its part, Canada might experience serious crosspressures
concerning all these regional authorities, given the recent evolution of
Canadian policies relating to marine affairs.[75]

Beyond this, the attitude of each of the major actors toward a regime
for Beringia based on functional authorities would undoubtedly be
sharply affected by expectations concerning alternative arrangements
for the region. Given the pace of change in the usage of the region's
resources, judgments about the attractiveness of a regime of this type
would rest on projections concerning probable future developments
rather than static comparisons with the present situation. This suggests
that a system of functional authorities should not be ruled out in the
Beringian region.

Critics of the idea of a regime based on functional authorities for
Beringia are likely to assert that such a regime would exhibit serious
weaknesses in the realm of compliance. Under such a regime, responsibility for compliance would generally be allocated partly to the
various functional authorities themselves and partly to the individual
members of these authorities. Specifically, it seems safe to assume that

201

direct enforcement would be largely decentralized to the individual states.[76] There is no doubt that this would generate real problems for the regional authorities. Though national enforcement has often been proposed in conjunction with international agreements and though some such system seems desirable in comparison with a total abandonment of enforcement, arrangements of this type have seldom been highly effective in the realm of international relations.[77]

In the case of resource management in Beringia, however, there are intrinsic problems with enforcement as a basis of compliance and regional authorities might be able to achieve considerable success in the realm of compliance without resorting to direct or overt enforcement. There is the possibility of negotiating arrangements that amount to equilibrium solutions in specific functional areas.[78] The basic idea here is to generate situations in which individual members would be reluctant to violate the decisions of functional authorities on a unilateral basis for fear of precipitating retaliatory actions on the part of others and initiating a chain of events that would leave them worse off than they were at the outset.[79] Similarly, individual functional authorities under such a regime might well be able to use selective incentives extensively in efforts to achieve compliance.[80] Depending upon the exact arrangements introduced, several of these functional authorities might acquire considerable revenues that could be used effectively as a source of selective incentives. In effect, individual authorities might be able to make it worthwhile in cost-benefit terms for individual members to adhere to the decisions of the authority. Finally, it is not unreasonable to suppose that such authorities could occasionally appeal to their members on the basis of claims to legitimacy within their respective functional domains. Any given authority of this type would not be imposed on its members, and it would certainly be unlikely to become a captive of one or a few of its members with respect to its regulatory and distributive decisions.

Would a regime based on functional authorities prove stable or durable in Beringia? Complications arising from interdependencies among the various functional areas within the region might pose serious threats to the stability of such a regime. A system characterized by sharply differentiated agencies may not be able to cope effectively with trade-offs arising from conflicting claims in such areas as commercial fishing and hydrocarbon production. Nor is such a system necessarily capable of facilitating the use of side payments and package deals to help with bargaining relating to the distribution of the proceeds of resource exploitation in a region like Beringia. Moreover, previous chapters of this study suggest that interdependencies of the type under consideration here are likely to increase quite rapidly in Beringia in the near future. To the extent that this occurs, the introduction of an umbrella agency or overarching coordination mechanism might be necessary for the maintenance of a system of functional authorities, though a qualitative change to some other type of regime might not be necessary.

Such a regime would also harbor certain latent political threats to its stability. There would typically be a substantial gap between the ideal and the actual with respect to the performance of individual functional authorities. Both the political difficulties and the technical complexities associated with resource management at the international level are sufficiently great to ensure that actual performance would always fall short of even the most lenient conceptions of optimality. Also, there would inevitably be cases of discontent with specific allocative formulas. Though discontent of this type is a normal feature of politics, it can pose particularly serious threats to the stability of any regime characterized by a high degree of decentralization with respect to effective power. Finally, the regime under consideration here would undoubtedly be vulnerable to charges concerning distributive injustices on the part of outsiders. In conjunction with the type of internal discontent with allocative formulas mentioned above, such external opposition might become a real threat to the stability of the regime.[81] There is no reason to conclude that political problems of this sort would inevitably destroy a Beringian regime based on functional authorities, but it would certainly be shortsighted to ignore potentialities of this kind, thereby failing to take steps designed to minimize their chances of bringing down the regime.

C. A Beringian Regional Authority

Without raising questions about federation, it is possible to consider a regime for the management of natural resources in an international region like Beringia characterized by loose confederal arrangements. Such a regime would involve conscious efforts to treat the region as an integrated unit from the perspectives of resource management and the maintenance of environmental quality. But the required transfers of power and authority would be minimized and regulated carefully under an arrangement of this type.

In essence, a Beringian regional authority would encompass a set of specific institutional arrangements for the individual functional areas tied together and integrated through the operation of an overarching umbrella agency. There would be considerable room for variation with respect to the details of such a system. In general, however, it would mean specific functional agencies for renewable resources, flow resources, and, perhaps, hydrocarbons coupled with an umbrella agency focusing on environmental resources, regionwide interdependencies, and external relations. A regime of this type would require greater centralization of power and authority than a regime based on a set of sharply differentiated functional authorities. But it would still leave considerable scope for autonomous action on the part of constituent members, especially with respect to issues like enforcement. Like other confederal systems, such a regime in Beringia would feature prominent restrictions on the authority and power of the regional authority together with an explicit emphasis on the retention of residual authority and power by the member states.

It would be perfectly feasible for a regional authority of the type under consideration here to acquire some relationship to the United Nations.[82] In the particular case of Beringia, however, it is quite unlikely that any such development would occur. This is so not only because the members of the regional authority would be apt to find an affiliation with the United Nations politically embarrassing but also because a link of this type would significantly increase the transactions costs of making important decisions within the Beringian regional authority.[83] Under the cirumstances, the principal members of the Beringian regional authority would have compelling reasons to establish the authority on a completely autonomous basis.

There are also questions concerning the demarcation of boundaries for a regional authority in Beringia. This can become a complex matter where the individual functional components of a regional authority are not congruent with regard to optimal geographical scope and there are no obvious geopolitical landmarks to coordinate expectations as there often are in the case of national boundaries. In a resource region like Beringia, the most probable solution would be to employ the boundaries of the functional area with the widest geographical scope. For the most part, over-inclusiveness with respect to some functional areas would be less troublesome from the point of view of managing natural resources than truncating the natural geographical domain of any important functional area.

As with the other regime types, the idea of a Beringian regional authority identifies a family of possibilities all of which exhibit a number of common features. In this section, I shall focus on the

204

probable consequences of a regional authority for Beringia with the following major characteristics. The principal members of the authority would be the United States, the Soviet Union, Canada, and Japan. In addition, the authority would include several minor members such as Korea, Taiwan, and Poland. The geographical scope of the authority would follow that of the most extensive functional area delineated in Chapter III. That is, the boundaries of the authority's domain would be roughly similar to those outlined in Figure V. The Beringian regional authority would have extensive regulatory capabilities and it would be able to raise revenues on its own. However, it would be relatively weak in the realm of direct enforcement and it would not be an operating authority in any functional area. That is, it would not itself engage in harvesting or producing operations with respect to any of Beringia's natural resources. Finally, the authority would have no official link to the United Nations or to any other global insitutions.

1. *Social (or group) consequences.* In the realm of production, the effects of introducing a Beringian regional authority would be much the same as those associated with a regime based on differentiated functional authorities. A regional authority would be in an ideal position to institute unified management systems for the exploitation of the region's natural resources. Moreover, the geographical scope of the authority would make it possible, in principle, to approach economic efficiency in the utilization of Beringia's resources. It is certainly not obvious, however, that the authority would always choose to pursue the goal of efficiency in the sense of profit or rent maximization.[84] Such an authority would be stronger in institutional terms than a set of differentiated functional agencies and it might gradually acquire a variety of influential political interests in its own right. It is unlikely that these interests would have to do with such things as security and energy independence. Instead, they might pertain to the achievement of environmental goals like the preservation of the habitat or to the pursuit of distributive goals like assisting the less developed countries of the world. In any case, developments along these lines could easily produce a situation in which the regional authority would not always place top priority on the achievement of economic efficiency in managing Beringia's resources.[85]

A regional authority would undoubtedly take steps to reduce current harvests in many of Beringia's marine fisheries. Nevertheless, it might well find the goal of maximum sustained yield more attractive politically than the goal of profit maximization so that reductions in most harvests would not be drastic. The orientation of such an authority toward the production of hydrocarbons in the region would unquestionably be a major political issue within the authority. Some of its members (e.g. the United States) would almost certainly bring pressures to bear on the authority to move rapidly toward large-scale production of oil and natural gas. But others would be less interested in such an outcome, and the authority would probably be more sensitive to the implications of such production for environmental resources than in the case of a sharply differentiated hydrocarbon authority. Under the circumstances, the level of hydrocarbon production under a regime of this type would be more a matter of bargaining among the members of the authority than of pursuing technical calculations relating to economic efficiency. Beyond this, a regional authority would no doubt be favorable to the expansion of maritime commerce in Beringia. It would be well suited to handling matters pertaining to upkeep and improvements and it would be able to establish a consistent system of regulations in this functional area. But there is no reason to expect maritime commerce to expand beyond the level associated with economic efficiency under a regime of this type.

The most distinctive advantage of a Beringian regional authority is that it would have the capacity to deal effectively with intra-regional interdependencies in a situation characterized by increasingly heavy usage of the natural resources of the region. It would be able to pay attention to the effects of other activities on various environmental resources. It could engage in regionwide planning concerning desirable levels and rates of use for the region's resources. And above all, it would constitute an appropriate forum in which to confront the numerous value trade-offs necessitated by heavy resource usage in the context of interdependent functional areas. There would, however, be a price to be paid for the achievement of these advantages. Specifically, the activities of a regional authority regarding these matters would involve substantial transactions costs.[86] That is, it would be costly to negotiate the necessary agreements, set up the relevant institutions, hammer out major decisions, and implement the resultant policies. The fact that the number of members of the regional authority would be small would help to keep these transactions costs down.[87] Nevertheless, such costs would most likely rise as a function of the geographical scope of the regional authority. Presumably, there would be some geographical domain over which the benefits produced by the authority in this realm would exceed the relevant transactions costs, though opponents of this regime

206

might deny this. But there is clearly no basis for arguing that the geographical scope of such an authority should be expanded indefinitely.

Figure XII clarifies this relationship graphically.[88] The y axis measures costs, while the x axis represents the geographical scope of a regional authority. The curve a—a' reflects transactions costs of the type discussed in the preceding paragraph, and the curve b—b' represents the expected social (or group) costs of failing to deal with interdependencies in the realm of resource management.[89] The case portrayed in Figure XII rests on the assumptions that increasing marginal transactions costs will set in after some point and that geographical extension will eventually produce declining marginal returns in terms of coping with interdependencies in the realm of resource management. Though the shapes of these curves may vary considerably, there is little reason to posit other fundamental forms in a resource region like Beringia. Under the circumstances, it would be socially rational to expand the geographical scope of a regional authority to the point labelled X_1 in Figure XII and no farther.[90]

Figure XII

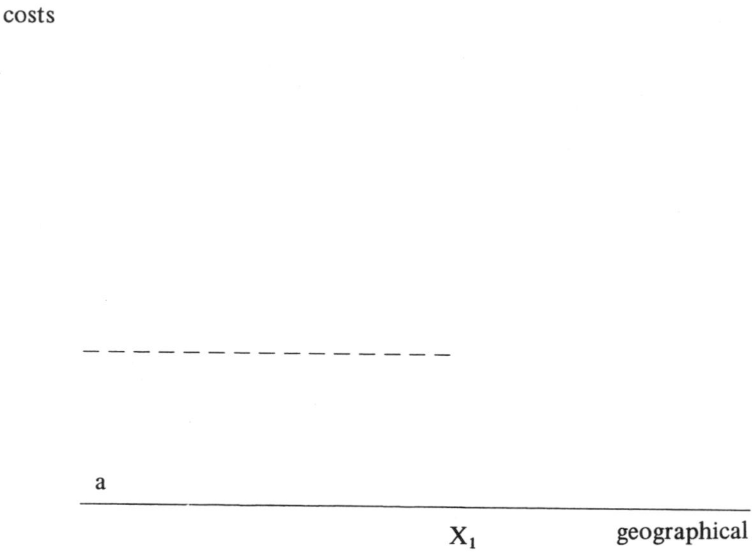

costs

- - - - - - - - - - - - - -

a

X_1 geographical
                         scope

The optimal Size of a Resource Region

207

Operationalizing this argument under the specific conditions of Beringia would obviously require substantial research. But I believe it is improbable that such an analysis would suggest expanding the geographical scope of a Beringian regional authority beyond the boundaries suggested earlier in this section.

2. *Distributive implications.* What implications would a regime of this type have for the distribution of the wealth emanating from the exploitation of Beringia's natural resources? In the first instance, I assume that a regional authority would institute some sort of market in entry rights for the marine fisheries, a system of competitive leasing for oil and gas reserves, and some form of user's fees for the region's marine highways. This would have the effect of distributing rights to exploit the region's resources to those willing to pay the highest prices for them.[91] In the case of fisheries, the relevant rights might be auctioned off on an annual basis, and transportation fees would presumably be levied only on vessels actually using the marine highways. With respect to oil and natural gas, however, it would be desirable to auction off leases that would be valid for longer periods of time.[92] Note also that a system of this type would tend to distribute the relevant exploitation rights to private corporations, except in cases where state-owned enterprises actually competed with others for the entry rights or leases in question.

Beyond this, the really distinctive feature of a regional authority for Beringia is that it would in effect acquire a public sector. The bulk of this sector would not stem from the imposition of taxes as in the case of most states. Instead, it would flow from the sale of entry rights, competitive bidding for leases, and the imposition of user's fees. The size of the public sector of this regional authority would depend on the extent to which the authority took steps to capture the profits or rents associated with the exploitation of resources in Beringia. It is improbable that all such profits or rents would accrue to the regional authority, especially in the realm of hydrocarbons. Nevertheless, it is important to note that the absolute size of this public sector might be quite large in a resource region like Beringia.

Some of the revenues in this public sector would presumably be allocated to such things as upkeep and improvements in the realm of the marine highways and measures aimed at the conservation of stocks in the area of renewable resources. But public sector revenues would also be available for other purposes such as research and development, programs to maintain environmental quality, distribution

208

to the members of the authority, and assistance to less developed countries. Ultimate outcomes in this connection would flow from bargaining processes among the members of the regional authority quite similar to those referred to in the discussion of differentiated functional authorities. The distinctive feature of distributive bargaining under a regional authority is that this system would permit logrolling and the formulation of package deals across the whole set of issues associated with the management of natural resources in Beringia.[93] This would of course make the resultant bargaining processes somewhat more complex. But it would presumably increase the chances of arriving at mutually agreeable deals, and it would not generate excessive transactions costs if the regional authority were able to introduce reasonably efficient procedures to govern these bargaining processes.[94] Under a system of this type the major actors would make trades with each other to maximize the chances of achieving their highest priorities in the region. And as with other authorities encompassing public sectors, the distributive results of this system would change from time to time as a function of shifts in the bargaining positions of the major actors.

To what extent would the distributive results of a system of this type be fair or just? With respect to the members of the regional authority, this question raises once again the problems of assessing the fairness of the outcomes of a bargaining process. It is probable that there would be difficulties under a regime of this type in gaining substantial allocations for such things as research and development and the maintenance of environmental quality. Nevertheless, the system under discussion here might yield fairer distributive results for the members of the authority than the regimes outlined in the preceding sections. It would maximize opportunities for the principal actors to make mutually beneficial exchanges, and it would not arbitrarily place the initial stocks of the resources in question in the hands of some subset of the region's members (e.g. the coastal states). Moreover, to the extent that the actual bargaining went on within the institutional framework of the regional authority, it might prove possible to develop rules of the game designed to avoid the occurrence of blatantly unfair outcomes.

New entrants could be accommodated under a system of this type, whether or not they were associated with a member of the regional authority. The fact that oil and gas leases would have to run for a considerable period of time would make it difficult for the authority to respond to the needs of new entrants in this realm over the short run.[95] Additionally, market imperfections could emerge which would have the effect of discriminating against corporations or state-owned enterprises from states that were not members of the regional authority. However, a system of this type would almost certainly be fairer from the point of view of new entrants than the alternative regimes considered in the preceding sections. In fact, it could be used to make special concessions to new entrants from less developed countries, though it is probable that most new entrants would be large corporations or state-owned enterprises from developed countries with no compelling claims to special treatment.

As in the cases discussed in previous sections, the distributive consequences of a Beringian regional authority would probably exhibit a certain 'conservative' bias in connection with the global distribution of wealth. That is, it would be a mistake to assume that large chunks of the authority's public sector revenues would be allocated to the less developed countries of the world through revenue sharing mechanisms.[96] However, the prospects of achieving some redistributive shifts would almost certainly be greater under this regime than under any of the others considered so far. Transfers of wealth from the public sector of the authority to various less developed countries would not occur directly at the expense of some other interested public. Accordingly, it might well be easier politically for countries like the United States, the Soviet Union, and Japan to respond to the rising chorus of redistributive demands at the global level by tapping this source of revenues than by dipping into their own national budgets. Moreover, it is quite possible that many recipients would find it far more desirable politically to receive assistance from a regional authority of this type than directly from various powerful states.

3. *Feasibility*. Would a regional authority be acceptable politically to the major actors in the region? It is possible to divide this issue into attitudes regarding the outcomes such a regime would yield on the one hand and problems of transition on the other. Assuming a regional authority were introduced successfully, there is no obvious reason to conclude that it would produce unacceptable results. Relative to the present situation, there is little doubt that it would greatly improve the prospects of maximizing social welfare with respect to the exploitation of natural resources in Beringia.[97] Moreover, though such a system would be characterized by hard bargaining over the distribution of wealth, the eventual distributive outcomes might well prove acceptable to the principal actors, especially over the long run. It is well known that 'Joint maximization policies are

210

not necessarily preferable, from the standpoint of any single participating country, to those yielding a lower aggregate rent with a greater individual share.'[98] Nevertheless, joint maximization policies have the advantage of generating the largest pool of wealth to be used in efforts to arrange side payments and to strike mutually agreeable bargains. Despite the political rigidities and problems of imperfect information that plague real-world situations, there is at leas a weak presumption that a system yielding joint maximization will dominate other arrangements among rational actors.

The crucial problems of acceptability facing a Beringian regional authority undoubtedly lie in the realm of transition rather than eventual outcomes. Above all, the introduction of such an authority would pose a contractarian problem under conditions of partial information.[99] Movement toward a regime of this type, in contrast to the emergence of other regime types, would require relatively coordinated and self-conscious actions. That is, the relevant actors would have to arrive at something akin to a social contract pertaining to the management of the region's natural resources. Politically, this would constitute an extaordinary hurdle to surmount in the context of an international region like Beringia. Beyond this, there would be serious problems associated with the actual transfer of jurisdictional prerogatives to a new regional authority, even if an initial agreement along these lines were negotiated. A number of specific interest groups (e.g. Alaskan fishermen, certain major oil companies?) would undoubtedly oppose and attempt to impede this transition. It is generally a traumatic process for states overtly to transfer jurisdiction to a supranational authority, even when the transfer involves numerous caveats and restrictions. Consequently, it is hard to foresee the emergence of this type of regime under calm or routine conditions. In all probability, an effective Beringian regional authority would only emerge in the wake of a series of dramatic disruptive events.

What sort of compliance mechanisms would it be reasonable to expect in conjunction with the introduction of such a regional authority? A regime of this type would be characterized by a somewhat greater degree of centralization of authority than a system of sharply differentiated functional authorities. Nevertheless, it would likely exhibit the weaknesses of most confederal systems in the realm of compliance. Specifically, it is hard to imagine the members of the authority transferring substantial coercive capabilities to the central authority, though there is reason to believe that the regional authority would acquire extensive capabilities in the areas of monitoring, information gathering, and analysis. Accordingly, such an authority would be hard pressed to enforce its regulatory rules and distributive decisions against those who chose to back their violations with force. To the extent that direct enforcement became important, then, it would be necessary to rely on national enforcement systems, a notoriously ineffective arrangement in the context of supranational organizations.[100]

At the same time, a regional authority might well achieve considerable success in the realm of compliance without resorting to direct enforcement. Major policies under such a system would emerge from bargaining processes involving all members of the authority. The fact that these actors would expect to bargain with each other on a continuing basis within the framework of the authority would give them strong incentives to carry out the terms of any given agreement.[101] Moreover, to the extent that the regional authority were effective, it would acquire extensive revenues that could be utilized to operate a system of selective incentives; this is clearly one of the primary devices employed by all public authorities in efforts to elicit compliance from their constituent members. It is also possible that the operation of a Beringian regional authority would encourage gradual shifts in patterns of human loyalties relating to the region. Thus, individuals and interest groups might come to embue the actions of the regional authority with a sense of legitimacy, and this would of course mitigate the compliance problems of this regime.

Assuming a regional authority with an appropriate geographical domain, there is no reason to conclude that a confederal regime for the management of natural resources in Beringia would collapse under the weight of non-political problems. Some commentators argue that global interdependencies have become so extensive in the contemporary world that it is infeasible to cope with regulatory problems below the level of the international system as a whole.[102] Although the Beringian region exhibits significant economic interdependencies with other regions of the world, these issues are not decisive in determining the optimal geographical scope for the region from the point of view of managing the exploitation of its natural resources. In this connection, the crucial interdependencies are those relating to such matters as efficient production processes, biological conservation, and pollution control. These matters may lead to disagreements concerning appropriate jurisdictional boundaries for a Beringian regional authority, but they certainly do not indicate that resource regions are inappropriate units when dealing with the international relations of resource management and environmental quality.[103]

The most serious threats to the stability of such a regime would stem from more immediate political issues. The introduction of a regional authority might generate great expectations and subsequent disillusionment on the basis of actual performance. This would be particularly true if the regional institutions were not accorded adequate authority at the outset or if individual members failed to make the necessary transfers of authority to set up the regional institutions called for in the original agreement. It is also easy to imagine severe conflicts arising from time to time within the regional authority in the realm of distributive bargaining. The experience of the European Communities in such areas as agricultural policy is suggestive in this connection, though it does not demonstrate that it is impossible to work out acceptable allocative formulas within the framework of supranational organizations.[104] Beyond this, it is worth noting that the component parts of the regime under consideration here would be more highly interdependent than in the case of a system of differentiated functional authorities. Therefore, disruptive crises within a system of this type would be more likely to generate ripple effects threatening the stability of the regime itself than they would in more decentralized regimes. It seems probable that the long-run stability of a regime of this type would depend heavily on the results achieved during its early phases. A solidly entrenched regional authority might prove quite durable over time, though the viability of the authority would be far more questionable during the early phases while it was attempting to gain a foothold in a political situation dominated by other actors.

D. Three Minor Options

The regimes assessed in the preceding sections constitute the principal alternatives for Beringia in the sense that they are the options that lie within reasonable bounds of feasibility. They do not, however, exhaust the range of logically possible regimes for an international resource region like Beringia. The purpose of this section is to comment briefly on three additional options for Beringia. The probability that any one of these alternatives will actually emerge is extremely small. Current trends are running in different directions at the international level, and it is difficult ot imagine the development of an effective constituency for options of this kind. Nevertheless, it seems worthwhile to devote a little thought to these lesser alternatives. It serves to identify the full extent of the alternative set with respect to future

213

regimes for Beringia while shedding additional light on the nature of regimes in general.

1. *A wilderness area.* There are those who wish to convert Beringia (and perhaps the remainder of the Arctic as well) into a large-scale wilderness area. The objective here would be to exempt Beringia from commercial exploitation or large-scale economic development and to preserve the region in an essentially natural state.[105] In fact, there are already some relatively large wilderness areas within the Beringian region. These include the Bering Sea National Wildlife Refuge on St. Matthew Island, the Nunivak National Wildlife Refuge, the Clarence Rhode National Wildlife Refuge, the Aleutian Islands National Wildlife Refuge, the Kodiak National Wildlife Refuge, and the Arctic National Wildlife Refuge. A general Beringian wilderness area would extend the conditions sought in these specific areas to the region as a whole. A variety of approaches to the management of such a wilderness area would be possible.[106] Some might advocate letting nature take its course with a minimum of human interference along any dimension. On the other hand, it might seem desirable to formulate specific goals for a wilderness area of this type involving standards like the preservation of species. But in all cases, human activity relating to commercial exploitation or extensive economic development would be excluded.

A regime of this type for Beringia as a whole is undoubtedly unacceptable politically during the foreseeable future. Certain individuals and groups strongly support ideas of this kind.[107] But their constituency is not large, and they typically encounter serious problems in achieving political efficacy due to organizational deficiencies, limited resources, and the fact that most people find their goals rather intangible. By contrast, there are well-organized and powerful interest groups opposed to a regime of this type in Beringia, and the claims of some of these groups are apt to have mass appeal. For example, there is no doubt that pressures associated with the 'energy crisis' are playing a major role in the evolution of American policy toward offshore drilling for oil and natural gas in Beringia.[108] Similarly, it is clear that commercial pressures relating to the marine fisheries of Beringia are extremely difficult to resist. In short, the existence of extensive natural resources in Beringia coupled with the demands for mass consumption in highly industrialized societies guarantees that the introduction of a wilderness regime will be politically unacceptable for a geographical region as large as Beringia.[109]

A brief comparison with the Alaskan d−2 lands, set aside under the terms of the Alaska Native Claims Settlement Act of 1971, may be instructive in this connection, though the area covered by the d−2 lands is small compared with the total area of Beringia.[110] The passage of the 1971 Act initiated an extraordinary competition for jurisdictional control over the d−2 lands, which is still in full swing at this time.[111] However, it has already served to demonstrate the political power of interest groups concerned with economic development in Alaska. Though such groups are unlikely to be totally opposed to small wilderness areas, they obviously are not interested in massive extensions of such areas and their power is such that their views are not likely to be dramatically over-ridden. If anything, a marine region like Beringia is less promising as a potential wilderness area than the Alaskan d−2 lands. Not only is Beringia far larger geographically, it also involves numerous problems of international coordination which are not present at the domestic level.

2. *Decentralization without rules.* Both common property regimes and regimes based on national zones are highly decentralized in terms of the distribution of authority and power. Nevertheless, they need not be lacking in well-developed systems of rights and regulatory rules governing the actions of the principal actors involved.[112] For example, the common property regime for the oceans encapsulated in the Geneva Conventions of 1958 involves a set of highly specific rights and rules. On the other hand, it is possible to imagine a regime for an international region like Beringia in which the decentralization of authority and power would be combined with a lack of generally accepted rights and rules. In such a system, there would be no zones in which the jurisdictional prerogatives of individual actors would be widely accepted and there would be no regulatory institutions at the international level. The only general rule would be the axiom that each actor with an interest in the region should engage in any activity it found profitable in cost-benefit terms. The result would be a situation of unrestricted competition resembling the state of nature described by political philosophers.[113]

Perhaps the most important observation to make about such a regime is that it would constitute a radical departure from the current situation in the international system. While it is common to describe the internationa polity as an anarchically organized political system, it would be quite erroneous to assert that this system exhibits a complete lack of accepted rights and rules governing the day-to-day behavior of the actors.[114] In fact, occasional dramatic examples of ruleless behavior in the war/peace area obscure the fact that the great bulk of international interactions occur in a setting characterized by an extensive system of rights and rules.

A regime based on decentralization without rules could only emerge in the wake of dramatic disruptions in the existing regime in Beringia. Nor is there any evidence to suggest that a transition of this type would be remotely acceptable to the principal actors and interest groups in Beringia. On the contrary, there is a distinct trend in the opposite direction in Beringia, as well as in the international system as a whole, though this should not be taken as an indication of growing interest in supranational institutions at the level of international regions. Briefly, policy makers are becoming more acutely aware of the importance of being able to count on certain fundamental elements of predictability in the behavior of others in an increasingly interdependent world. Moreover, the need for rules designed to minimize the probability of international disasters in the areas of food, population, and environmental quality is coming to be accepted as a fact of life. These incentives to maintain an operative system of rights and rules will become more and more effective in the case of Beringia as the region's natural resources are subjected to heavier usage. Therefore, regardless of the institutional characteristics of Beringia's future regime, it is highly improbable that the region will move toward a system based on decentralization without rules.

3. *A Beringian federation.* At the opposite end of the spectrum, it is possible to imagine a regime for the region featuring a much higher degree of centralization with respect to authority and power than in the case of a Beringian regional authority. In essence, this would mean the emergence of a Beringian government in the formal institutional sense. Such a government would undoubtedly be organized federally rather than as a unitary system.[115] But it would constitute a radical departure from the loose confederal regime discussed earlier in this chapter in the sense that a Beringian federal government would have considerable authority to make rules, the capacity to make distributive decisions independently, the ability to raise revenues directly, and the resources to play an active role in the realm of enforcement.[116] A regime of this type would involve the creation of something akin to a new state in Beringia, though it would focus primarily on problems associated with the management of natural resources and the maintenance of environmental quality.

If anything, a regime of this type would require an even more drastic departure from current arrangements at the international level than a regime characterized by decentralization without rules. The probability of such departures occurring during the foreseeable future is minimal. It is true that there has been a recent upsurge of attention devoted to the hypothesis that the nation state has entered a period of decline. But it would be a serious mistake to overemphasize the impact of various threats to existing states,[117] and the emergence of a Beringian regional government would hardly symbolize the development of a system based on units other than states in any case. Recent years have also witnessed a growing disillusionment with the efficacy of formal institutions at the international level.[118] In part, this is a function of the evident inability of the United Nations to cope adequately with critical problems at the level of the international system. Thus, a Beringian federation would run directly counter to the tide of current thinking about appropriate forms of organization at the international level.

Quite apart from general trends in the international system as a whole, central features of the Beringia region itself would make such a regime improbable. The political sensitivities of major actors in the region, like the United States and the Soviet Union, are such that they would certainly oppose vigorously the development of a Beringian government, even if it were rigidly restricted to well-defined functional areas. Since it is far from clear what the constituency of such a government would be, serious difficulties would arise in working out appropriate arrangements for the representation of relevant interests. The contractarian problem in this case would be far greater than in the case of a Beringian regional authority organized along loose confederal lines. Therefore, there is no reason to conclude that a federal regime is a live option for Beringia at this time.

E. Conclusion

Constructs like those employed in this chapter are of great value in efforts to understand complex issues, but real-world situations seldom coincide with the images associated with such 'extreme types' or 'ideal types'. Regimes typically emerge *ad hoc* from streams of specific events and choices. In effect, they constitute an accumulated response to large numbers of concrete problems arising over time. What is unusual in this realm is the occurrence of anything resembling a consitutional convention designed to map out a consistent regime for a given social structure or region.[119] Accordingly, actual international regimes are apt to be hybrids that do not conform precisely to the essential features of any analytic type. Beyond this, all regimes are dynamic rather than static. They change continuously in response to shifts in the underlying social, economic, and political realities of the relevant social structures.

This does not mean that guided change with respect to the future regime of Beringia is out of the question. It merely suggests that the formulation of grand designs intended for submission to something resembling a constitutional convention is not likely to constitute an effective strategy in this area.[120] Effective efforts to guide the development of Beringia's regime during the foreseeable future will probably have to focus on the problems of specific functional areas and to proceed through the formation of transnational coalitions of interest groups aimed at bringing pressure to bear on the relevant national governments with respect to concrete problems. While the resultant regime may not be analytically neat, there is no *a priori* reason to conclude that it is impossible to achieve improved results in managing Beringia's natural resources and maintaining the quality of the region's environment.

Finally, this chapter has largely ignored the transition problem (i.e. the problem of mapping out specific strategies for the achievement of desired changes in the Beringian regime). This problem raises a variety of complex issues that cannot be treated definitively in an essay of this kind. But to pass over these issues altogether would constitute a serious oversight. Therefore, the next chapter turns explicitly to the concrete policy implications for Beringia of the arguments concerning the management of natural resources at the international level advanced in the preceding pages.

Notes

1. Robert Brown, *Explanation in Social Science*, (Chicago 1963), 177–185. Ideal types are empirically empty constructs (e.g. frictionless planes); extreme types are empirically feasible, though they seldom occur in pure form.
2. See, for example, the comments in John R. Stevenson and Bernard H. Oxman, 'The Preparations for the Law of the Sea Conference', *AJIL*, 68 (1974), 1–32.
3. For a general discussion of rules or behavioral prescriptions in the context of decentralized social structures see Michael Barkun, *Law Without Sanctions*, (New Haven 1968).
4. See also the comments of John R. Stevenson in *Emergency Marine Fisheries Protection Act of 1974*, Hearing before the Foreign Relations Committee of the United States Senate, (Washington 1974), 37–42.
5. Robert L. Friedheim, 'Understanding the Debate on Ocean Resources', *University of Denver Monograph Series in World Affairs*, (Denver 1969),

esp. 7–10.

6. For example, 200-mile zones would leave certain areas of Beringia outside the jurisdiction of the relevant coastal states.

7. See, for example, Lawrence G. Mallon, 'A Multi-Disciplinary Analysis of the Various Proposals Presented for the 1974 Law of the Sea Conference on Exclusive Fisheries Zones', Sea Grant Technical Bulletin No. 28, University of Miami Sea Grant Program (1974).

8. In recent years, the United States has been a particularly vigorous advocate of including clearcut arrangements for dispute settlement in any new regime for maritime areas. For background consult Stevenson and Oxman, *op. cit.*

9. For a general discussion of property rights see Eirik Furubotn and Svetozar Pejovich, 'Property Rights and Economic Theory: A Survey of Recent Literature', *Journal of Economic Literature*, X (1972), 1137–1162.

10. With respect to highly migratory species this regime would still amount to a common property system at the international level. For background see - Francis T. Christy, Jr. and Anthony Scott, *The Common Wealth in Ocean Fisheries*, (Baltimore 1965).

11. A system designed to overcome these problems is discussed in Arlon R. Tussing, 'The Place of Trade with Japan and Japanese Investment in Alaska's Economic Development', Arlon R. Tussing *et. al., Alaska-Japan Economic Relations*, (Fairbanks 1968), esp. 42–49.

12. James Crutchfield, 'The Marine Fisheries: A Problem in International Cooperation', *American Economic Review*, LIV (1964), 207–218.

13. Tussing, *op. cit.*

14. Lewis M. Alexander, 'National Jurisdiction and the Use of the Sea', *Natural Resources Journal*, 8 (1968), 387 and Hiroshi Kasahara and William Burke, 'North Pacific Fisheries Management', *RfF Program of International Studies of Fishery Arrangements*, Paper No. 2, (Washington 1973), 70.

15. William M. Terry, 'International Facets', Sidney Shapiro ed., *Our Changing Fisheries*, (Washington 1971), 146–166.

16. Richard James Sweeney, Robert D. Tollison, and Thomas D. Willett, 'Market Failure, the Common-Pool Problem, and Ocean Resource Exploitation', *Journal of Law and Economics*, XVII (1974), 179–192.

17. This would be the case whenever foreign firms were lower-cost producers than domestic firms.

18. See, for example, Dmitri Belousov, 'Russians Announce New Discoveries in Siberia', *Alaska Industry*, VI (October 1974), 26–27.

19. There are, however, some possibilities along these lines. See 'Siberian Gas-Development Pact Revealed', *Oil and Gas Journal*, 72 (2 December 1974), 47.

20. J. W. Devanney III, *The OCS Petroleum Pie*, MIT Sea Grant Program, Report No. MITSG 75–10, (1975).

21. Arlon R. Tussing, 'New Priorities for Energy and the Environment', mimeographed copy of a lecture delivered at Evanston, Illinois, 2 April 1974, 8.

22. For a general discussion of the prospects for maritime commerce in the region consult, *Arctic Marine Commerce*, Final Report, Contract No. 2-36288 (Maritime Administration, United States Department of Commerce), Arctic Institute of North America, (August 1973).

23. On problems of this kind see Thomas A. Clingan, Jr. and Lewis M. Alexander eds., *Hazards of Marine Transit*, (Cambridge 1973).

24. *Arctic Marine Commerce, op. cit.*

25. Oscar Schachter and Daniel Serwer, 'Marine Pollution Problems and

Remedies', *AJIL*, 65 (1971), 84–111. For a highly relevant case study see William M. Ross, *Oil Pollution as an International Problem*, (Seattle 1973).

26. See, for example, the comments of R. Sage Murphy, 'Pollution Control in the Arctic', mimeographed copy of a lecture delivered at Lenexa, Kentucky, 11 May 1972.

27. See the comments in Donat Pharand, *The Law of the Sea of the Arctic with Special Reference to Canada*, (Ottawa 1973), 309–310.

28. Francis T. Christy, Jr., 'Alternative Arrangements for Marine Fisheries: An Overview', *RfF Program of International Studies of Fishery Arrangements*, Paper No. 1, (Washington 1973), 49–61.

29. Investments of this type might allow outsiders to obtain some of the profits or rents associated with marine fisheries in a national zone without engaging in direct harvesting operations.

30. Devanney, *op. cit.*

31. Soviet attitudes toward the use of the Northern Sea Route should be viewed in the light of this proposition. For background see Pharand, *op. cit.*, Part I.

32. Christy, *op. cit.*, 44–61.

33. Philip E. Chitwood, 'Japanese, Soviet, and South Korean Fisheries Off Alaska', Circular No. 310, Fish and Wildlife Service, United States Department of the Interior, (Washington 1969).

34. For a general discussion of the problem of 'new entrants' see Crutchfield, *op. cit.*, esp. 214–215.

35. In this realm, new entrants would ordinarily be large, multinational firms rather than countries.

36. For an indication of the magnitude of the resources at stake consult Charles C. Bates and Paul Yost, 'Where Trends the Flow of Merchant Ships?', John K. Gamble and Giulio Pontecorvo eds., *Law of the Sea: the Emerging Regime of the Oceans*, (Cambridge 1974), 249–276.

37. This would of course depend on the extent to which substitutes for these goods were available to the relevant groups of consumers.

38. For a discussion which emphasizes the distinction between the productive consequences and the distributive consequences of regimes see Alan Randall, 'Coase Externality Theory in a Policy Context', *Natural Resources Journal*, 14 (1974), 35–54.

39. On the distinctions among conceptions of justice see John Rawls, *A Theory of Justice*, (Cambridge 1971), esp. Ch. 1.

40. For a discussion of these issues as they arise in the context of marine fisheries see Edward Miles, 'Organizational Arrangements to Facilitate Global Management of Fisheries', *RfF Program of International Studies of Fishery Arrangements*, Paper No. 4, (Washington 1974).

41. For background see *Emergency Marine Fisheries Protection Act of 1974*, *op. cit.*

42. Allan Gotlieb and Charles Dalfen, 'National Jurisdiction and International Responsibility: New Canadian Approaches to International Law', *AJIL*, 67 (1973), 229–258.

43. William E. Butler, *The Soviet Union and the Law of the Sea*, (Baltimore 1971).

44. William T. Burke, 'Some Thoughts on Fisheries and a New Conference on the Law of the Sea', Brian J. Rothschild ed., *World Fisheries Policy*, (Seattle 1972), 61.

45. Gotlieb and Dalfen, *op. cit.*, 256.

46. Richard B. Bilder, 'The Emerging Right of Physical Enforcement of Fisheries Measures Beyond Territorial Limits', University of Wisconsin Sea

Grant College Program, Technical Report No. 222, (1974), esp. 20–21.
47. In this case, enforcement is a joint responsibility of the offices of the National Marine Fisheries Service and the United States Coast Guard Service in Juneau, Alaska.
48. For a general discussion of this subject see H.L.A. Hart, *The Concept of Law*, (Oxford 1961).
49. For background on this perspective concerning the issue of compliance see Gary S. Becker, 'Crime and Punishment: An Economic Approach', *Journal of Political Economy*, 76 (1968), 169–217.
50. For a collection of materials relating to these issues see Robert O. Keohane and Joseph S. Nye, Jr., eds., *Transnational Relations and World Politics*, (Cambridge 1972).
51. Menno T. Kamminga, 'Building "Railroads on the Sea": China's Attitude Toward Maritime Law', *China Quarterly*, 59 (1974), 544–558.
52. S.M. Olenicoff, 'Territorial Waters in the Arctic: the Soviet Position', Rand R-907-ARPA, 1972.
53. There has, however, been some experience with international river basins along these lines. See, for example, Allen V. Kneese, *The Economics of Regional Water Quality Management*, (Baltimore 1964).
54. See the essays in Leon Lindberg and Stuart Scheingold eds., *Regional Integration: Theory and Research*, (Cambridge 1971).
55. For general studies of functionalism at the international level see Ernst B. Haas, *Beyond the Nation State*, (Stanford 1964), and James P. Sewell, *Functionalism and World Politics*, (Princeton 1966).
56. See also the discussion in Ernst B. Haas, *The Uniting of Europe*, (Stanford 1958).
57. James A. Crutchfield, 'Economic and Political Objectives in Fishery Management', Rothschild ed., *op. cit.*, 74–89.
58. Terry, *op. cit.*
59. For a discussion of the impact of the 'energy crisis' on American policy toward the outer continental shelf in Beringia see Nancy Munro, 'OCS Development – What it Means', *Alaska Seas and Coasts*, 3 (15 April 1975), 1–4.
60. For a general discussion of the problem of transactions costs see E.J. Mishan, 'The Postwar Literature on Externalities: An Interpretative Essay', *Journal of Economic Literature*, IX (1971), 21–24.
61. Such actions would involve procedures like entry restrictions, a major concern of the regional fisheries authority.
62. It is conceivable, though probably unlikely, that the environmental authority could generate substantial revenues on its own through such devices as the creation of markets in pollution rights. See, for example, J.H. Dales, *Pollution, Property and Prices*, (Toronto 1968).
63. For an interesting discussion of markets in rights see *ibid.*, esp. Ch. VI.
64. Devanney, *op. cit.* discusses these problems thoroughly, though he does not apply his analysis to the case of a regional authority.
65. For a general discussion of bureaucratic politics see Graham Allison, *The Essence of Decision*, (Boston 1971).
66. For a sophisticated treatment of this problem see R. Duncan Luce and Howard Raiffa, *Games and Decisions*, (New York 1957), esp. Ch. 6.
67. See, for example, Ross D. Eckert, 'Exploitation of Deep Ocean Minerals: Regulatory Mechanisms and United States Policy', *Journal of Law and Economics*, 17 (1974), esp. 152.
68. For a variety of theoretical perspectives on bargaining consult Oran R. Young editor and contributor, *Bargaining: Formal Theories of Negotiation*,

221

(Urbana 1975).

69. It is worth noting, however, that at least in the United States much of the exploratory work in this realm is not carried out by the corporations that actually produce oil and natural gas.

70. Revenues of the order of $1 billion a year would certainly not be out of the question in this context.

71. For a wealth of background information see *Arctic Marine Commerce, op. cit.*

72. Haas, *Beyond the Nation State, op. cit.*

73. The collaborative efforts undertaken under the terms of the Soviet-American Agreement on Cooperation in the Field of Environmental Protection are highly interesting in this connection. See Weldon L. Merritt, 'The Soviet-U.S. Environmental Protection Agreement', *Natural Resources Journal*, 14 (1974), 275–281.

74. Though a common property regime for renewable resources might be optimal for the Japanese, they would undoubtedly prefer a functional authority in this area to a system of national zones.

75. See Gotlieb and Dalfen, *op. cit.*

76. See also the discussion in Bilder, *op. cit.*

77. For example, arrangements of this type have been discussed quite extensively in the realm of arms control and disarmament agreements. For a collection of relevant materials consult Richard Barnet and Richard A. Falk eds., *Security in Disarmament*, (Princeton 1965), Part 2.

78. On the concept of an equilibrium solution in the theory of games see Luce and Raiffa, *op. cit.*, 65–71.

79. So, for example, arguments against competitive monetary devaluations and actions that could precipitate tariff wars seldom relate to questions of enforcement. There are good reasons for rational actors to avoid taking steps of this kind which have little to do with enforcement as such.

80. On the concept of selective incentives see Mancur Olson, Jr., *The Logic of Collective Action*, (Cambridge 1965), Ch. VI.

81. For a discussion of similar issues in the context of the European Communities see Leon Lindberg and Stuart Scheingold, *Europe's Would Be Polity*, (Englewood Cliffs 1970).

82. A regional authority of this type would fall under the terms of Articles 52–54 of the United Nations Charter. But more specific institutional relationships would also be possible.

83. For a parallel argument in the case of deepsea mining consult Eckert, *op. cit.*, 167–168.

84. See Crutchfield, 'Economic and Political Objectives . . . ', *op. cit.* and J. A. Gulland, *The Management of Marine Fisheries*, (Seattle 1974).

85. For example, such interests might be reflected in efforts to achieve maximum sustained yield from the region's fisheries in contrast to economic efficiency.

86. On transactions costs consult Mishan, *op. cit.*, 21–24. See also the argument developed in Eckert, *op. cit.*, 167–168.

87. Most commentators would undoubtedly agree with Mishan's statement that transactions costs ' . . . increase with the numbers involved, probably at an exponential rate', (Mishan, *op. cit.*, 22).

88. Analytically, this argument resembles certain points raised by Buchanan and Tullock in their discussion of the selection of constitutional decision rules. See James Buchanan and Gordon Tullock, *The Calculus of Consent*, (Ann Arbor 1962), esp. Ch. 6.

89. The b–b' curve actually refers to expected costs. That is, it combines the

social costs of failing to deal with interdependencies with the probability that they will in fact be left unregulated.

90. That is, the intersection of the two curves is an equilibrium point from the perspective of marginal analysis.

91. It would also be possible for the holders of such rights to transfer them to others by means of private exchanges. For a helpful discussion of these issues consult Dales, *op. cit.*

92. This is so because the exploration and development phases with respect to oil and gas production typically extend over considerable periods of time.

93. See also Fred C. Iklè, *How Nations Negotiate*, (New York 1964).

94. Procedures of this type are discussed in *ibid.*, esp. Ch. 7. Note that the number of major participants in these bargaining processes would be small.

95. However, it would be possible to develop a system in which new entrants could purchase exploitation rights directly from the initial holders of the leases.

96. There are various technical procedures that could be used to make a transfer payment of this kind. Accordingly, the essential problems are political rather than procedural.

97. That is, it would improve the prospects of achieving Pareto optimal outcomes. In game-theoretic terminology, this would imply maximizing the probability of obtaining solutions in the 'negotiation set' (Luce and Raiffa, *op. cit.*, 115–119).

98. Crutchfield, 'The Marine Fisheries . . . ' , *op. cit.*, 214.

99. In other words, the situation would not be characterized by what Rawls calls a 'veil of ignorance'. For a discussion of information conditions in the context of contractarian thinking see Rawls, *op. cit.*, esp. Ch. III.

100. But see also the discussion of mixed enforcement systems in Bilder, *op. cit.*

101. That is, they might refrain from cheating with respect to any given agreement in order to foster an atmosphere of trust or confidence in which to negotiate subsequent agreements.

102. See also the discussion in John Gerard Ruggie and Ernst B. Haas, 'Environmental and Resource Interdependencies: Reorganizing for the Evolution of International Regimes', paper prepared for the Murphy Commission, (Berkeley 1975).

103. See also Christy, *op. cit.*, 66–69 and Crutchfield, 'The Marine Fisheries . . .', *op. cit.*, 214–216.

104. For a discussion of the experiences of the European Communities with agricultural policy see Lindberg and Scheingold, *Europe's Would Be Polity, op. cit.*

105. On the concept of wilderness areas consult John C. Hendee, 'A Scientist's Views on Some Current Wilderness Management Issues', *Western Wildlands*, 1 (1974), 27–32.

106. *Loc. cit.*

107. See Richard Pollack, 'Introduction', Tom Brown, *Oil on Ice*, (San Francisco 1971), 9–24. Pollack's statement reflects the position of the Sierra Club.

108. See the comments in Munro, *op. cit.*

109. See the essays in George Rogers ed., *Change in Alaska*, (College and Seattle 1970), esp. Parts IV and V.

110. This is the Alaska Native Claims Settlement Act, 18 December 1971 (PL 92–203; 85 Stat. 688). The d–2 lands, encompassing approximately 80 million acres, have been set aside to be considered for various public uses.

111. The Secretary of the Interior submitted a plan for the use of these lands to Congress in 1974. However, it is expected that it will take 4–5 years to make final decisions concerning all these lands.

112. See Daniel Guérin, *Anarchism: From Theory to Practice*, (New York 1970).

113. It is not self-evident whether the resultant situation would resemble Hobbes' conception of the state of nature rather than that of other philosophers like Locke or Rousseau.

114. See Hedley Bull, 'Society and Anarchy in International Relations', Herbert Butterfield and Martin Wight eds., *Diplomatic Investigations*, (London 1966), 35–50.

115. On the nature of federal governments see K.C. Wheare, *Federal Government*, 4th ed., (New York 1963).

116. In fact, federalism and confederalism should undoubtedly be thought of in terms of a spectrum (rather than a simple dichotomy) with respect to the distribution of power and authoirty. The idea of a Beringian federation under discussion here would fall a considerable distance farther along the spectrum in the direction of centralization than a regime based on a Beringian regional authority.

117. See Oran R. Young, 'The Actors in World Politics', James Rosenau, Vincent Davis, and Maurice East eds., *The Analysis of International Politics*, (New York 1972), 125–144.

118. See, for example, Robert O. Keohane, 'International Organization and the Crisis of Interdependence', *International Organization*, 29 (1975), 357–365.

119. That is, the activities discussed by contractarian thinkers like Rawls are not common in the real world. For Rawls' own views on this point see Rawls, *op. cit.*

120. Some may argue that the new Law of the Sea Conference resembles a constitutional convention. But it is questionable whether this is an appropriate way to think about the Conference, and it is unlikely to produce anything more than the barest outlines of a new regime for the oceans.

CHAPTER VI

POLICY IMPLICATIONS: WHAT IS TO BE DONE?

The argument of the previous chapter constitutes a form of comparative statics. It merely assesses the probable consequences of introducing alternative regimes in a resource region like Beringia; it does not advocate the adoption of any particular alternative or discuss its implementation. However, it strikes me as both appropriate and desirable at this stage to draw out explicitly the policy implications of the analysis presented in this essay.[1] The purpose of this final chapter, then, is to offer a set of proposals relating to new institutions for the management of natural resources in Beringia and to discuss the problems of implementing these arrangements.

Two preliminary comments will lend perspective to this exercise. I shall adopt the viewpoint of Beringia as an international resource region rather than the perspective of any individual actor, such as the United States or the Soviet Union, in this discussion. That is, my proposals concerning Beringia's regime are not aimed primarily at promoting the interests of any particular actor, though I am convinced that each of the major actors in the region should find them preferable to the existing state of affairs. This posture may pose problems for efforts to induce policy making elites in individual countries to espouse these proposals and to press for their acceptance in international negotiations. However, a major objective of the argument advanced in this essay is to establish the position of international regions as distinguishable entities raising issues in the realm of resource management which are not identical with efforts to secure the interests of

225

individual actors.

This discussion also assumes the occurrence of large-scale resource exploitation in Beringia. Therefore, the proposals formulated in this chapter are not designed to avoid or even to reduce such activities in the Beringian region. Instead, the objective is to introduce a regime that will facilitate the exploitation of resources in such a way as to avoid both inefficiency and damage to the environmental resources of the region. Thus, a desirable regime for the region would be one that: 1) allowed for a reasonable approximation of economic efficiency in the exploitation of Beringia's natural resources, 2) yielded a normatively justifiable distribution of wealth among the relevant actors,[2] and 3) safeguarded the principal environmental resources of Beringia. The critical problem is to develop a regime that is politically acceptable to the region's major actors as well as capable of fulfilling these objectives.

A. The Problem

Social structures possess regimes at all times, though they may produce results that are negatively evaluated by many and though they may be experiencing rapid change at any given moment in time. Therefore, the relevant questions to ask about a particular case like Beringia concern the nature of the outcomes associated with the existing regime and the extent to which alterations in the regime would produce preferred results. In this connection, the argument of this essay licenses the conclusion that the existing regime in Beringia leaves a great deal to be desired.

The essential features of the existing regime in Beringia emerged some time ago during an era of relatively light usage of the region's resources. For the most part, this regime yielded acceptable outcomes under the conditions prevailing at the time.[3] But conditions in the region have changed dramatically during recent years and there is every reason to expect continuing changes. An era of heavy usage of the region's resources is upon us, and fundamental asymmetries have arisen with respect to the interests of the principal actors in the region so that it is no longer sensible to treat them identically for purposes of managing natural resources.[4] These developments have given rise to a growing sense of malaise concerning the Beringian regime. More specifically, they are leading to outcomes that are both highly in-efficient (e.g. overinvestment in commercial fisheries) and destructive to the environmental resources of the region (e.g. serious depletions of fish stocks).[5] At the same time, distributive conflicts among the major actors of the region are growing (e.g. Japanese-American conflicts over the salmon fisheries). Consequently, the region is now experiencing a growth of claims and counter-claims which the existing regime is unable to cope with effectively. Unilateral actions of various kinds (e.g. the Canadian Arctic Waters Pollution Prevention Act of 1970) have become more prominent, and there is a rising feeling that major changes in the existing regime will inevitably occur during the near future. Though the prospect of continuing increases in the usage of the region's resources only serves to exacerbate this situation, little conscious effort has been made so far to come to grips with the problems of adapting the Beringian regime to current and probable future circumstances.

These comments raise the following teleological question. Is it possible to identify with any precision the essential characteristics of a preferred regime for Beringia under current conditions? As mentioned previously, the region is experiencing a period of rapid and extensive change which is likely to continue for some time. It is never easy to make confident predictions concerning the consequences of alternative regimes. The desirability of any given regime depends heavily on the extent to which its key provisions are actually complied with by the principal actors involved. Moreover, it is important to bear in mind the limits of political acceptability in making recommendations pertaining to the future of the Beringian regime. Even leaving aside detailed questions relating to the transition from the existing situation to an alternative regime, therefore, it is hard to describe clearly and without hesitation a preferred alternative for Beringia.

It is relatively easy, however, to identify critical defects in some of the alternatives that are often suggested not only for international resource regions like Beringia but also for the oceans as a whole. Perhaps the most widely discussed of these alternatives rests on the idea of extending the jurisdiction of coastal states far out into maritime areas.[6] In the case of Beringia, there is no compelling reason to believe that a system of this type would resolve the problems of overinvestment in fishing and excessive usage of fish stocks, facilitate the development of a coherent set of regulations to cope with marine pollution in the region, or yield solutions for the emerging conflicts arising from interdependencies among the resources of the region. Nor is it easy to construct a persuasive justification of the probable distributive consequences of such a system, since the relevant coastal states do not have any compelling claims to the gains they would reap under such an arrangement. On the other hand, any regime involving dramatic shifts toward the centralization of authority and/or power in the Beringian region would suffer from serious problems in the realm of political acceptability. Moreover, it is not self-evident that such a regime would invariably serve to maximize social welfare in the region or to produce distributive outcomes preferable to those flowing from the current rather inchoate regime in Beringia. Relatively centralized regimes sometimes involve high transactions costs and they can lead to the dominance by one or a few powerful members of the social structure with respect to distributive issues. All this suggests the importance of steering clear of certain major pitfalls in proposing a new regime for Beringia, even if it is difficult to specify precisely the characteristics of an optimal alternative.

B. A Proposed Regime for Beringia

This section outlines a set of concrete proposals relating to the regime of Beringia, leaving a discussion of the problems of implementation to the following section. Taken together, these proposals amount to the suggestion that a mixed system be adopted for the governance of Beringia. This system would feature a combination of several functional agencies with a loose regional authority capable of coping with certain problems cutting across the domains of the individual functional agencies. Specifically, I wish to suggest that the following institutional arrangements constitute the most desirable alterantive for Beringia which is likely to be politically acceptable.

The single most important task is to create a regional functional agency to manage the marine fisheries of Beringia. The management problems in this area are complex, and the need for effective regulation is increasingly urgent in an era of heavy usage of the stocks of fish and marine mammals. There is a compelling argument to be made for the region as an appropriate managerial unit in the case of Beringia.[7] The crucial task of a functional agency in this area would be to regulate entry into the marine fisheries of Beringia, a process that would also have far-reaching implications for the distribution of the harvest.[8] An attractive method of handling this task would be to determine maximum permissible harvests for various stocks and then to create annual markets in entry rights. This would produce desirable results from the point of view of economic efficiency, and it would serve to resolve the relevant distributive problems without protracted international negotiations.[9] Such markets could be organized in such a way as to allow new entrants from outside the original organizing group to acquire shares of the annual harvests. These could be utilized to raise revenue for the fisheries agency itself. However, markets in entry rights may not be politically acceptable during the early phases of this arrangement. In that case, it would be necessary to introduce some system of work permits and this would lead to more overt processes of distributional bargaining among the principal actors in the region.

It is highly unlikely, for political reasons, that a regional agency for hydrocarbons will soon emerge in Beringia. Beringian practice in this functional area will probably follow the pattern that has developed in the case of the North Sea.[10] The principle of coastal state jurisdiction over the resources of the continental shelf is now firmly embedded in international doctrine as well as in recent state practice.

On the other hand, a functional agency for the flow resources of Beringia seems desirable and at least potentially acceptable in political terms.[11] It is important to steer clear of the sensitivities of major actors, such as the United States and the Soviet Union, concerning the use of marine regions for security purposes. It would be pointless at this time, for example, to place pressure on the superpowers to remove their anti-submarine warfare devices from Beringia. However, Beringia has considerable potential in the realm of maritime commerce, especially as usage of the region's other resources expands.[12] In this connection, a functional agency could serve several useful purposes. It might play a major role in the development of a consistent set of rules governing maritime commerce in the region.[13] It could serve to alleviate the tendency toward underinvestment in upkeep and improvements with respect to marine highways. Moreover, it would be able to introduce traffic patterns to cope with congestion in the event that overuse became a problem on any of Beringia's marine highways. The activities of this agency could be financed through the development of a system of user's fees. Though such fees might be set initially in such a way that they just offset upkeep and improvement costs, they could be raised later on to give the agency a certain amount of latitude to pursue innovative policies.

The establishment of a Beringian regional authority over and above these specific functional agencies also seems desirable. This would constitute a major innovation at the international level and would have to be pursued with great care. It would no doubt be politically necessary to organize this authority on a highly voluntaristic basis, at least at first. Even so, it might perform several important functions. It could deal with problems involving conflicts between or among specific functional activities in Beringia. Relevant situations would include conflicts between activities associated with offshore production of hydrocarbons and the pursuit of fishing operations and conflicts between the use of certain marine highways and commercial fishing activities. A regional authority would also be well suited to cope with environmental problems that have regionwide implications and that are difficult to confine to a specialized functional agency. Presumably, the fisheries agency would play a key role in problems relating to the conservation of renewable resources. But the regional authority would be in a better position to deal with problems pertaining to marine pollution and the preservation of the Beringian habitat.[14] Furthermore, a Beringian regional authority would be more appropriate than individual functional agencies as a vehicle for handling relations between the major actors in Beringia and various outside actors concerning the exploitation of the region's natural resources. It is to be hoped that the Beringian institutions proposed here could be prevented from becoming as protectionist or exclusionary as some other functional arrangements have become in recent years. Given the fact that the Beringian institutions will focus on resource management rather than trade and monetary problems, these tendencies may not be as pronounced as they have been in many customs unions and common markets.[15] Nevertheless, the problem of new entrants is a well-known one in situations involving the exploitation of resources,[16] and it certainly cannot be taken for granted that functional arrangements for Beringia will produce significant benefits for those outside the initial club. Under the circumstances, there is a persuasive case to be made for the creation of a Beringian regional authority above the specific functional agencies, even if the politics of the region require it to be loosely structured.

The implementation of these proposals will raise certain standard issues in the realm of international organization which deserve some comment at this point. There are of course administrative questions concerning such matters as formal institutionalization, staffing, and the development of headquarters facilities. While formal institutionalization is currently rather unfashionable at the international level,[17] the arrangements proposed in this section would necessitate some degree of formal organization since they would have to cope with a variety of complex technical issues (e.g. monitoring fish stocks) on a continuous basis. Moreover, some element of formal institutionalization is indicated by the fact that these agencies would require a considerable staff, especially in the scientific, technical, and information processing areas. Note, however, that these arrangements would not necessitate elaborate or continuously operating institutions of a specifically political nature.[18] Thus, organization might well follow the model suggested by agencies like the International North Pacific Fisheries Commission, though the substantive content of the underlying international agreements would be considerably different. Beyond this, it would be helpful to locate the headquarters of all these agencies in the same place both to facilitate coordination among them and to lend salience to these new institutions for the management of Beringia's natural resources.[19] A site like Gambell on St. Lawrence Island would be attractive because of its central location, though it has serious drawbacks with respect to accessibility and weather conditions. A site like Cold Bay, on the other hand, would offer greater accessibility and better facilities,[20] but it is rather closely associated with the United States and does not exemplify the natural features of Beringia as clearly as Gambell.

There are also the usual questions about revenues which arise in connection with international organizations. That is, the operation of such institutions is costly, and it is typically difficult to induce individual members to make substantial voluntary contributions to their maintenance.[21] In the case at hand, there are unusual prospects for the acquisition of revenues on an autonomous basis, assuming that the principal actors in the region would find the resultant arrangements politically acceptable. Markets in entry rights for harvests of renewable resources could yield substantial revenues. It would be reasonable to levy user's fees in conjunction with the use of Beringia's marine highways. It would also be interesting to consider the prospects of establishing markets in pollution rights or taxing the sources of various forms of pollution affecting the region, whether these sources are national governments or corporate enterprises.[22] If all such sources of revenue proved politically unacceptable, the Beringian institutions would have to fall back on a more precarious system of voluntary national contributions. Experiences with arrangements of this type in other situations suggest that every effort should be made to provide the Beringian institutions with autonomous sources of revenues, even if these sources are highly restricted at the outset.

Another standard problem of international organization, which would arise in connection with Beringian regional institutions, concerns the matter of compliance. There is a major gap between inducing various actors to accept international institutions in principle and ensuring that they will adhere to the rules and decisions subsequently promulgated by such institutions.[23] With respect to

Beringia the following comments about the compliance problem seem relevant at this juncture. First, it would be highly desirable (and not necessarily infeasible) to organize a new regime for Beringia in such a way as to give each of the members strong incentives on the basis of self-interest to contribute to the maintenance of the system.[24] Second, it would be advantageous to deal with distributive issues either through the introduction of markets or on the basis of open negotiations so that each member would be encouraged to regard the outcomes as generally fair, though not necessarily optimal for itself. In this context, it would almost certainly help to make provisions for regular renegotiations concerning distributive arrangements so that no member would feel locked into a given arrangement indefinitely and so that changing circumstances could be reflected in altered formulas. Third, it would help if the regional institutions had certain autonomous sources of revenues. This would permit the use of selective incentives to elicit compliance from individual members.[25] There is no doubt that compliance would constitute a major, ongoing problem under a regime of the type proposed in this section for Beringia. However, it is important to bear in mind that compliance is typically a continuous phenomenon rather than a dichotomous one so that it is not necessary to approach the problem on an all-or-nothing basis.

Finally, there is the matter of dealing with outsiders or non-members on an equitable basis. Regional organizations exhibit an inherent tendency to behave in a discriminatory fashion toward outsiders.[26] Though I believe this problem would be more severe in connection with regimes featuring either extensive centralization at the regional level or full-scale coastal state jurisdiction, I would expect the occurrence of some developments along these lines under the system proposed for Beringia in this section. It would undoubtedly be tempting simply to divide up the natural resources of Beringia among the initial members of the regional club and then to exclude outsiders from participating directly in the exploitation of these resources or receiving any of the benefits.[27] But it is virtually impossible to construct a persuasive justification for such an outcome, especially in light of the fact that the principal members of the Beringian club would be highly industrialized states whereas many of the outsiders would be less developed countries. There is of course no magic solution to this problem of combatting the inherent discriminatory tendencies of regional organizations. Nevertheless, I believe this is a matter that should be thought about seriously and persistently in conjunction with the development of a regime for Beringia of the type proposed in this section.

C. The Process of Implementation

Implementation of the proposals advanced above can be pursued on either of two distinct levels. On the one hand, this problem can be approached from a full-blown contractarian point of view.[28] The idea here would be to induce the principal actors in the region to draw up something amounting to a social contract laying out a new regime for Beringia in some detail. Presumably, this process would yield clear-cut agreements about the major features of the new regime and it would resolve the implementation problem in a single stage. On the other hand, the problem of implementation can be dealt with by stages or in a piecemeal fashion.[29] Here the idea would be to focus on the negotiation of certain *ad hoc* agreements pertaining to specific institutional arrangements in Beringia, avoiding the issues associated with efforts to formulate an overall social contract for the region. The presumption here would be that the steps taken at the outset would precipitate a dynamic process involving the evolution of a new regime over time.

Each of these approaches has serious drawbacks. As I suggested at the end of the preceding chapter, the contractarian approach is not likely to be politically acceptable, at least in the case of Beringia. It is difficult enough to strike *ad hoc* bargains in international negotiations among major powers, let alone articulating the details of a social contract for a whole international region. The piecemeal approach, by contrast, rests on the somewhat questionable assumption that initial agreements will in fact precipitate a process of task expansion or 'spillover' leading to the evolution of a relatively comprehensive new regime over time.[30] Recent experiences with economic and political integration at the regional level suggest serious reservations about the plausibility of this assumption.[31] Therefore, it seems necessary to conclude that there is no simple or self-evident method of implementing the proposed regime for Beringia outlined in the preceding section. Nevertheless, I am inclined to believe that it is desirable to concentrate on some version of the piecemeal approach at this juncture. It should at least prove politically acceptable, even though it does not carry with it any guarantee of producing an effective new regime for Beringia.

Regardless of the level at which the problem of implementation is approached, decisions pertaining to the regime of a well-defined social structure, such as an international resource region, constitute social choices.[32] This is true no matter how the relevant actors and the other essential features of the region are specified. Several distinguishable (though complementary) theoretical perspectives lend themselves to an understanding of social choice problems. Thus, the choice of a regime can be conceptualized in terms of efforts to aggregate non-identical preference structures into a collective choice or a social welfare function.[33] Market mechanisms are not likely to be useful in coping with social choice problems of this type because the selection of a regime does not involve the production and exchange of standard economic goods. Moreover, since voting will not be an effective mode of aggregation in an international region like Beringia, this perspective leads to an emphasis on other mechanisms of social choice such as bargaining.

Similarly, it would be feasible to model the problem of selecting a regime for an international region like Beringia as an N-person, non-zero-sum, cooperative game.[34] Even a cursory inspection of the situation makes it clear that there are some outcomes that would be jointly preferred to others by the relevant actors but that there is also considerable conflict among the actors concerning the matter of preferred outcomes. Once again, this suggests that bargaining is likely to be a central feature of any efforts to develop a new regime for Beringia. It indicates that the study of the relevant bargaining processes will involve an examination of such things as coalition formation, side payments, logrolling, and enforcement mechanisms.

Note also that the selection and implementation of a new regime for Beringia would involve the supply of what amounts to a collective good.[35] In fact, a regime will ordinarily constitute a relatively pure collective good in the sense that it will exhibit the attributes of jointness of supply and non-excludability to a high degree within the relevant social structure.[36] This means that the classic problems of free-rider incentives and tendencies toward underinvestment must be taken into account when analyzing the prospects of implementing an alternative regime for Beringia.[37] That is, even if the principal actors in the region should arrive at an agreement concerning the essential features of a preferred regime, there will remain serious problems in eliciting the contributions of resources (including political will) required to implement the regime. Since there is no reason to believe that Beringia constitutes an Olsonian privileged group, one could not expect one of the principal actors unilaterally to supply a viable regime for the region.[38] But the region does involve a relatively small number of major actors,

234

however these actors are conceptualized. Unlike the case of international organization at the global level, therefore, it makes sense to think of efforts to supply an effective regime for Beringia as an explicit bargaining problem.[39] This does not mean that the resultant regime will be optimal, but it does indicate that the problem of guided change with respect to the future regime in Beringia is not a hopeless one.

The repeated references to bargaining in the preceding paragraphs suggest that some general comments on international bargaining are in order at this juncture.[40] Bargaining is of great importance at the international level precisely because other modes of social choice, such as voting, are typically infeasible in this context. Nevertheless, international bargaining about issues like the regime of a resource region is often affected by impediments that are more severe than those arising at the domestic level.[41] There is a relative lack of well-established institutional frameworks to facilitate the bargaining process at the international level. Linkages among issues are apt to be emphasized persistently at this level, thereby making it difficult to subdivide problems and to cope with them piecemeal rather than attempting to resolve them all at once. Moreover, conflicts of the moment (e.g. the current controversy over Bristol Bay salmon in Beringia) have a tendency to foster particularly emotional responses and short-run perspectives at the international level which seriously impede efforts to strike effective bargains concerning longer-run issues. None of this indicates that it is impossible to bargain successfully over a matter like the selection and implementation of a new regime for Beringia. It merely suggests that a healthy respect for the difficulties inherent in such processes is in order.[42 2]

Is there a meaningful role for the individual publicist in the bargaining processes I have been describing? Given the complexities of the external behavior of major states, like the United State and the Soviet Union, it is easy to arrive at pessimistic conclusions about the ability of the individual publicist to affect policymaking concerning an issue like the development of a new regime for the management of natural resources in Beringia. Furthermore, the case at hand raises additional problems since I have articulated proposals from the perspective of the region as a whole rather than from the narrower perspective of efforts to promote the interests of one of the major actors in Beringia. In a sense, this is like playing the role of policy advisor to a currently non-existent Beringian regional authority, a posture that is obviously subject to serious doubts in the realm of efficacy. Therefore, it would clearly be a mistake to overemphasize the ability of the individual publicist to influence the implementation of the proposals outlined in the preceding section of this chapter.

Nevertheless, I want to argue that it would also be erroneous to conclude that the individual publicist is totally lacking in efficacy with respect to matters of this kind. The relevant policy making processes within the major actors generally take the form of complex patterns of bureaucratic politics.[43] Under the circumstances, the central problem in pursuing proposals such as those under consideration here frequently is not one of overcoming deep-seated, principled opposition to the basic ideas involved. Instead, the problem is apt to be one of intervening in the processes of bureaucratic politics with sufficient sophistication to facilitate the formation of a winning coalition in support of the proposals in question.

The detailed problems of advancing these proposals for Beringia will vary in the specific policy making processes of the United States, the Soviet Union, Japan, and Canada. Nevertheless, several general comments about the nature of policy making strike me as relevant to all these cases. To begin with, individual publicists sometimes exercise considerable influence in the realm of what I have elsewhere described as 'sensitization'.[44] Bureaucratic interactions frequently become stuck on shopworn themes so that a new point of view or perspective introduced from outside can come as a sudden breath of fresh air, even if it does not take the form of a fully articulated set of policy proposals. Something of this sort seems to have occurred with respect to the concept of global interdependence during the last several years in the United States.[45] Beyond this, where bureaucratic battle-lines are evenly drawn or bureaucratic processes have failed to turn up any attractive proposals in a given area, the suggestions of informed outsiders can suddenly achieve a high degree of salience almost irrespective of their intrinsic merits. This seems to be what happened, for example, in the case of the original American proposal for a Multilateral Force during the early 1960s.[46] In my judgment, there is a fair chance that similar conditions will arise during the near future with respect to the international relations of managing natural resources and maintaining the quality of the environment. Publicists who wish to influence policy making in this realm must pay careful attention to the dynamics of the relevant bureaucratic processes. But those who are willing to do so may have an opportunity to advance well-timed proposals that achieve a surprising impact on the actual content of subsequent policy.

Finally, I believe the key to success in pursuing the proposals for

236

Beringia advanced in this chapter lies in inducing the United States and the Soviet Union to undertake joint or coordinated initiatives in this area. Given recent developments in the external policies of Canada,[47] it is not reasonable to expect the Canadians to take any initiatives with respect to a new regime for Beringia and they may actually oppose some of the proposals advanced in this essay. For its part, Japan is not a central Beringian power in geopolitical terms, though it has extensive interests in the exploitation of the region's resources.[48] On the other hand, it is not far-fetched to imagine the United States and the Soviet Union taking the lead in this area during the foreseeable future. While the two countries have certain actual or potential disagreements concerning the allocation of Beringian resources, they also possess substantial common interests relating to the region. Both are highly industrialized states with extensive requirements for natural resources and with common interests in their dealings with the less developed countries of the world. As time passes, the two countries are acquiring increasingly similar postures concerning the governance of marine regions in general. So, for example, the United States and the Soviet Union now find themselves on the same side of numerous issues arising in the context of the new Law of the Sea Conference. Moreover, initiatives pertaining to a new regime for Beringia may well seem attractive as a method of bolstering the spirit of detente between the two countries.[49] Such initiatives would be important enough to have considerable symbolic value as an indicator of the continued viability of detente, but they would not require drastic alterations in the fundamental postures of the two countries as in the case of genuinely effective arms control agreements. Consequently, it does not seem unreasonable to think of inducing the United States and the Soviet Union to assume a joint leadership role in supplying the collective good of a new regime for Beringia. What I am suggesting here is the possibility of supplying the collective good in question as an externality of the mutual desire of the two countries to take periodic steps designed to maintain their current relationship of detente.[50]

Should it prove possible to persuade the United States and the Soviet Union to serve as joint sponsors, it would undoubtedly be desirable to organize an international conference on Beringia (or on Beringia and the Arctic) during the near future.[51] Such a conference could follow the pattern of the conference that produced the Antarctic Treaty in 1959.[52] The objective of the exercise would *not* be to promulgate an elaborate social contract dealing with all aspects of the future regime for Beringia. In fact, it would be preferable for the major actors to reach informal agreements in advance on a small number of basic principles applicable to the region. In this context, the formal international conference would serve to give symbolic significance to these new developments with respect to Beringia's regime. That is, the purpose of the conference would be to lend salience to an important transition in the evolution of Beringia's governing arrangements rather than to lay out in detail a new set of institutions for the region. The timing of such a conference would of course depend on the progress of the antecedent negotiations concerning the major issues involved, especially between the United States and the Soviet Union. However, it strikes me as perfectly reasonable to think of convening such a conference sometime during the remaining years of the 1970s.

Notes

1. The argument of this chapter is fundamentally normative. While this makes it different in kind than the material presented in previous chapters, it is nevertheless based squarely on the empirical analyses of those chapters.
2. This is a complex objective since numerous criteria have been suggested to evaluate the justice or fairness of any given distributive formula. For an important recent discussion see John Rawls, *A Theory of Justice*, (Cambridge 1971).
3. On the divergent consequences of common-property regimes under conditions of light usage and heavy usage see H. Scott Gordon, 'The Economic Theory of a Common Property Resource: the Fishery', *Journal of Political Economy*, LXII (1954), 124–142.
4. For example, there are sharp asymmetries between the interests of distant-water states (e.g. Japan and the Soviet Union) and the interests of coastal states (e.g. the United States and Canada) with respect to the marine fisheries of Beringia.
5. Though their occurrence is not probable, it is possible to imagine conditions under which it would be rational for certain actors deliberately to deplete specified stocks. For a discussion of these conditions see Frank T. Bachmura, 'The Economics of Vanishing Species', *Natural Resources Journal*, 11 (1971), 674–692.
6. See, for example, John R. Stevenson and Bernard H. Oxman, 'The Preparations for the Law of the Sea Conference', *AJIL*, 68 (1974), 1–32.
7. In addition to the arguments advanced in previous chapters of this essay, see James Crutchfield, 'The Marine Fisheries: A Problem in International Cooperation', *American Economic Review*, LIV (1964), 207–218; Hiroshi Kasahara and William Burke, 'North Pacific Fisheries Management', *RfF Program of International Studies of Fishery Arrangements*, Paper No. 2, (Washington 1973), esp. xiii, 62, and 88, and Ole A. Mathisen and Donald E. Bevan, 'Some International Aspects of Soviet Fisheries', *Mershon Center Pamphlet Series No. 7*, (September 1968), esp. 51–52.
8. See also Thomas A. Morehouse and Jack Hession, 'Politics and Management:

The Problem of Limited Entry', Arlon Tussing, Thomas A. Morehouse, and James D. Babb, Jr. eds., *Alaska Fisheries Policy*, (Fairbanks 1972), 279–331.

9. For a related discussion consult Ross D. Eckert, 'Exploitation of Deep Ocean Minerals: Regulatory Mechanisms and United States Policy', *Journal of Law and Economics*, 17 (1974), esp. 151–154.

10. Irvin L. White, Don E. Kash, Michael A. Chartock, Michael D. Devine, and R. Leon Leonard, *North Sea Oil and Gas*, (Norman, Oklahoma 1973).

11. For background information on the probable future usage of the region's flow resources see *Arctic Marine Commerce*, Final Report, Contract No. 2-36288 (Maritime Administration, United States Department of Commerce), Arctic Institute of North America, (August 1973).

12. See also Terence Armstrong, 'International Transport Routes in the Arctic', *Polar Record*, 16 (1972), 375–382.

13. On problems of this kind see the essays in Thomas A. Clingan, Jr. and Lewis M. Alexander eds., *Hazards of Marine Transit*, (Cambridge 1973).

14. On the importance of regional perspectives regarding issues of this type see Oscar Schachter and Daniel Serwer, 'Marine Pollution Problems and Remedies', *AJIL*, 66 (1972), esp. 111 and Ross' case study of the Puget Sound-Straits of Georgia area [William M. Ross, *Oil Pollution as an International Problem*, (Seattle 1973)].

15. Jacob Viner, *The Customs Union Issue*, (New York 1950).

16. See, for example, Crutchfield, *op. cit.*, esp. 213–215.

17. Consider, for example, the comments in Robert O. Keohane, '*International Organization* and the Crisis of Interdependence', *International Organization*, XXIX (1975), 357–365.

18. That is, it might well be feasible to follow the pattern of organizations like the European Common Market in which a council of ministers meets periodically to deal with major political issues while an administrative branch operates continuously. For further details see Leon Lindberg and Stuart Scheingold, *Europe's Would Be Polity*, (Englewood Cliffs 1970).

19. An alternative arrangement would be to distribute the headquarters facilities among the principal member states in order to give each of them a tangible sense of participation. Though this arrangement has certain virtues in short-run political terms, the pattern suggested in the text seems preferable from the point of view of developing a viable new regime for Beringia.

20. Specifically, Cold Bay is south of the boundaries of winter sea ice; it has a large all-weather airfield, and it already has an extensive collection of buildings.

21. See John C. Stoessinger and Associates, *Financing the United Nations System*, (Washington 1964).

22. On the idea of markets in pollution rights see J. H. Dales, *Pollution, Property and Prices*, (Toronto 1968).

23. For a fuller discussion of this point see Oran R. Young, 'Compliance and Politics', mimeographed essay, (Austin 1974).

24. In more formal terms, the idea would be to create a situation in which compliance would constitute a preferred strategy for each participant so that mutual compliance would become an *equilibrium* point. On this usage of the concept of equilibrium see R. Duncan Luce and Howard Raiffa, *Games and Decisions*, (New York 1957), Ch. 3.

25. On selective incentives see Mancur Olson, Jr., *The Logic of Collective Action*, (Cambridge 1965), Ch. VI.

26. For an analysis that explores some of the bases of this phenomenon in a

sophisticated fashion see Jeffrey A. Smith, 'Coalition Formation in the International Market: A Game Theoretic Model of Economic Integration', mimeographed essay, (Austin 1974).

27. See also William T. Burke, 'Some Thoughts on Fisheries and a New Conference on the Law of the Sea', Brian J. Rothschild ed., *World Fisheries Policy*, (Seattle 1972), esp. 72.
28. For an extensive exposition of contractarian thinking consult Rawls, *op. cit.*
29. This orientation resembles what is known as the functionalist or neo-functionalist point of view among students of international relations. For a good survey see Ernst B. Haas, *Beyond the Nation State*, (Stanford 1964), Pt. I.
30. On the ideas of task expansion and 'spillover' see the essays in Leon Lindberg and Stuart Scheingold eds., *Regional Integration: Theory and Research*, (Cambridge 1971).
31. See, for example, Lindberg and Scheingold, *Europe's Would Be Polity, op. cit.*
32. For a discussion of the selection of constitutional rules which raises a number of the same issues see James Buchanan and Gordon Tullock, *The Calculus of Consent*, (Ann Arbor 1962).
33. Perhaps the classic contemporary work dealing with issues of this kind is Kenneth Arrow, *Social Choice and Individual Values*, 2nd. ed., (New York 1963).
34. For a good introduction see Anatol Rapoport, *N-Person Game Theory*, (Ann Arbor 1970).
35. For relevant theoreticl material consult, *inter alia*, Olson, *op. cit.* and Norman Frohlich, Joe A. Oppenheimer, and Oran R. Young, *Political Leadership and Collective Goods,* (Princeton 1971).
36. On these concepts see Norman Frohlich and Joe A. Oppenheimer, *An Entrepreneurial Theory of Politics,* unpublished Ph.D. dissertation, (Princeton University 1971), Ch. 2.
37. On these problems consult Olson, *op. cit.*; Frohlich, Oppenheimer, and Young, *op. cit.*, and Eckert, *op. cit.*
38. Olson, *op. cit.*, 48–50. Note also that a regime supplied by a single member of a group might well be valued negatively by the other members of the group precisely because of the unilateral nature of its supply.
39. *Ibid.*, Ch. I.
40. On the special problems of bargaining in the international arena see Thomas C. Schelling, *The Strategy of Conflict*, (Cambridge 1960) and Oran R. Young, *The Politics of Force*, (Princeton 1968).
41. For further discussion of these issues see Young, *The Politics of Force, op. cit.*, Ch. 10.
42. For a general survey of theoretical models of bargaining consult Oran R. Young editor and contributor, *Bargaining: Formal Models of Negotiation*, (Urbana 1975).
43. For an extensive account of American bureaucratic politics in the realm of foreign policy see Morton Halperin, *Bureaucratic Politics and Foreign Policy*, (Washington 1974).
44. Oran R. Young, 'The Perils of Odysseus: Problems of Theory Construction in International Relations', Raymond Tanter and Richard H. Ullman eds., *Theory and Policy in International Relations*, (Princeton 1972), 179–203.
45. See, for example, the essays in Robert O. Keohane and Joseph S. Nye eds., *Transnational Relations and World Politics*, (Cambridge 1972).
46. John Steinbrunner, *The Cybernetic Theory of Decision*, (Princeton 1974).
47. Allan Gotlieb and Charles Dalfen, 'National Jurisdiction and International

Responsibility: New Canadian Approaches to International Law', *AJIL*, 67 (1973), 229–258.

48. Specifically, it is not a coastal state in any part of Beringia and does not have direct claims to jurisdiction over any of the Beringian continental shelves.

49. On the origins and development of Soviet-American detente see John Spanier, *World Politics in an Age of Revolution*, (New York 1967).

50. That is, the new regime for Beringia would be a by-product of Soviet-American policy initiatives whose guiding purpose had little to do with the development of governing arrangements for Beringia.

51. Related suggestions have been advanced from time to time. See, for example, 'Arctic Pact Sought by U.S. and Canada', *Polar Times*, 70 (June 1970), 24 (reprinted from the *New York Times*) and Malcolm F. Baldwin, 'Public Policy on Oil – An Ecological Perspective', *Ecology Law Quarterly*, 1 (1971), 245–303.

52. See Howard J. Taubenfeld, 'A Treaty for Antarctica', *International Conciliation*, No. 531 (1961).

NAME INDEX

Alexander, Lewis M., 51, 171, 177, 219, 239
Allison, Graham, 221
Alonso, William, 50
Anderson, Raymond, 127
Anderson, William R., 127
Andrassy, Juraj, 171
Armstrong, Terence, 19, 51, 53, 54, 125–127, 131, 239
Arrow, Kenneth, 240

Babb, James D., 119, 170, 172, 176, 239
Bachmura, Frank T., 19, 56, 128, 130, 238
Baldwin, Malcolm T., 124, 129, 241
Barkun, Michael, 218
Barnet, Richard, 222
Barry, Roger G., 129
Bates, Charles C., 126, 220
Becker, Gary S., 221
Belousov, Dmitri, 219
Bennett, Gordon, 9
Benson, Carl S., 128
Bevan, Donald E., 53, 132, 173, 238
Bilder, Richard B., 126, 170, 174–176, 220, 222
Bleicher, Samuel A., 176
Borgstrom, Georg, 51, 53, 173
Brent, Stephen M., 54, 99
Brockett, Lester, 9, 124
Brown, Robert, 218
Brown, Tom, 51, 54, 125, 127, 130, 223
Buchanan, James, 56, 222, 240
Buck, Eugene H., 9, 55, 119, 121, 122
Bull, Hedley, 224
Burke, William, 51–53, 121, 122, 132, 143, 172, 176, 219, 220, 238, 240
Burns, John, 9
Butler, William E., 51, 53, 55, 131, 153, 170, 174, 220
Butterfield, Herbert, 224

Chartock, Michael A., 54, 123, 239
Chasen, Robert E., 131
Chitwood, Philip E., 53, 120, 220
Christy, Francis T., 55, 62, 64, 116,

120, 130, 131, 170–175, 219, 220, 223
Clingan, Thomas A., 170, 177, 219, 239
Coase, Ronald H., 56, 128
Comitini, Salvatore, 121, 176
Conroy, Michael, 9
Cooper, Bryan, 54, 130
Cooper, Richard N., 55, 130
Crommelin, Michael, 53
Crutchfield, James A., 120, 121, 130–132, 172, 175, 176, 219–223, 239

Dales, J.H., 128, 221, 223, 239
Dalfen, Charles, 51, 122, 127, 170, 177, 220, 222, 240
Davis, Vincent, 224
Devanney, J.W., 122, 124, 219–221
Devine, Michael D., 54, 123, 239
Dickstein, H.L., 51, 176, 177
Dobey, Patrick L., 88, 125
Dorfman, Nancy, 50
Dorfman, Robert, 50
Dunbar, M.J., 128
Dworsky, Leonard B., 50

East, Maurice, 224
Easton, David, 56
Eckert, Ross D., 55, 126, 221, 222, 239
Edel, Matthew, 50

Falk, Richard A., 222
Fay, Francis, 9, 122
Finnie, Richard S., 124, 125
Foote, Don C., 54, 122, 129, 174
Franies, George R., 50
French, Stewart, 125
Friedheim, Robert L., 9, 218
Friedmann, John, 50
Frohlich, Norman, 121, 126, 128, 240
Furubotn, Eirik, 55, 120, 219

Gamble, John K., 126, 170, 171, 220
Gardner, Frank, 123
Goldberg, Robert M., 54, 99
Gordon, H. Scott, 54, 120, 131, 238
Gorelick, Jeffrey A., 121

242

243

SUBJECT INDEX

Standard Oil of California, 83

Taiyo Gyogyo, 37
Tanner crab, 72, 148, 158
Terminal facilities, 41, 91, 97, 98, 106
Territorial sea, 16, 29, 43, 97, 133–142, 149, 152, 154–156, 167, 190
Test Ban Treaty, 112
Texas, 10
Timber, 31, 96
Tokyo, 98
Torrey Canyon, 106
Tourism, 38, 39, 100, 101
Transactions costs, 24, 94, 103, 195, 204, 206, 207, 209, 228
Trans-arctic routes, 97, 98
Transistion area, 70
Trash fish, 72
Triad concept, 138
Tuna, 28, 60, 70
Turbot, 72

U-2, 112
User's fees, 167, 184, 186, 188, 189, 195, 196, 198, 200, 208, 229, 231
Unimak Island, 144
Union, 35
Union of Soviet Socialist Republics, 16, 18, 24, 28–30, 32, 34–36, 40, 41, 43, 44, 62, 65–68, 70–74, 77, 84, 86, 87, 94–96, 100, 107, 111–114, 134, 136, 137, 139, 142–146, 148–150, 152–156, 158–162, 164, 165, 267, 169, 181, 183, 185, 188, 190, 193, 195, 201, 205, 217, 225, 229, 236–238
fishing fleets, 34, 37
Navy, 34
United Kingdom of Great Britain and Northern Ireland, 158
United Nations, 134, 204, 205, 217
United States of America, 21, 28–32, 35–37, 39–41, 43, 44, 60, 67, 69, 73, 77, 78, 86, 94, 95, 100, 106, 111–113, 134–137, 139, 142, 143, 145–150, 152, 154, 156, 158–163, 165, 167, 169, 181, 183, 185, 187, 189, 192, 193, 194, 201, 205, 206, 210, 217, 225, 229, 231, 235–238

fishing industry, 36
U.S. Coast and Geodetic Survey, 20
U.S. Coast Guard Service, 40, 221
U.S. Geological Survey, 87
U.S. Navy, 34, 35, 82, 154
U.S. Senate, 170, 218
Foreign Relations Committee, 170, 218
U.S. Supreme Court, 33, 85, 154
Unitization agreements, 183
University of Alaska, 9, 51, 55, 122
University of British Columbia, 53
University of Miami Sea Grant Program, 175, 219
University of Texas, 9
University of Wisconsin Sea Grant College Program, 220, 221
University Research Institute, 9

Vancouver, 147
Vertical domains, 42
Vilkitski Strait, 34, 167

Western hemisphere, 15
Wilderness areas, 19, 26, 27, 48, 79,
Wilderness Society, 38
World Order Program, 9
World War II, 29, 30, 100, 112
World Wildlife Fund, 38
Wrangel Island, 15

Yamal Peninsula, 30, 84
Yellow Sea, 15
Yellowfin, 72
Yokohama, 96
Yukon, 32
Yukon River, 86
Kandik, 88